The Congressional Endgame

The Congressional Endgame

Interchamber Bargaining and Compromise

JOSH M. RYAN

THE UNIVERSITY OF CHICAGO PRESS   CHICAGO AND LONDON

The University of Chicago Press, Chicago 60637
The University of Chicago Press, Ltd., London
© 2018 by The University of Chicago
All rights reserved. No part of this book may be used or reproduced in any manner
whatsoever without written permission, except in the case of brief quotations in critical
articles and reviews. For more information, contact the University of Chicago Press,
1427 E. 60th St., Chicago, IL 60637.
Published 2018
Printed in the United States of America

27 26 25 24 23 22 21 20 19 18   1 2 3 4 5

ISBN-13: 978-0-226-58206-1 (cloth)
ISBN-13: 978-0-226-58223-8 (paper)
ISBN-13: 978-0-226-58237-5 (e-book)
DOI: https://doi.org/10.7208/chicago/9780226582375.001.0001

Library of Congress Cataloging-in-Publication Data

Names: Ryan, Josh M., author.
Title: The congressional endgame : interchamber bargaining and compromise /
    Josh M. Ryan.
Description: Chicago ; London : The University of Chicago Press, 2018. |
    Includes bibliographical references and index.
Identifiers: LCCN 2018019132 | ISBN 9780226582061 (cloth : alk. paper) |
    ISBN 9780226582238 (pbk. : alk. paper) | ISBN 9780226582375 (e-book)
Subjects: LCSH: United States. Congress—Conference committees. |
    United States. Congress—Resolutions. | Legislation—United States. |
    United States—Politics and government.
Classification: LCC JK1111 .R93 2018 | DDC 328.73/0775—dc23
LC record available at https://lccn.loc.gov/2018019132

♾ This paper meets the requirements of ANSI/NISO Z39.48-1992 (Permanence of Paper).

Contents

Acknowledgments

I wish to thank my colleagues at Bradley University, where I began this project, and at Utah State University, where I completed it. At Bradley, I am especially grateful to Ed Burmila, Tom Carty, and Lori Wiebold, each of whom provided substantive suggestions and encouragement. At Utah State, I owe Damon Cann, Robert Ross, Anna Pechenkina, Laura Gamboa, and Michael Lyons a debt of gratitude. Greg Goelzhauser entertained my sometimes long-winded questions and always offered thoughtful advice on various aspects of the project.

Thanks also go to numerous others who read versions of the manuscript over the last few years. Scott Adler, Anand Sokhey, Ken Bickers, and Scott Wolford have each helped me mature as a scholar, and I am indebted to their guidance. Greg Koger, Jim Curry, Phil Arena, Mike Crespin, and Nate Monroe all offered helpful comments on various chapter drafts. Jon Rogowski, Rob McGrath, Dave Doherty, Mike Touchton, Scott Minkoff, and Jeff Lyons kept me motivated via phone conversations, email exchanges, and not-frequent-enough get-togethers. All of these people are brilliant political scientists; more importantly, I am privileged to call them friends.

The University of Chicago Press has made the process as enjoyable and painless as possible. I owe thanks to my editor, Charles Myers, and his entire staff. Chuck not only made valuable comments on the manuscript but answered all of my questions with patience and thoughtfulness. He also guided the book through a very useful review process.

I would not have finished the project without the support of my family, Greg and Sue Ryan, and my brother, Sean Ryan. They have given me unending support during this process. Finally, my partner Kristin has put up with my stress, complaints, and frustrations with incredible optimism and enthusiasm. Her interests do not include political science, and for that I am very grateful.

CHAPTER ONE

Does Bicameralism Work in the Modern Congress?

People are trying to remain open for negotiation, but I don't really know how we ever reconcile where the House is and where the Senate is.—Sen. Mary Landrieu, speaking about climate change legislation, June 23, 2009

In the summer of 2017, Republicans in the Senate believed they had finally hit upon a successful strategy to repeal and replace the Patient Protection and Affordable Care Act (commonly called the ACA or Obamacare). The House had previously passed a very conservative bill that stood little chance of attracting even fifty-one votes in the Senate, so the Senate had spent the last few months searching for a bill that could both pass the chamber and receive sufficient support in the House.[1] After not being able to agree, the process looked dead until the party leadership advanced the idea of "skinny repeal," a bill that, among other things, would have repealed the ACA's mandate that Americans must purchase insurance on the private market. The bill avoided other controversial topics, such as cuts to Medicaid, but most policy experts agreed that it would have destabilized the health care market, potentially causing the system to collapse.

The idea behind skinny repeal was to pass something to move the chambers to a conference committee, where the details could be hammered out and, eventually, a take-it-or-leave-it offer could be sent back to both chambers. Lindsey Graham, Republican from South Carolina, called the bill "terrible policy and horrible politics." Ron Johnson, Republican of Wisconsin, implored the House, "Just give us the assurance that whatever we pass tonight will go to conference, so the good ideas . . . can get scored and have a chance to be argued."[2] Senators were concerned that the House might pass the bill without any modifications, and in fact there would have been little stopping the chamber from doing just that. Paul Ryan's qualified statement that the House would be "willing" to go to conference[3] reassured the senators enough that both Graham and Johnson ended up voting for the bill hours later, though John McCain, along with Senators Collins and Murkowski, cast dramatic no votes that sank the plan.

The Senate was right to be concerned. Skinny repeal would have given the House majority much of what it wanted. If policy experts were correct, and the Obamacare markets collapsed, the law would have effectively been repealed. The bill also prevented the House from taking additional tough votes on specific, popular provisions and placed much of the blame on the Senate. Procedurally, this would not have been all that uncommon. The chambers frequently pass legislation without modifying the bill, especially when postpassage bargaining is likely to be difficult and costly. Even if the House agreed to conference, there was no guarantee the committee would produce a satisfactory compromise, and the House could have then voted for skinny repeal. Despite these important policy implications, there is, at present, little theory that offers guidance on how these different paths to resolution might work, and what types of policy might be produced.

Or, consider the 2014 Farm Bill, which was successfully enacted after a conference committee. The Farm Bill's reauthorization is not the type of legislative activity that typically attracts media headlines. The bill, which must be passed every five years, is Congress's main vehicle for agricultural and food policy and is an important, if wonkish, legislative item. Among other things, each Farm Bill renewal manages crop subsidies and insurance programs, implements trade regulations that allow American crops to be sold overseas, and imposes environmental and conservation regulations on farmers. Passage has traditionally been bipartisan because the bill authorizes spending for key constituencies across many legislative districts and because it does not deal with any hot-button social issues. The 2002 version of the bill, enacted only a few weeks after the previous version expired, passed with 280 votes in the House and 64 votes in the Senate and was approved in both chambers after a conference committee negotiated the bill for about three months. Most of the opposition to the bill was driven by conservative Republicans concerned about earmarks and the overall cost of the legislation.[4] The 2008 version was enacted with large bipartisan majorities and required Congress to override a presidential veto.[5]

The 2014 process, by contrast, took over two years to complete and faced stiff opposition from members of both parties in the House and Senate. Because of a historical need to generate urban support for farm programs and rural support for a poverty-based food program, the Department of Agriculture is responsible not only for farm policy but also for implementation of the federal food stamp program known as the Supplemental Nutrition Assistance Program (SNAP). In fact, in 2014, the SNAP program was by far the largest portion of Farm Bill spending, responsible for about $756 billion of the overall bill cost of $956 billion. In 2014 both chambers agreed on cutting funding for SNAP but disagreed strongly about how much to cut. The Democratic-led Senate, as is typical, substituted their own language into the House-passed version of the bill and agreed on a cut of about $4 billion while the Republican-led House had previously cut food stamp funding by nearly $21 billion. For months, the chambers could not even agree to meet, and the bill languished without action during the summer and fall of 2013.

Observers were unsure which chamber would be successful during conference negotiations and looked to the public pronouncements of the leadership, the conferees, and key members. House Republicans originally wanted to separate food stamps from farm subsidy reauthorizations, presumably to make it easier to cut food stamps in the future, but that was a nonstarter for the Senate and would have likely triggered a presidential veto. Instead, the chambers squared off over the size of food stamp cuts, with both sides seemingly committed to their position. In the end, the bill was much closer to the Senate's preference, with cuts of about $8 billion in food stamps but with some additional funding for food banks, much to the dismay of many House Republicans, some of whom voted against the final version of the bill, despite support from both the Republican Speaker and Majority Leader.

Bicameral negotiations significantly and fundamentally affect policy outcomes and comprise a crucial and necessary step in the lawmaking process in Congress. Yet, most existing theories, and the accompanying empirical research on congressional action, do not adequately take into account the central role of bicameralism in lawmaking or the implications thereof. While there is a substantial literature on how congressional committees develop legislation, how party leaders push or block bills, and how the president uses his influence to affect legislative outcomes, the ability of conferees to drastically change legislation after initial passage and with virtually unlimited autonomy is underappreciated. For cases like the Farm Bill reauthorization, political science offers little help in understanding how conference committee negotiations take place, how chambers resolve their differences, or how and why one chamber is likely to be more successful in achieving its preferences. Each conference outcome seems idiosyncratic, seemingly determined by the shrewdness of one chamber's bargainers or by a more impassioned and resolute group of members.

In this book, I argue that conference committees and an alternative resolution mechanism—amendment trading—can be explained by a coherent theoretical framework. Rather than focusing on ad hoc explanations driven by individual statements, personality-driven politics, or leadership characteristics, bargaining outcomes are structured by the same institutional factors that structure other bargaining situations. Stronger bargainers are those that are more willing to walk away from a deal because they receive a larger share of the benefits from not compromising. When the House and Senate disagree on legislation, one chamber can receive more of what it wants as a result of institutional factors that empower it during the bargaining process. Legislative failure is caused by the costs of negotiating a compromise and by the uncertainty of what the winning coalitions within each chamber will accept.

Constitutional Design and Bicameral Bargaining in the Modern Congress

Bicameralism with two truly equal chambers is relatively rare among democracies. Even those countries with a two-chambered legislature typically provide substantial proposal or amending rights to only one. The House and Senate, despite some minor differences in their constitutional roles, are equal partners in the legislative process, and this unique institutional design gives each chamber the same ability to shape legislative outcomes.

When writing the Constitution, Madison and others sought to create a stronger national government that would not fall victim to the same problems that plagued the Continental Congress under the Articles of Confederation. It was too difficult to reach agreement in that system, and, importantly, the national government had no power to compel the states to act, a situation that made the country economically and militarily weak. Madison makes the case in *Federalist* 39, arguing that a more vigorous national government is not only necessary but unavoidable if the country is to succeed. Despite the necessity of a stronger central government, there was substantial fear that the new congress would be too strong and would too quickly and recklessly carry out the whims of the majority (Hammond and Miller 1987). Madison recognizes this danger in *Federalist* 48, pointing out that, "[T]he legislative department is everywhere extending the sphere of its activity, and drawing all power into its impetuous vortex."

Bicameralism offers one protection against overreach. Through a two-chambered legislature, the framers sought to create additional institutional checks against the nefarious intentions of a legislative majority determined to use its lawmaking power as a tool of tyranny. As Madison famously said in *Federalist* 51, "In framing a government which is to be administered by men over men, the great difficulty lies in this: You must first enable the government to control the governed; and in the next place oblige it to control itself." The design of the Senate in particular, with longer terms and appointment by state legislatures, was seen by many framers as a necessary curb on the more imperious tendencies of the House (Binder 2003). In *Federalist* 62 Madison recognizes the tension inherent in a bicameral congress, saying, "No law or resolution can now be passed without the concurrence, first, of a majority of the people, and then, of a majority of the States. It must be acknowledged that this complicated check on legislation may in some instances be injurious as well as beneficial." But he notes that the Senate "doubles the security to the people, by requiring the concurrence of two distinct bodies in schemes of usurpation or perfidy, where the ambition or corruption of one would otherwise be sufficient." Not only were the framers aware that bicameralism would slow down and complicate lawmaking, they explicitly endorsed this effect.

Thus, Madison justified the creation of a bicameral legislature on the grounds that it would take action but not too quickly, be responsive to the people without falling victim to majority tyranny, and make policy changes when both the citizens (the House) and the states (the Senate) agreed. Madison and the other framers also expected bicameralism to promote conservative lawmaking; that is, policy change would be made not just slowly but also incrementally even though popular, legitimate, or desirable legislation would have a harder time winning approval. Still, they advocated for such a system, claiming the inherent status quo bias of a bicameral legislature promotes stability, a desirable result in republican government. In *Federalist* 62 Madison says of laws, "if they be repealed or revised before they are promulgated, or undergo such incessant changes that no man, who knows what the law is to-day, can guess what it will be to-morrow," the effects would be "calamitous." He goes on to say, "Law is defined to be a rule of action; but how can that be a rule, which is little known, and less fixed? Another effect of public instability is the unreasonable advantage it gives to the sagacious, the enterprising, and the moneyed few over the industrious and uniformed mass of the people." Legislative stability was clearly an important goal of the designers and informs our understanding of how Congress operates today. Unlike parliamentary systems, where action is not only swift but also quite dramatic, American lawmaking seems to be characterized by slow *and* incremental action.

Is Bicameralism Effective?

Bicameralism almost certainly achieves the first goal of the framers by making it harder to accomplish policy change. As compared to a unicameral system, it promotes the status quo and makes policy action slower and more difficult to accomplish (Muthoo and Shepsle 2008; Tsebelis and Money 1997). The logic behind this claim is simple. In bicameral systems, instead of one chamber agreeing to policy change, two must agree. While it is difficult to show empirically that bicameralism reduces legislative productivity, some indirect evidence has been found. In the American context, there is support for the claim that legislative gridlock is more likely as the preferences of the two chambers diverge (Binder 2003).

As William Riker (1992) points out, bicameralism is often criticized on normative grounds. Populists condemn the system because it is not as responsive to public demands as unicameralism. Additionally, most bicameral systems include an "upper" chamber that is not proportionally representative and therefore magnifies the power of the minority (Heller 2007). Minority coalitions that are overrepresented may have a disproportionate influence on policy and, in many cases, allow the minority a veto over policy change supported by the other chamber (Cutrone and McCarty 2006). Riker (1992), in finding that bicameralism prevents lawmaking in the absence of a stable majority (as opposed to unicameralism), says that bicameralism is, "now, unfortunately, often regarded as a rather old-fashioned constitutional structure."

But, more importantly, does bicameralism justify the trade-off made by the framers that, despite its more onerous structure, it helps moderate or limit policy change? There are some good reasons to be skeptical. First, the Senate no longer represents states "as political and coequal societies" (*Federalist* 39), as senators are directly elected by the people and, hence, more influenced by popular passions. Though six-year terms still distance senators from their constituents more than the two-year terms of House members, there is no doubt senators have become more responsive to the public than the framers originally imagined.

Second, political parties play a much more important role now than during the founding and in recent years have been more consequential than at perhaps any time in American history. The rise of partisan polarization is well documented in both the House and the Senate, and, as members become more ideologically separated and parties grow more powerful, it is unclear whether one chamber is able to moderate the other's more extreme preference or whether an ideologically strong and unified party can force its positions on an ideologically moderate or heterogeneous chamber.

In recent years, this debate about whether institutional rules help produce moderation or extremity has been at the forefront of political science research and popular accounts of Congress. Legislative fights between House Republicans and Senate Democrats were common in the 112th and 113th Congresses over virtually all important legislative proposals. The inability to resolve interchamber disagreements led, at least indirectly, to a government shutdown in 2013. Even in the 115th Congress, with unified Republican government, interchamber compromise was difficult. Polarization has also led political observers to wonder whether the institutional design of Congress is up to the challenges of governing such an enormous and complex country during periods of intense partisanship. Unicameral chambers are seen by many as more effective and efficient institutions, and calls to reform Congress are common. Indeed, the *New York Times* reported in 2012 that developing countries designing new constitutions look to European parliamentary systems rather than the American system for a simple reason: it is simply too difficult to get things done.[6]

Summary of the Findings

In this book, I focus not on the amount of legislation passed, though bargaining failure has implications for legislation productivity, but on the resolution process itself and how it changes bills. That is, what outcomes are to be expected given the preferences of winning coalitions in both the House and the Senate? In answering this question, I also explore the different types of resolution mechanisms used and whether their effects on bills differ. Despite the apparent procedurally difficulty the chambers have resolving their differences, they are remarkably successful. More than 90 percent of legislation on which the chambers begin the bargaining process is ultimately sent to the president. I also explain why some bills fail, even when they are passed with large bipartisan majorities in their respective chambers.

Broadly, I find that the result of House-Senate negotiations is a bill that approximates the more moderate chamber's preference but that neither chamber receives exactly what it wants, especially from a conference committee. This occurs because more moderate coalitions are more willing to walk away from the resolution process, giving it enormous sway over the conferees. As a result, the conferees ensure the preferences of these coalitions are met, resulting in more moderate policy outcomes. This is true even under conditions of strong partisan control of the House and Senate, when the leadership might be expected to exert its influence over individual members. I find little evidence that legislative outcomes depend on the partisan strength or control of the institutions.

A similar dynamic applies to the other major resolution process used by Congress, amendment trading or "ping-ponging." In this process, the chambers make iterative policy proposals to each other until agreement is ultimately reached. There has been virtually no research on this process, but some observers, including some members of Congress, seem to think this empowers the party leadership to create more ideological bills (Sinclair 2012). The empirical tests of bill outcomes in this book, for perhaps the first time, examine amendment trading's effects on policy outcomes. Again, I find little evidence that parties dominate the process, even in recent congresses and during unified partisan control of the chambers.

The theory predicts that the institutional rules of conferences and amendment trading produce different outcomes despite their overall moderating effects, though the empirical evidence for both is very similar. The conferees are empowered to create a take-it-or-leave-it proposal, which cannot be changed, while amendment trading is a sequential process that involves the revelation of preferences across multiple policy offers. The result is that conference bills sometimes allocate more than might be expected to the more extreme chamber, while amendment trading also favors the more moderate chamber, though policies do not collapse to its exact ideal point.

These findings suggest the framers' goals are largely met. Policy results are closer to the status quo than they would be if there was a single, more extreme chamber. Ideological cohesiveness within a chamber does not necessarily make that chamber a stronger bargainer, and being more extreme, while appearing more resolute, actually makes a chamber weaker. Winning coalitions made up of extreme members are simply unwilling to reject an offer and, as a result, must conform to the preferences of the winning coalition willing to walk away from the compromise. Strong parties are ineffective insofar as they make individual chambers more extreme, but polarization in general increases the costs of resolution and makes immediate acceptance of a bill and amendment trading more common. There is also evidence that interchamber negotiations allow the conferees to expand the distribution of benefits for certain types of bills. Some bills, it seems, are distributive in nature, and conferences are willing to ensure that most members are able to take advantage of the particularized benefits. Again, this is not inconsistent with the goals of the framers when they designed the Constitution.

Before examining bill outcomes, I begin by explaining how and why the House and Senate choose to use amendment trading or conferencing. Historically, conferencing has been far more important and far more common, especially for important legislation. Many have noted the decline of conferencing and a rise in amendment trading, which is usually attributed to the party leadership or an inability to generate sufficient support for conferencing. First, I show that conferences are still used for important bills at the same frequency they have been in the past, but there are far fewer important bills passed in recent congresses. Second, I develop a coherent theoretical framework that explains why conferencing or amendment trading is used. A conference is almost always the preferred venue because of its low-cost nature; it is an efficient way for the chambers to resolve their differences because it does not use floor time or require the wrangling of votes across multiple issues. However, congressional rules, up until very recently, made it difficult to actually go to conference, and as a result amendment trading became the default option. Amendment trading produces similar legislative outcomes and is comparably successful to conferences, but it seems to require more of the winning coalition.

Plan of the Book

In the next chapter, I discuss bicameral resolution processes in historical context and the modern resolution process. The structure of the House and Senate is largely based on legislatures in the colonies prior to the

Constitution, which themselves are modeled after the British Parliament. In the modern Congress, there are well-defined procedures for conferencing and for amendment trading, and I explore some important questions related to these congressional procedures, which no longer resemble the textbook approach. This chapter also shows the relative frequency of conferences and amendment trading over the last forty years and indicates how bill importance matters with respect to postpassage resolution venues.

In chapter 3, I develop a theory of interchamber resolution that relies on a noncooperative bargaining model. In this type of model, two actors, in this case the House and Senate winning coalitions, compete for a share of the total benefits available from reaching a compromise. If they do not agree, both actors receive some benefits from disagreement as well—for example, support from a particular constituency group opposed to the legislation. In these noncooperative bargaining situations, both actors are made better off by agreement but disagree on how large a share of the benefits they receive, meaning bargaining is not zero-sum but instead allows both bargainers to receive something from the end result. The bargaining game allows inferences to be made about the trade-off between conferencing and amendment trading and about the size of the share of the benefits each chamber will accept. In particular, I focus on the relative benefits of rejection compared to those of acceptance—and the costs of bargaining—to draw inferences about policy outcomes.

The empirical analyses begin in chapter 4. Applying the logic of the bargaining game, I generate hypotheses about the selection of conferencing or amendment trading while also accounting for bills that are passed in the same form by both chambers and skip the postpassage bargaining process altogether. Using data from the 93rd to 111th Congresses, selection and logit models are used to predict first whether a bill went to postpassage bargaining and, if so, whether it was resolved in conference or through amendment trading. Predictors of bargaining venue include bill importance, coalition support on passage, and if the bill made appropriations.

Before exploring how much conferees change legislation from that originally passed by the chambers, chapter 5 examines how much room or discretion the conferees have when negotiating a bill. In some cases the House and Senate are relatively insensitive to changes made by the conferees and will accept almost any proposal, while in other cases even small changes made by the conferees to a chamber's original bill may result in rejection, substantially limiting their discretion. I treat discretion separately from outcomes because it affects the amount of possible change and because, according to the noncooperative bargaining model, bill failure during the conference process represents a misuse of discretion when the conferees move policy too far from one chamber's preferences. Though failure is rare, it is most likely to occur when a chamber has very diverse preferences and a small coalition, creating uncertainty and little margin for error on the part of the conferees, who in turn propose an unacceptable bill.

Chapter 6 uses characteristics of the winning coalition, such as overall support, majority and minority party support, and ideological extremity, to compare bills on passage to those postconference. In this way, I can determine, indirectly, how bills change as a result of a conference relative to what was originally passed in each chamber. This chapter also connects the theory of postpassage bargaining to existing theories of legislative organization and describes how consistent each is with the theoretical model and with the empirical results. The evidence is clear that bills become more moderate relative to the more extreme chamber but slightly more extreme relative to the more moderate chamber. This result is due to the necessity of giving a share of the benefits to the more extreme chamber and the inability of a majority within the more moderate chamber to change the bill. Though outcomes are more moderate than they would be if the more extreme chamber could dictate its preference, they are not exactly at the more moderate chamber's ideal point.

Amendment trading is analyzed in chapter 7 using a similar technique to compare bills passed in each chamber originally to those passed by each chamber during the amendment trading process. Remarkably, the results look very similar to those for conference committees. Bills passed by extreme winning coalitions become more moderate ideologically, have larger coalitions, and have greater support from both the majority and minority party. Despite the iterative nature of amendment trading, which should produce outcomes nearly identical to the more moderate chamber's preference, policy ends up slightly closer to the extreme chamber as well. Coalition ideology in the more moderate chamber becomes slightly more extreme both after a conference and after amendment trading, suggesting that the winning coalition on passage and voting for the amended bill postpassage are very similar though not identical.

Finally, chapter 8 concludes by discussing the implications of postpassage bargaining for our understanding of theories of legislative organizations, the power of parties on the process, and bill outcomes. The results largely support the framers' intuition about how bicameral bargaining would work and about its "cooling" effects on legislation.

CHAPTER TWO

Postpassage Resolution in Historical and Contemporary Context

Process, Procedures, and Controversies

Virtually all bicameral legislatures require some mechanism of settling their differences prior to legislative enactment. This process differs depending on the institutional context, with some systems providing for formal mechanisms while others use well-established but more informal procedures. In many state legislatures, the situations when a conference committee must be used, the number of members who serve on the committee, and the voting rules within the conference committee are written directly into the legislative procedures of each chamber. The same is not true in Congress, which retains relatively flexible and informal procedures for resolving differences.

A significant number of legislative systems around the world are bicameral, at least in principle. In many of these countries, however, bicameralism does not mean two truly equal chambers like those in the US Congress. Some parliamentary systems, including those in Great Britain and Australia, only allow the second chamber veto rights and reserve proposal rights and the ability to debate and amend legislation to one chamber. Yet, despite the weakness of these second chambers, they can still have a substantial effect on legislative outcomes and the government. Upper chambers, because they typically empower minority coalitions, can serve as a crucial gatekeeper on majoritarian legislation (Bradbury and Crain 2002); the unwillingness of the Australian Senate to pass appropriations legislation led to a constitutional crisis in the country in 1975 (Bach 2003).

Likewise, there is evidence that if the same majority coalition does not control both the upper and lower chambers, then legislative productivity decreases, and the government becomes more likely to fail (Druckman, Martin, and Thies 2005).

Bicameral legislatures in the United States differ from most other countries in important ways. Terms of service for the members of each chamber are fixed (and are different in each chamber), and the executive is not a member of the legislature. There are fewer shared incentives for the winning coalitions in Congress to work together as there is no risk of collapse for the ruling coalition, and in many cases, such as when the chambers are controlled by different parties, the majorities in each work at cross-purposes. Finally, in Congress, unlike the states and many other bicameral systems, representation in the chambers is determined through different mechanisms. As a result of the Great Compromise, the population-based House must negotiate with a chamber based upon the principle of equal representation within different geographic districts (states).

In the following sections, I begin with a brief discussion of the historical evolution of bicameralism in the United States and follow with the unique institutional rules that exist in Congress. The important question, as detailed in the first chapter, is whether bicameralism empowers moderates or extremists, especially in an era of strong parties and an increasingly ineffective Congress. There are concerns that House-Senate differences hinder the ability of the national government to deal with serious issues in a timely manner. Are the roadblocks to lawmaking created by a bicameral legislature worth the trade-off of protecting minority interests, and are the republican goals of the framers served by current congressional processes?

As I will argue, we know very little about how well the bicameral resolution process works in our partisan age. Studies of congressional postpassage resolution continue to rely on the paradigm of what congressional scholars call the "textbook" Congress: the postwar period of congressional development that began with the Legislative Reorganization Act of 1946 and ended with the rise of party polarization in the late 1970s and 1980s. Until we understand how the House and Senate negotiate with each other during the current era of divided government and divided chambers under strong party leadership, rather than through nearly autonomous standing committees, we cannot understand whether our two-chambered legislature is now an antiquated system or whether it continues to ensure informed policy.

A Brief History of Bicameralism in the United States

The framers fully expected the House and Senate to generate different versions of the same bill and that negotiations over the exact language to send to the president would be necessary. The delegates to the Constitutional Convention had experience with this process in their own state legislatures, which themselves borrowed heavily from the British Parliament. The constitutional requirement that only one version of a bill be sent to the president has proven to be a crucial, yet little understood, feature of American lawmaking.

As Peverill Squire (2006) details, the roots of bicameralism can be traced to the structure of the colonial legislatures that took root in the mid-1600s. Nearly all the assemblies at the time quickly developed dual chambers because of two distinct factors. First, much of the structure and many of the procedures in the new legislatures were imported from Parliament. At the time, some members of the state legislatures had been to England and observed the legislative procedures there, informing their view about how a republican body should work. Once a few chambers adopted certain institutional structures based on the British model, similar rules and procedures diffused slowly across the colonies. Though Parliament provided a rough outline of a functioning legislature, the colonists quickly made the assemblies their own by incorporating many different features not seen in Great Britain, largely driven by the geographic and representational challenges present in many of the colonies (Squire 2012).

Bicameralism in Parliament ensured representation for the different social classes, and the House of Lords consisted of members who achieved their appointment through hereditary means (Lijphart 1999). The upper chamber then was not necessarily loyal to the King but instead protected the class interests of the aristocracy as one of three parts of the "classical theory of mixed government" (the other two being the monarchy and the public) (Shell 2001, 7). In the colonies, bicameral differences were based more on policy disagreements as the councilors sought to protect the interests of the appointing royal governors, who in turn represented the Crown on economic issues (Lipset and Lakin 2004; Squire 2012). Because the colonies did not have a long-standing social structure, they lacked an aristocracy with significant political power.

The development of the second chamber has also given rise to the belief that the Senate is, in some ways, the House's better. Even today there is a tendency to refer to the Senate as the "upper chamber," but there is no historical or constitutional justification for this, and it assumes colonial deference to the preferences of the second chamber that never, in fact, existed. Squire (2012) says that the colonists viewed both chambers as equal; he quotes a reply made by the Speaker of the South Carolina Assembly when the governor sent a message addressed to "Mr. Speaker and Gentlemen of the Lower-House of Assembly." The Speaker responded, "The style of Lower-House is by no means applicable to us; it implies, that there is another House in this Colony, dignified with the appellation of Upper-House of Assembly, which we absolutely deny" (25).

When conflict arose over the design of the new federal legislature, bicameralism seemed like an obvious choice. Many of the framers had experience with bicameralism as, by 1787, it had been a fixture in most state legislatures for over one hundred years. Developing a House based on population[1] and a Senate based on geographic representation also provided a convenient solution to simultaneously reconciling the critical divisions between small and large population states and slave and nonslave states (Pope and Treier 2011). By creating a two-chambered legislature based on two different representation rules, the Constitutional Convention won support from a majority of state delegates, even after a vote on a similar proposal had failed only about a month before.[2]

While the Constitution does not prescribe a specific mechanism for Congress to reconcile the chambers' differing versions, the conference committee quickly developed as one of the main vehicles for reaching agreement on legislation. Conference committees then, as now, were ad hoc committees created after the passage of a bill and consisting of members appointed to represent the interests of their parent chamber in negotiations with the other chamber. The conference committee was another development that borrowed heavily from colonial legislatures. John Winthrop discusses a joint committee to resolve differences between the two chambers in 1636 in Massachusetts (Squire 2012, 17), and their common usage within the colony can be traced to 1645 (Volger 1970, 3). They were used in other colonial legislatures as early as the seventeenth century (Longley and Oleszek 1989), and members of the first congresses must have participated in them during their previous roles as members of colonial assemblies. The use of conferences continued in early congresses and became much more common in the years leading up to the Civil War (Volger 1970).

An Overview of the Bicameral Resolution Process

In the 220 years since the First Congress, the body has become increasingly institutionalized (Polsby 1968); members are more professional, career oriented, and educated, and the institution itself has added numerous rules and procedures, undergone significant reforms and reorganization (Adler 2002), and become more reliant on parties and committees to organize legislative activity and increase efficiency (Cox and McCubbins 2005; Weingast and Marshall 1988).

Yet, in many ways, the bicameral resolution process has resisted many of these trends. Today, the majority party seems to have more control over the process, but this control is often indirect, through the appointment of friendly conferees rather than through writing policy. Even prior to the development of the current strong party system, when standing committees had significant discretion over conference outcomes, the parent chamber still had recourse if the conference committee stepped too far out of line. This power was implied and inherent to the process but rarely exercised. In short, resolving differences seems less institutionalized than many aspects of the modern Congress and remains something of an ad hoc process. The postpassage action taken on a bill depends enormously on its content, the degree of ideological alignment between the chambers, and the distribution of preferences within the chambers. Within Congress, resolving differences has not, like many other procedural activities (say, passing rules in the House), become an exact science, and as a result Congress seems to continually tinker with the associated rules and procedures.

Examples of recent changes in postpassage bargaining abound. For example, amendment trading, little mentioned in the historical record and little studied, seems to have become a much more common practice, even for substantively important bills. The House recently changed its rules about modifying conference reports because of its own germaneness requirements and the ability of the Senate to force the House to accept nongermane items. In the other chamber, the Senate has struggled with rules designed to limit the scope of the bargaining, with different rules being adopted in the 106th and 110th Congresses. Finally, the Senate recently changed the process of approving a conference with the House because of a new willingness by the minority to filibuster procedural motions necessary to the postpassage resolution process. None of these changes constitute wholesale revision, but adjustments on the margin, meant to facilitate compromise between the chambers, are frequently made.

The process is more notable for the changes that have not occurred. Congress could have developed standing joint committees with the sole purpose of reconciling differences. Or, alternatively, the chambers could have developed more formal and institutionalized internal procedures dictating the resolution process or the structure of the bicameral give-and-take with their counterparts in the other house. None of these possible reforms have occurred, and, perhaps by necessity, resolving bicameral differences remains a remarkably informal and flexible process.

Because of the weak institutional rules and continued reliance on norms and tradition to develop compromises, political science remains without an overarching theory to explain postpassage reconciliation, and, as a result, it is nearly impossible for observers to predict how Congress will resolve differences for a particular bill (i.e., a conference committee or amendment trading), which bills are likely to fail during the process, and how different institutional factors produce different policy outcomes. Frequently, common beliefs about House-Senate negotiations are folk wisdom; many important claims have not been tested empirically, nor are they supported by evidence.

Modern Resolution Procedures in a Polarized Congress

As previously noted, conference committees in the modern Congress are used most frequently on complicated, salient, or important legislation. Not all important bills go to conference, but nearly all conferences deal with important bills. Conferences offer the chambers efficiency, as members do not have to spend precious floor time reconciling legislation, and they ensure the process is insulated from the whims of the rank and file. On the other hand, the outcomes produced by conference committees are controlled by small groups of legislators who may not represent the broader wishes of their chamber, and can be difficult to predict even for seasoned observers.

The other main resolution mechanism is amendment trading, or what is sometimes called ping-ponging, so named because the two chambers shuttle the bill back and forth, each amending the legislation to move it closer to the other chamber's preferences. Amendment trading has become more prominent in recent years and is thought to reduce deliberation but increase party power. Instead of delegating negotiations to a set of conferees, the party leaders seem to maintain substantial power over the process by controlling the floor and, as a result, the amending process.

Members seem to prefer conference committees, based on recent public statements by senators and representatives advocating for conferences over amendment trading and describing conferences as "regular order" (the procedures that should be normally followed according to the formal rules of the chamber).[3] In 2013, the Democrats actually used the Republicans' obstruction of a budget conference committee as a political talking point. Democratic leader Harry Reid said at the time, "It seems House Republicans don't want to be seen even discussing the possibility of compromise with the Democrats for fear of a Tea Party revolt. They're no longer interested in regular order even though they preached that for years."[4] Whether or not amendment trading confers more power on the leadership is unclear and is a subject taken up in subsequent chapters.

Postpassage resolution can only begin after both chambers have passed an initial version of the legislation. Though bills do not move sequentially through each chamber, the House is the more frequent first mover in recent congresses, probably because in the modern era of polarization and the rise of the implied filibuster, the House simply has an easier time getting things done than the Senate. The sixty-vote threshold required on most substantive bills has slowed legislative action significantly in the Senate, and, with the new willingness by small groups of senators to deploy the filibuster against procedural votes (Theriault 2008), the Senate seems reluctant to take up bills without first receiving a blueprint from the House.

A bill sent to the House or Senate by the other chamber may be considered under regular order by that body or may not be considered at all. In fact, a significant number of bills passed by one chamber are never considered by the other. Many of these bills are passed as position-taking measures for constituents, such as the numerous attempts by House Republicans to repeal the Affordable Care Act between 2011 and 2014, as they were certainly aware that the Democratic-led Senate was not going to act on their legislation. Even during unified government, a significant number of bills passed by one chamber may not be taken up by the other chamber due to time constraints, differences in agenda priorities, or a lack of support for the measure.

In recent congresses, the Senate has been the place where House bills have died, rather than the other way around, because of the difficulty in passing legislation in a closely divided and partisan Senate. The House acts with relative ease if a unified majority exists.[5] When the Democrats had unified control after the election of Barack Obama in 2008 and a huge majority in the chamber, the House was fairly successful at passing much of its wish list, including a bill to combat climate change and single-payer health care legislation, only to see much of its work rejected or be substantially modified by the Senate. Democratic House member Jerrold Nadler said at the time, "There's a lot of anger toward the Senate. We pass a lot of good things, and it goes over there to die."[6] On the other hand, a senior Democratic aide in the Senate characterized the Senate's frustration with the public statements of House members: "It's like none of these guys ever took a civics class, they get to ram stuff down the throats of the minority; we do not. We are as frustrated as they are."[7]

For those bills that are acted upon in the other chamber, most considered minor or nonsubstantive in nature may be passed by the House on the consent calendar or by unanimous consent in the Senate. In these cases, the second-acting chamber does not change any of the language in the bill, and as a result no bicameral negotiating is needed, and the bill is sent directly to the president. Though the received wisdom is that unmodified bills are unimportant bills, sometimes even substantive legislation is passed, unchanged, by the second-acting chamber. I explore this phenomenon in chapter 4 and argue it occurs because the potential benefits from changing the legislation are not worth the extra costs associated with additional negotiations. The passage of the same version of a bill in the second-acting chamber is not necessarily indicative of its importance; there are numerous examples of salient legislation passed in the same form by both chambers.

When either chamber takes up and amends the other chamber's bill, they have a number of options to begin the postpassage resolution process. The chambers can either deal with the amendments individually and begin the process known as amendment trading, or the first-acting chamber can disagree with the amendments made by the second-acting chamber and move to initiate a conference. For example, if the House receives its own bill back from the Senate with amendments, it may concur in those amendments; concur and then add its own additional amendments, which begins the amendment trading process, and send the bill to the Senate; or disagree with the amendments and request a conference (Davis 2014).

Frequently, the Senate and House will begin committee work on an agenda item at the same time, but, in practice, most legislation that eventually becomes law starts in the House and is given an H.R. number before being modified in the Senate (Longley and Oleszek 1989; Rogers 1998;

Strom and Rundquist 1977). In fact, for scheduling reasons, the Senate sometimes takes an entirely different House bill from the Senate calendar and insert its own language. A bill previously received from the House may already be on the calendar, whereas consideration of a different bill reported from Senate committee and with the Senate's version of the text (or the bill of interest most recently passed by the House) may wait on the calendar for a substantial period of time. This often leads the Senate to strike all the language of a different bill previously passed by the House already on the calendar and insert the Senate's version of the text into that bill as a way of creating a shared legislative vehicle on which the House and Senate can negotiate.

When the Senate amends the House bill, typically the Senate Majority Leader, using his right of first recognition, is able to offer an amendment that strikes all the language from the House's version after the enacting clause and inserts the Senate's new language. This version is also subject to additional amendments made on the floor if the requisite Senate majority supports the proposed amendment. Thus, after going to the Senate, the bill is either a somewhat modified version of the bill that passed the House, or it is an entirely new version of the legislation with the Senate's language of the proposed law but with an H.R. number instead of an S. number.

The vehicle for the Affordable Care Act was originally the Service Members Home Ownership Tax Act, which passed 416–0 in the House. Because this bill had already been passed by the House and was already on the Senate calendar, it became the vehicle by which the Senate could consider the health care bill more expeditiously. The Senate pulled that bill off the calendar, inserted its own language, then sent the bill back to the House for debate and final approval.[8]

Going to Conference

Data on the number of bills that go to conference are scarce. Somewhere between 5 percent and 30 percent of all bills are sent to conference, but virtually everything sent to conference is considered "major" or important legislation (Rybicki 2007; Volger 1970), and nearly all appropriations bills are settled in conference as well (Fenno 1966; Volger 1970). The choice by Congress to use conference committees to reconcile differences seems to be a good one as they have traditionally been highly successful in reaching agreement. Approximately 97 percent of measures sent to conference are eventually reported back to both chambers for final approval

(Rybicki 2003). Once the conference report is sent back to the chambers, a take-it-or-leave-it vote is held in both the House and Senate. Amendments are not allowed to the bill at this stage.[9]

The formal rules of selecting conferees vary by chamber, but typically the party leaders consult with committee leaders to select appropriate members. This means that those selected for the conference committee are both majority and minority party members from the relevant standing committee, with members from different committees being appointed if more than one standing committee has jurisdiction over the bill. Members appointed as conferees should be in favor of the bill or at least willing to work toward resolving differences with the other chamber.[10] Occasionally, the Speaker will appoint members from committees that do not have jurisdiction or additional committee members who closely match the Speaker's preferences. This is done to ensure the party leadership's position is represented, in addition to, or instead of, the standing committee's position. Still, the party leadership in each chamber seeks to accord with the rules that require any conferee to be in agreement with the legislation (Krehbiel, Shepsle, and Weingast 1987; Lazarus and Monroe 2007; McQuillan and Ortega 1992).

While the House motion to disagree with the Senate allows the Speaker to appoint conferees of his choosing, the process is more complicated in the Senate. Prior to reforms made early in 2013, there were actually three different motions required in the Senate: a motion to disagree with the House amendments, a motion to request a conference with the House, and a motion to appoint conferees. Like most legislative action in the Senate, each of these three motions was debatable and, as a result, could be filibustered or require the passage of a sixty-vote majority to invoke cloture (see Riddick and Frumin 1992, 449–493, 731–733). Senate norms and institutional comity previously meant these motions were pro forma, but this no longer seems to be true. Walter Oleszek recounts how Republican senators filibustered each of these three motions for a campaign finance bill in 1993 and quotes then Senate Majority Leader George Mitchell as saying, "In the 210 years in the history of the United States Senate, never—until last week—has there been a series of filibusters on taking a bill to conference." Oleszek goes on to say, "By the early 2000s, given an environment of sharper partisan conflict, what had been precedent-shattering to Majority Leader Mitchell in 1994 became a fairly common occurrence in the Senate" (2007, 262).

While "talking" filibusters of conference motions are still rare, cloture votes have become a necessity on many motions to avoid even the threat of a filibuster. As has been well documented in the recent literature, a senator or group of senators need not actually engage in a filibuster to obstruct; because the Senate now suffers from serious time constraints, the threat is just as effective as the practice (Koger 2010). Anecdotally, congressional observers have noted a steep decline in the number of conferences in the last few congresses, and the willingness to threaten a filibuster using procedural motions gets much of the blame; not because the Senate could not overcome the filibusters—after all, the bill was likely passed with sixty votes—but because the time required to invoke cloture makes using a conference extraordinarily costly to the majority. Even senators who approve of the bill and vote for it on passage are less willing to vote for the conference motions, as the party leadership generally expects their caucus to stick together on procedural votes regardless of their feelings about the substance of the legislation (Theriault 2008). In addition, because a cloture motion must "ripen"—once it is filed the Senate must wait an additional full day then wait an additional thirty hours for debate to conclude—being forced to invoke cloture three times could effectively delay or even prevent a conference from occurring if the majority was not willing to make the substantial time commitment required.

As part of the move toward reforming the use (or abuse) of the filibuster threat, the Senate took a number of steps to curb procedural roadblocks in 2013. One of these reforms combined the three separate motions to go to conference into a single motion. This change still allows for a filibuster and requires a sixty-vote threshold to invoke cloture, but it does not require cloture three separate times.[11] In theory, requiring one cloture vote should make the majority more willing to use a conference and, as a result, once again make conferences the more attractive postpassage bargaining venue.

Resolution within Conference

Once the procedural hurdles are overcome the conferees can begin their deliberations. Typically, a particular conferee or set of conferees is authorized to bargain with the other chamber only on specific titles or provisions within the bill, and conferees are limited to the "scope of the differences," meaning only those issues on which the chambers disagreed. This limitation has proven to be unimportant in both practice and theory. I was told by a former member of both chambers that conferees interpret this restriction very loosely. He said, " 'within the scope of the differences' is kind of lip service in the House."[12] Further, if the Senate inserts its own language after the enacting statement, then the scope of the differences effectively includes the entire bill. Legislation that was referred to multiple committees in the House, more common because of an increase in omnibus legislation (Krutz 2000, 2001), may have hundreds of House members on the conference committee, with each set of members bargaining on their jurisdictional slice of the bill. The slate of Senate conferees is typically smaller as there are fewer senators, fewer multiple referrals, and senators generally exercise less jurisdictional control than their House counterparts.

Conferees, once appointed, have nearly total control over the content of the bill. The Speaker does have the ability to replace conferees, and, though replacement is exceedingly rare, it may make conferees more willing to toe the party line. In the Senate, replacing the conferees would be subject to a motion and another vote on the slate of conferees. More common is the practice of instructing conferees. Members of the minority are given the first opportunity to introduce a motion to instruct, which in essence expresses the will of the chamber. However, conferees do not have to follow the instructions, and there is no way for either the House or Senate to enforce their instructions. For this reason, motions to instruct have been viewed as relatively unimportant to the final conference outcome though their frequency raises the question as to why chambers would spend time debating and passing them.

Once a conference is formed and chamber differences are resolved, the compromise bill sent back to both chambers is privileged business and may be dealt with at any time the chamber is not considering other legislation. Along with the bill, the conferees submit a report that outlines the changes made to the bill and may also submit a narrative that explains the reasons behind each change. The formal procedure for reporting a bill out of conference requires that a majority of each chamber's delegation sign the conference report.

The conferees may also submit amendments in disagreement—issues on which the conferees could not reach agreement and which are sent back to the two houses. These outstanding issues must be resolved prior to the passage of the bill, so the chambers will approve the conference report and then begin the amendment trading process on the items that were not resolved in conference. It is not altogether uncommon for amendment trading to occur after conferencing, nor is it uncommon for the chambers to start with amendment trading, realize the differences may be better addressed in conference, and then switch to that venue. This complicates measurement of the frequency of conferences and amendment trading as they are not mutually exclusive. Amendments in disagreement are usually solved by amendment trading after a conference and typically do not pose a significant hurdle to resolving differences.

Crucially, once the bill is returned from conference, the members of each chamber are not allowed to amend the bill to any significant degree. The chamber can either reject the bill outright, pass a concurrent resolution changing parts of the bill that both chambers find unpalatable, or vote to recommit to conference. Rejecting or recommitting legislation after a conference committee is exceedingly rare. Almost anything offered will improve on the status quo for a majority of members because the conferees are selected from among the members who agreed with the first version of the bill passed. In other words, it is unlikely members selected to the conference committee would attempt to sabotage the negotiations or present a bill that moved policy in the opposite direction from the preferences of the chamber coalitions. It is also highly unlikely the majority party leadership would allow conferees to report a bill that does not have the support of a majority of the chamber members. Rejection of a conference bill does happen, however, and understanding why these important bills fail must be included in any theory of postpassage resolution.

The Importance of Conference Committees

Conferences offer a number of advantages over the amendment trading process and traditionally the majority coalitions have preferred to use them, if possible, with amendment trading the venue of last resort. Conferences allow committee chairs and committee members to negotiate on the legislation exclusively, saving the chamber time and energy while allowing the most interested and expert members to bargain with the other chamber on the legislation. In this sense, conference committees, though they are formed only temporarily, operate much like the standing committees in the chamber in that they empower select groups of legislators with jurisdictional preferences. Conferences provide a venue in which these members can work to improve the proposed policy, allowing standing committee members to realize particularized benefits while increasing the overall efficiency of the entire chamber.

Reconciling legislation quickly and efficiently is important for the chambers because initial passage is frequently a complex and difficult process, and forcing the two chambers to resolve their differences through a collective process delays the processing of other legislation. This is especially true in the modern Congress, where the policy agenda exceeds lawmaking capacity, and time has become the major constraint on majority coalitions seeking to build legislative accomplishments (Cox 2006). Conferences bypass the inherent costliness of chamber action by delegating to a small group of legislators who are then able to force the parent body to cast a final, take-it-or-leave-it vote on the compromise bill.

Because of their central role in postpassage bargaining and their larger role within the legislature, conferences have long been the exclusive focus of scholars studying the process. Kenneth Shepsle and Barry Weingast (1987) developed one of the first theories of conference committees by tying their function into larger claims about legislative organization. As the authors note, conference committees had been made up almost exclusively of members of the standing committee, presumably, according to previous analyses, because the chamber as a whole trusted those members to get the best deal for the chamber. Shepsle and Weingast, however, view the committee system as one that allows individual members to deliver particularized goods to their district and enforce logrolling opportunities across the chamber, solving the collective action problems associated with the distribution of individual benefits.[13] Conference committees play a critical role in this process because they allow the conferees—standing committee members—one final chance to ensure their preferences are enacted. The particularized benefits for committee members may be stripped out of a bill during the amending and passage stage, but, by exercising the power to negotiate over the final compromise version of the bill, committee members have the opportunity to restore their lost benefits. This ex post veto ensures the chamber majority will not amend the bill in a way that is unfavorable to the standing committee members. This theory has long been the dominant view of conference committees, but more recently party-based explanations have become prominent. These theories, and a view of conferences as serving the chamber median, are detailed in chapter 5.

The Decline of Conferences?

Despite the scholarly focus on conference committees, they are not always used as the method of reconciliation. In fact, much of the recent commentary on Congress suggests that conferences are being used with less regularity, while amendment trading has become more prominent, used either exclusively or in combination with conferences. This is also true when chambers must reconcile important, complicated legislation. Walter Oleszek of the Congressional Research Service exemplifies this view, saying, "In short, the current reality is that major bills often cannot reach the conference stage, leaving informal negotiations and 'amendments between the houses' as the alternative methods for resolving bicameral differences on major legislation" (2008, 5).

The cause of the decline in conference committees is usually attributed to Senate procedures and polarization. Senate procedures are much more onerous than those of the House and offer greater opportunity for a small group of members to block a conference. When an intense partisan battle occurs over a bill, senators are more willing to forgo unanimous consent and force time-consuming debates and cloture votes. A statement by former Senate parliamentarian Robert Dove reflects this position: "There's no question that amendments between the houses has been used more [today] than it has in the past, but that's because Senators blocking [legislation] from going to conference has happened more often."[14]

The raw number of conferences seems to support the assertion that they are much less frequent than in previous congresses. The 110th Congress (2007–2008) used the conference committee exclusively only sixteen times out of 277 total bills subject to chamber reconciliation. Amazingly, only seven bills went exclusively to conference in the 112th Congress, and only one bill in the 113th Congress went to conference exclusively, though another two bills used both a conference and amendment trading. In the 1970s, conferences were used over one hundred times per congress with regularity.

Figure 2.1 shows the percentage of bills from the 93rd through 113th Congresses that went to conference, amendment trading, both venues, or were passed in the same version by the second-acting chamber, thus not requiring postpassage bargaining.[15] The four categories are mutually exclusive and add to 100 percent, and though not all bills bargained on by the chambers became law, most did. The graph shows clearly that, as a percentage of all bills bargained on, the frequency of conferences has been in approximately linear decline since the 93rd Congress, excepting a brief spike in the 104th Congress when the Republicans took control of the House and Senate for the first time in over fifty years.

There has also been a less dramatic decline in the frequency of amendment trading and a sharp increase in the number of bills that are simply passed by the second-acting chamber and skip postpassage bargaining altogether. Perhaps even amendment trading has become costly, causing

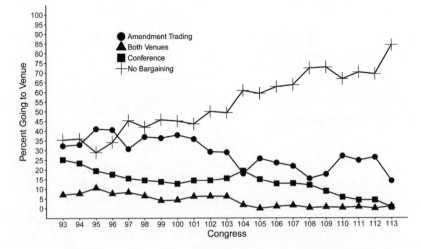

FIGURE 2.1. The frequency of postpassage bargaining venues for all bills passed by both chambers from the 93rd through 113th Congresses. The four categories are mutually exclusive and add to 100 percent.

chambers to more or less accept the proposal of the other chamber so as to avoid having to reconcile legislation. To be sure, many of the bills passed in the same form by both chambers are not substantively important, but the increase in the number of bills that did not go to either resolution venue, especially since the 104th Congress, is surprising.

The claim that polarization, at least indirectly, has decreased the number of conferences can be evaluated by comparing measures of congressional polarization to the frequency of conferences. Figure 2.2 plots the percentage of bills going to conference out of all bills passed by both chambers, along with the distance between the chamber medians as measured by common-space DW-NOMINATE scores (Poole and Rosenthal 1997),[16] the number of moderates in the Senate,[17] and the number of moderates in the House. Aside from a decrease in interchamber distance in the 111th Congress, when Democrats had one term of unified government, each of these measures shows an increase in polarization that corresponds well with a decrease in conferencing. In fact, conferencing is correlated with interchamber distance at −.58, with the number of Senate moderates at .75, and with the number of House moderates at .71. It is also clear that there is little relationship between divided government, when at least one chamber of Congress is controlled by a different party from that

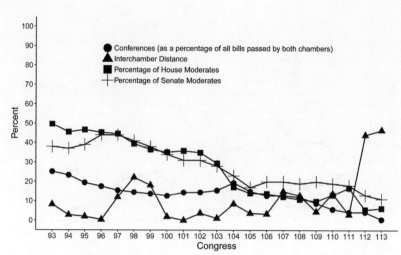

FIGURE 2.2. Conference committees and congressional polarization. Interchamber distance is calculated as the absolute difference from the Senate median to the House median as measured by common-space DW-NOMINATE scores. This score ranges from 0 to 1 and is multiplied by 100 to place it on the same scale as the other measures. House and Senate moderates are defined as members having DW-NOMINATE scores between −.25 and .25.

of the president, and conferencing. That is, the president's party relative to Congress does not seem to have much of a role, as might be expected. The sample is long enough to cover periods of unified and divided government, with little discernible effect on conferencing. The two correlate at only .05. The limitation of analyzing the percentage of bills going to conference with measures of ideological polarization is that, as has been well documented, polarization has been increasing in a nearly linear manner for the past thirty or so years, but it is not clear that the downward trend in conferencing is causally related to polarization or some other factor.

The number of conferences shown so far has included all bills. Yet, most bills passed by Congress are not substantively important and produce only minor policy changes. Further, one of the major claims of many observers has been that conferences are being used with less frequency for the most important pieces of legislation. To evaluate this claim, I use two measures of legislative importance.[18] One is taken from the Congressional Policy Agendas Project[19] and uses the number of article lines written about the bill in the *Congressional Quarterly Almanac* (*CQA*), a reference published at the end of each year. These data extend only to the 111th Congress, but the sample of cases covers all possible bills, though only very important ones receive any coverage. The second measure I use captures the importance of all laws, extending to the 103rd Congress. This measure was developed by Joshua Clinton and John Lapinski (2006) and uses an item-response scaling method to produce a relative value for all laws.

Figure 2.3 shows the percentage of bills going to one of the two resolution venues, going to both venues, or that were not bargained on because the bill was passed in the same form by both chambers. However, it includes only those bills that had at least one line of coverage in *CQA*, representing about 42 percent of all bills that were passed by both chambers. As the data show, there has not been a substantial decline in the number of conferences for noteworthy bills. In fact, there was more conferencing between the 104th and 109th congresses than during the 1970s, at least for important bills. The percentage of important bills resolved in amendment trading also does not seem to be noticeably rising, and there is no dramatic increase in the number of bills not bargained on at all by the chambers as there was when looking at all bills (see figure 2.1).

It is possible that the *CQA* may write about bills going to conference more frequently, though the magazine tends to cover the entire passage process, even before the chambers have used a postpassage bargaining venue, but it is useful to verify these results with additional data. Figure 2.4 shows postpassage resolution actions using only laws that are above

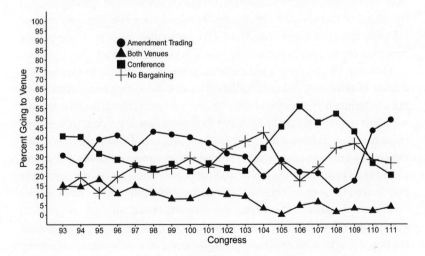

FIGURE 2.3. The frequency of postpassage bargaining venues for bills receiving *CQA* coverage. Only bills that received at least one line of coverage in *CQA* are included.

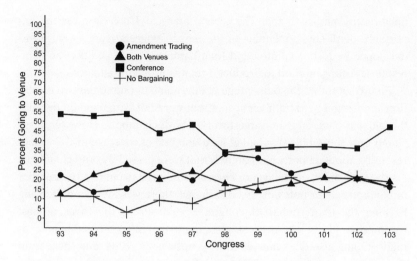

FIGURE 2.4. The frequency of postpassage bargaining venues for important laws. Clinton and Lapinski (2006) identify as "important laws" those that are above average on the Clinton-Lapinski measure of importance. The measure of importance extends only through the 103rd Congress.

average on the Clinton-Lapinski law importance measure. Again, there is no discernible decrease in the number of conference committees from the period 1973–1994. In fact, conferences look to have increased some over the last few congresses, while the use of amendment trading has not increased or decreased substantially. The limitations on this data are important, but, combined with the *CQA* data, they present a compelling case that conferencing is not as rare as it is perceived to be.

How can we reconcile the results from the first two graphs showing the decline in absolute number of conferences with the second two graphs showing no decline for important bills and laws? It seems that Congress is passing fewer important bills or laws and thus requiring fewer conferences, but there has been neither a large decline in conferencing nor a corresponding increase in amendment trading for substantively important bills. For example, in the 111th Congress, there were only nine conferences on important bills, but only forty-two bills were even mentioned by *CQA*. While polarization may be promoting the passage of unimportant bills, it does not seem to explain, at a macro level, the frequency of conferencing or amendment trading. Clearly, a more nuanced explanation of postpassage bargaining is needed, and the question of why some bills go to conference, some to amendment trading, and some to neither venue, is explored in more detail in chapter 4.

The Appropriations Process and Conference Committees

Together, appropriations and authorizations bills comprise most of the legislation related to the overall budgetary process responsible for funding the activities of the federal government on an annual basis. While authorizations are just beginning to receive more attention from congressional scholars and incorporated into larger theories of legislative organization (e.g., Adler and Wilkerson 2012), the appropriations process has historically been seen as one of the most important aspects of congressional committee work. And, as many observers have noted, conference committees have traditionally been the primary mechanism for creating compromise versions of appropriations bills (Fenno 1966).

Most of what we think of as government programs are categorized as discretionary spending and must be periodically reviewed by the standing committees and annually re-funded by the Appropriations Committees.[20] Discretionary spending includes money for the military, many of the programs administered through cabinet-level agencies, such as Education, Agriculture, and Energy, and funding for most other non-cabinet-level agencies and their programs like those in the FBI, EPA, or National Science Foundation. The federal budgeting process is probably the most important—and controversial—legislative activity the president and Congress undertake every year.

Congressional rules require that every program receive an authorization, while the Constitution requires that any money spent must be written into a bill that is enacted into law.[21] The authorization process occurs through the standing committees, which frequently review the programs within their jurisdiction and pass reauthorizing legislation when the program's old authorization expires or when Congress wishes to make significant changes to the programs. The authorization stage is when most policy-oriented substantive changes to government activities are made. For example, the Farm Bill, which reauthorizes agriculture programs and is one of the largest reauthorizations, is typically on a five-year cycle, whereas the Surface Transportation Bill is reauthorized about every two years.[22] Reauthorizations also tend to be controversial, involving negotiations on spending priorities, earmarks, and budgetary limitations, but they are usually passed successfully, and may be reconciled either in a conference or using amendment trading.

Appropriations have historically been less controversial within the chamber, but they can present challenges during the interchamber resolution process (Kiewiet and McCubbins 1991). While authorizations are completed by the standing committees with jurisdiction over the program, appropriations must be completed every year and are exclusively the domain of the Appropriations Committees in each chamber. Regular order involves the passage of approximately twelve (the number has changed slightly over time) appropriations bills that correspond to the twelve appropriations subcommittees in both the House and the Senate. Unlike most committees, the appropriations subcommittees in the House and Senate each have a counterpart in the other chamber with an overlapping jurisdiction.

Conferences have been used to resolve differences on appropriations bills because they provide the likeliest venue for success. Unlike most bills, even reauthorizations, appropriations are truly "must-pass" legislation. If additional spending is not enacted into law, funding for a program or agency will cease and a partial government shutdown will occur. During the Obama and Clinton administrations, the president and at least one chamber of Congress engaged in brinkmanship over appropriations legislation or supplemental appropriations used to temporarily fund a program to cover an annual shortfall. The results were government shutdowns that paralyzed important parts of the federal bureaucracy and had dire political consequences for congressional Republicans and the president.

In fact, Congress in recent years has frequently failed to pass the twelve annual appropriations bills. Instead, they have often passed supplemental or emergency appropriations bills that spend additional money on a program to ensure it does not lapse while negotiations continue on the annual appropriations bill. Congress is also combining appropriations bills into larger omnibus bills, appropriating money for programs across many jurisdictions all at once. For example, between the 110th and 113th Congresses, fewer than ten appropriations bills were passed in three of the four sessions. The exception was the 111th Congress, when a strong Democratic majority passed multiple spending bills to stimulate the economy in the wake of the economic downturn.

Polarization, as usual, is commonly blamed for the decline in appropriations bills. Congress must spend money to fund programs, but recent years have seen stalemates over federal funding, especially for programs implemented by the 2010 health care law. Republican attempts to use the appropriations process to force the defunding of programs making up "Obamacare" led to a shutdown for half a month, and other programs have suffered partial shutdowns as Congress has lurched from one funding crisis to another. The appropriations process has been another victim of unorthodox lawmaking and the decline of regular order, and, as a result, the bicameral resolution process on appropriations may be changing as well.

The centrality of conferences to the appropriations process is noted by Richard Fenno (1966). Conference negotiations over appropriations are the exclusive domain of the chair of the Appropriations Committee or the relevant subcommittee chair, who exercises substantial discretion to modify the legislation in the search for a compromise. Fenno emphasizes the twin goals of appropriators during the conference process: ensure a compromise is reached and fight for the chamber's position. Though the threat of a government shutdown due to an inability to agree on appropriations seems like a more recent phenomenon, its specter loomed large even over appropriations conferences in the 1960s. Wilson (1885), in his study of congressional government, seemed to take a dim view of conference negotiations on appropriations. He characterized the resolutions as "rushed" and "chaotic," "unintelligible" to non–committee members, and suggested that conferences are little more than an elaborate ritual. According to Wilson, "The House rejects the Senate's amendments without hearing them read; the Senate stoutly refuses to yield; a conference ensues, conducted by a committee of three members from each chamber; and a compromise is effected, by such a compounding of disagreeing propositions as gives neither party to quarrel the victory" (157).

Interestingly, there is a perception that, in both the House and Senate, the House acts as the guardian of the federal budget, sometimes provoking strong disagreements with the Senate. According to Fenno, "House members frequently allude to the assumption of the founding fathers that the Senate would be the more conservative of the two chambers. 'If ever there was a bad prediction, it was that one.' 'The House, not the Senate, is the more conservative body.' And, of course, 'the House' means the Appropriations Committee" (1966, 627). This was due in large part to the perception (in both chambers) that senators have less expertise than House members, but because of the informal and more consensual norms present in the Senate it was much easier to logroll and load up bills with special projects. The House viewed these actions as an abuse of the appropriations process and House appropriators saw it as their duty to try to rein in Senate spending, with mixed success. Part of the problem for the House in limiting Senate excesses was that the Senate historically has seemed much more unified on their version of the appropriations bill. Bargaining strength during the appropriations process, according to Fenno, is based on chamber cohesion, of which the Senate seemed to have more because logrolling facilitates the construction of oversize coalitions.

Conferences appear to be fundamental to the appropriations process, a claim supported by the data. Figure 2.5 shows bargaining venues for only

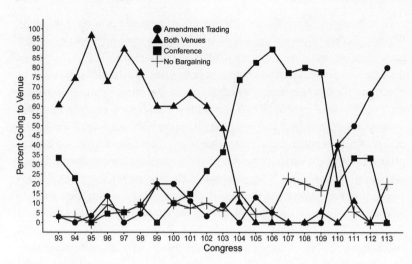

FIGURE 2.5. The frequency of postpassage bargaining venues for appropriations bills.

appropriations bills from the 93rd through 113th Congresses. The data include all appropriations bills, including supplemental and emergency bills, but excludes appropriations that were included in joint resolutions.[23]

Conferences are used for the vast majority of appropriations bills though a large percentage of bills were reconciled using both venues, especially during the 1970s. Many of these bills had only minor changes to be resolved in amendment trading and were likely modified due to the Senate's inclusion of extra spending or nongermane items. The number of bills resolved by a combined conference and amendment trading process began declining in the 104th Congress, but the use of conferences alone rose. Amendment trading, by itself, had not been a prominent bargaining venue until the 110th Congress, while it has become much more common since. Although there is not much evidence that more important bills are reconciled via amendment trading at a higher rate in more recent congresses, there is some support for the claim that the chambers are settling appropriations conflicts outside of the conference committee.

Who Wins in Conference?

Prior to the more recent focus on the role of conferences in theories of legislative organization, research on conference committees consisted of observational work exploring which members served on the conference, how the chamber delegations interacted with each other, and the performance of each coalition's conference delegation. In fact, the question of "Who wins?" in conference has been the defining theoretical motivation for studying bicameral bargaining and remains the focus of most work on postpassage bargaining. The question is a natural one given that most scholars seem to view House-Senate negotiations as a noncooperative bargaining process, even if scholars have not traditionally used this language.[24] Like formalized conceptions of noncooperative bargaining, past research examining which chamber "wins" assumes that a majority of both the House and Senate seek to achieve a legislative compromise and prefer the policy passed in their chamber to the policy passed in the other chamber and that, during negotiations, the conferees seek to protect their own chamber's policy.

As early as 1966, Fenno asserted, "The central question of conference committee decision-making is, 'Who Wins?' It must be answered before the other important questions of 'how' and 'why' can be broached" (611). The "Who wins?" question is so important because understanding which chamber majority's preferences are enacted speaks directly to the nature of policy outcomes, and the set of conditions that produce more powerful bargainers during negotiations. In the context of budgetary bargaining, understanding "who wins" has important implications for the funding and enforcement of federal programs and policies through the appropriations process. And, as the first chapter discusses, understanding "who wins" is crucial for determining whether or not American bicameralism systematically shapes policy outcomes in the way the framers intended. For example, the Senate may not be the "cooling saucer" the framers wanted if the House consistently wins in conference. Likewise, even if the Senate does win consistently, outcomes may not be moderated if the Senate is the more extreme chamber, as many scholars claimed in the 1960s and 1970s when the Senate seemed to take more liberal ideological positions and pursue federal spending more aggressively (Fenno 1966; Kernell 1973).

Though some early work used detailed case studies of a few conference committees to determine a winner, the typical approach to answering the question has been to compare the amounts requested in appropriations bills by the House and Senate and determine which proposal the final bill was closer to after conference. Using appropriations bills has an important advantage over using other types of bills when determining which chamber is more successful. Because the bills contain discrete dollar values, the difference between the proposed and enacted amount can be calculated empirically, avoiding the problem of interpreting legislative language as being closer to the House's or Senate's version. Gilbert Steiner (1951) conducted one of the first in-depth studies of conferences, and, typical of the case study approach, he examined the interaction of personalities and politics on a variety of bills in different policy areas between 1928 and 1948, leading him to conclude that the House wins more often than the Senate. More recent work typifies the empirical approach of comparing proposed and enacted spending, albeit with limited samples, and generally concludes the Senate does better in conference (Fenno 1966). In his study of the appropriations process, Fenno (1966) finds that the chamber favoring higher spending wins more frequently, an outcome that favored the Senate during the postwar era because of its willingness to distribute pork to members.

Any conclusions about the Senate winning more than the House are tentative at best, and the empirical approach of comparing each chamber's requests with the enacted budget has largely been discarded due to a number of limitations. Most prominently, the proposed amounts made by chambers likely do not reflect their true preferences. Losing some money on one line item for more spending on another line item might be a trade-off a chamber is willing to make if the second area is more important to the majority. There is evidence that appropriations bills contain many different policy components, and hence are multidimensional (Crespin and Rohde 2010). Chamber coalitions may "overask" prior to negotiations knowing they will need to accept some sort of cuts, as suggested by Wilson (1885) in the quote above. If a chamber's true preference is to increase spending from $10 million to $50 million, it may ask for an increase of $100 million, knowing that this amount is likely to produce a compromise at $50 million, exactly what the majority's preferences are, but observationally appearing as a loss. Strategic offers and counteroffers are an integral part of any bargaining process but cannot be captured by simply comparing amounts. Finally, the empirical analysis necessarily limits the sample to legislation with clearly stated monetary amounts and does not allow for the examination of bills without spending, which may still be important.

Setting aside these objections about the success of the dollar comparison approach, it provides little theoretical context. If the Senate is more successful, it is not at all clear why this should be the case. Fenno (1966) suggests the Senate may win because the conferees are closer to the parent body than House members, as a function of greater agreement in the Senate on spending. On the other hand, David Volger (1970) points out that members of the House are more specialized in that they serve on fewer committees, tend to have more expertise in their policy area than senators who, because of their lower number, are spread across multiple policy areas and committees, and have greater time demands on their service. Neither is a satisfactory explanation of bargaining strength in conference, and neither explanation accounts for changes to chamber rules and changes across time. Are the bargaining dynamics the same when the chambers are controlled by different parties, as they frequently are in recent congresses but were not during the 1950s, 1960s, and 1970s? With respect to chamber ideology, does a committed chamber defending a more extreme position prevail over a chamber that has weaker preferences and prefers policy closer to the status quo? And, is the winning chamber able to pull policy toward or away from the status quo? Even if it was clear which chamber did better in conference, there is no coherent theoretical story to explain the causes of strength or weakness or to incorporate these characteristics into the bargaining process writ large.

Postpassage Bargaining in a Changing Congress

Not only are the theoretical and empirical underpinnings of postpassage bargaining weak, most of our current understanding is based on the "textbook" Congress (Shepsle 1989), the period when congressional research came of age, loosely characterized as beginning in the postwar era and continuing through the late 1970s or 1980s.[25] In the textbook Congress, postpassage resolution is characterized by strong committees, the leadership role of committee chairmen, the weakness of the party leadership, and the adherence to conventional rules, or regular order (Shepsle and Weingast 1994). Fenno (1966) characterizes the party leadership as doing little more than "prodding" appropriators on conference committees when time ran short. The ex post veto theory developed by Shepsle and Weingast is the canonical work on postpassage bargaining in this tradition, but in many ways Congress is no longer an institution that relies on autonomous committees to develop legislation and shepherd it through the bicameral resolution process.

More recent congresses are far more partisan, and there is far more conflict both between and within the chambers. There has been a steep decline in the use of regular procedures, a dramatic increase in the use of closed rules in the House, and a dramatic rise in the role of the party leadership in the development of legislation (Aldrich and Rohde 1997; Sinclair 1994, 1997). Today, it is difficult to imagine the party leadership giving committee chairs carte blanche to produce legislation or distribute pork. Important bills are still developed in committees but with the guidance of the party and with an eye toward negotiations with the other chamber and the other party. Even the appropriations process, long considered one of the most consensual and least partisan congressional venues has become an important tool used by the party to achieve policy goals (Kiewiet and McCubbins 1991).

The potential reasons for congressional polarization are myriad and include geographic sorting (Abramowitz, Alexander, and Gunning 2006; Brewer, Mariani, and Stonecash 2002), the greater salience of social issues (Layman and Carsey 2002; Layman, Carsey, and Horowitz 2006), the collapse of the New Deal Coalition and increasing conservatism in the South (Jacobson 2000; Rohde 1991; Theriault 2008), the larger role of primary campaigns and the need for campaign funds (Fiorina, Abrams, and Pope 2005; Brady, Han, and Pope 2007; Burden 2001; Sinclair 2006), and increasing income inequality (McCarty, Poole, and Rosenthal 2006). Whatever the causes, the consequences for Congress and the legislative process are clear. Southern Democrats, who served as the bridge between the more liberal Northeastern Democrats and Republicans, have nearly disappeared. Congressional Republicans, marginalized during much of the New Deal postwar time frame, have now developed into a strong, cohesive party that is frequently in the majority, especially in the House, promoting intense two-party competition.

Congressional polarization has caused a decline in legislative productivity with each successive congressional term, as a result of obstructionist tactics. Once limited by chamber comity and norms, blocking bills through procedural tactics, especially in the Senate, has become accepted practice. The decline in regular order and legislative productivity has taken bicameral research from questions of "Who wins?" to understanding the types of legislation produced by the interchamber bargaining process. As Shepsle and Weingast (1987) show, legislation may reflect the priorities of preference outliers (committee members), due to the power of the procedural rules that govern bills returned from conference. Alternatively, given the majoritarian nature of congressional chambers, even legislation that goes to conference should converge to the median as predicted by median voter theory. After all, the median could reject the revised bill outright,[26] recommit the legislation to conference, remove the conferees and appoint new ones, or use amendment trading (Krehbiel, Shepsle, and Weingast 1987).

New work emphasizes that conference outcomes may reflect the preferences of the majority party rather than the preferences of the standing committee or the median. The conditional party government thesis predicts that, under conditions of ideologically coherent parties, leaders will accept responsibility for the crafting and passage of legislation. A significant amount of literature has sought to determine whether party influence exists in conference committees, usually through the analysis of conference committee membership. Despite the standing committees apparently having control over conferences, there is evidence that loyal party members are likely to be appointed to conferences, presumably to represent the party during the bargaining process (Lazarus and Monroe 2007; Vander Wielen and Smith 2011). Whether this translates into differences in policy outcomes is unclear, though the rules, combined with favorable conference membership, empower parties to produce nonmedian outcomes (Ryan 2014; Vander Wielen 2010).

Moving Toward a Comprehensive Theory of Interchamber Bargaining

Postpassage resolution is fundamental to the legislative process yet remains poorly understood. And, as has been shown, conferences are not the only mechanism through which the chambers resolve their differences. In this book, I create a comprehensive theory of postpassage bargaining that builds upon previous research but that encompasses both conferencing and amendment trading, as well as the decision by a chamber to forgo changes to the bill. The decision to use a conference committee or forgo it in favor of amendment trading is not well understood, nor is the decision to bypass bargaining altogether. It is critical that the theory offer an explanation of how policy is developed when the House and Senate seek compromise. In doing so, the theory can answer the "Who wins?" question and, more importantly, address whether policy outcomes reflect the preferences of the median, the party, the committee, or some other set of actors. Understanding these outcomes will inform theories of legislative organization and place postpassage bargaining squarely within other scholarly work on congressional procedures and outcomes.

CHAPTER THREE

A Bargaining Theory of Postpassage Resolution

Most research on bicameralism confirms the conventional wisdom and the framers' beliefs: in general, bills are more likely to fail as compared to legislation in unicameral systems. Though bicameralism makes policy agreement more difficult, this tells us little about how policy changes as a result of the negotiations between the chambers. Understanding both the resolution process and, more generally, how bicameralism affects lawmaking and policy outcomes requires a theory of how the House and the Senate compromise with each other. The theory should accomplish three goals. First, it needs to encompass all legislation passed by the chambers rather than limiting itself to an arbitrary definition of important or controversial legislation. Generally, only the most important bills go to conference, but many types of bills are resolved using amendment trading, and some bills, even those identified as important or meaningful by congressional observers, skip the postpassage bargaining process because the chambers simply agree during initial passage. The choice by the coalitions in each chamber to *not* use postpassage bargaining is itself an important strategic consideration. Excluding legislation not resolved in conference introduces selection bias because the strategic choice to use a conference committee is correlated with the policy outcomes produced when the chambers resolve their differences. By ignoring some types of bills, especially ones that do not go to postpassage bargaining or to a conference, an important part of the story would be missed.

Second, the theory must explain legislative failures as well as successes. The fundamental tension in the American political system is between its republican institutional design intended to respond to public policy demands while also privileging the status quo and promoting policy stability. Those bills that are not enacted despite passage by both the House and Senate are the most obvious examples of how bicameralism and the necessities of interchamber bargaining affect policy outcomes; when the chambers fail to agree, the status quo policy remains (a status quo that both chambers would apparently like to change).

Finally, the theory should be able to explain each procedural mechanism the House and Senate use to resolve their differences. Observers of Congress are familiar with the conference committee, the traditional method used to resolve important bills, but in recent congresses a different process— amendment trading—has become more common, even for important legislation (e.g., the 2010 Affordable Care Act, which was passed using amendment trading).

A Bicameral Bargaining Theoretical Framework

The standard approach when studying the relationship between different ideological actors in Congress and the approval of laws is to use a one-dimensional spatial model. These models have a rich history in economics and political science and have been used to model legislative outcomes in a variety of institutional contexts (Black 1948; Black et al. 1958; Downs 1957; Krehbiel 1998; Tsebelis 2002). While they have some important advantages, spatial models present significant limitations when seeking to understand postpassage bargaining. Bargaining occurs across multiple dimensions and, as already discussed, involves situations where both political actors have strong incentives to reach agreement and both benefit from a successful compromise. Spatial models, however, tend to view outcomes as zero-sum, where one player loses in direct proportion to the other player's gains. Finally, spatial models do an excellent job of defining the range of *possible* outcomes as a function of ideological preferences but are not as helpful in more precisely characterizing the final outcome as a result of other factors that affect bargaining, including the costs imposed by negotiating, the structure of institutional rules, and the ability of actors to trade policies across dimensions.

For these reasons, I borrow insights from noncooperative bargaining theory to develop an understanding of postpassage bargaining. Bargaining theory is frequently used in economics and political science to understand how negotiations between individuals or groups produce shared outcomes. These types of models are used to understand the relationship, for example, between a car dealer and a prospective buyer or between two countries on the brink of war (Fearon 1995). The noncooperative bargaining model[1] is appropriate when at least two actors try to reach some mutually agreeable compromise, and both try to maximize their shares of the benefits (Rubenstein 1982). For example, both the car dealer and buyer have a mutually beneficial interest: the dealer wants to sell the car and the buyer wants to purchase it, and if the two can agree on the price, components, loan terms, and other important factors, then both are left better off by a deal. However, each also has different interests: the dealer wants to sell the car for as much as possible, while the buyer wants to spend as little as possible. Bargaining may break down because, even though negotiators agree on the outcome, they disagree on how to achieve that outcome.

The key component of the bargaining model is that both actors receive a benefit from reaching an agreement. Since we are interested in the bargaining process between the House and Senate, we must exclude situations in which the chambers have opposing interests. Suppose that the Senate, controlled by Democrats, passes a bill to increase the minimum wage from $7.25 to $10.00 an hour (just such a situation occurred in the 113th Congress, when President Obama proposed and congressional Democrats supported a minimum wage increase to $10.10). Now suppose the House, controlled by Republicans, prefers to reduce the minimum wage from $7.25 to $5.00 an hour. Because Democrats want to increase the minimum wage and Republicans want to decrease it, no mutually agreeable solution leaves both parties better off than they are with the status quo policy. If another policy dimension were added to the process, where the chambers were bargaining over minimum wage and taxes on the wealthy at the same time, then Democrats might consider a small reduction in the minimum wage for a large increase in taxes on the wealthy (and vice versa for Republicans). If the overall benefits for both actors are positive, then the agreement is mutually beneficial, even if one actor does worse on one particular component of the compromise.

Situations—like the minimum wage example where neither bargainer realizes positive benefits—often occur and do not, under the definition used here, qualify as bargaining situations. With respect to the House and the Senate, if there is no agreement that leaves *both* coalitions better off than they were with the status quo, then they are not engaging in noncooperative bargaining. This is identical to saying that in a single-dimensional policy space the pivotal actors in both winning coalitions are on opposite sides of the status quo. Any movement from the status quo to the House's ideal point results in a utility loss for the Senate, and vice versa. The consequence is stalemate and the eventual failure of the bill.

But, when both the House and Senate agree that the minimum wage should be raised, the question is then which of the two receives policy closer to its preference, and why? While negotiating over the specific point at which the minimum wage should be raised seems trivial, this definition of a bargaining situation provides a context for much more complicated and substantively important legislation, including those bills which contain multiple issues. In 2009 and 2010 the Democratic House and Democratic Senate agreed that some change to the health care system was preferable to the status quo but disagreed about what that change should look like. Would it be a single-payer system (as the House majority seemed to prefer) or a market-based system? To take another example, there was political support in 1981 in both the Democratic-controlled House and Republican-controlled Senate for some sort of tax cut, but members from both sides argued over what would be included in the tax cut and how significantly it would change the tax code. On issues like tax cuts and health care policy there are, effectively, an infinite number of possible new policies and an infinite number of possible dimensions on which the chambers can bargain.

The use of this bargaining theoretical framework also provides the means to analyze other questions. Most significantly, if the House and Senate seem to agree on how to change policy, why do they sometimes fail to reach agreement? Accounts of why bargaining breaks down emphasize the role of commitment strategies, imperfect information, an unwillingness on the part of one actor to concede to the other (resoluteness), and the costliness (in that bargaining is not frictionless) of negotiating (Morrow 1989, 1992; Reiter 2004). As Elizabeth Rybicki (2007) says about the congressional bargaining process specifically, "the threat of failure is an inherent element of bicameral negotiations" (2) because the House and Senate try to maximize their respective benefits from the eventual compromise. Likewise, Oleszek (2007) characterizes the risk of failure during conference committees as important to the process. He describes the three difficult and competing "objectives" conferees undertake: sustain the position of their respective chamber on the bill, find a compromise the chamber will accept, and find a compromise acceptable to the other chamber and the president (270).

That the tactics of the coalitions, parties, and conferees should produce failure even in cases when there is bicameral agreement is not surprising to most observers of Congress, but the claim seems logically intractable. Any compromise bill, with *any* provisions on which both winning coalitions agree, makes the members in both chambers better off than the status quo. Any aspect of a bill on which there is no possible compromise could be dropped from the legislation, allowing the coalitions to secure the gains from only those matters on which they agree.

Consider the 2006 Lobbying Accountability and Transparency Act. Though the House and Senate could not agree on limits to 527 organizations, why would the House refuse to strip the provision from its version of the bill? If the Senate would not pass the legislation with that provision, the House and Senate would have both been better off passing a bill without the offending language in order to receive benefits for all the aspects of the bill on which the chambers did agree, language that constituted the vast majority of the bill. When a bill fails because of a disputed provision or set of provisions, neither chamber receives any benefits from the other legislative components on which compromise is possible, and both suffer costs from using time, energy, and political capital on legislation that fails to become law.

For other provisions, where disagreements exist between the chambers, heated rhetoric, bluffing, and attempts to commit to preferred policies are all standard tactics, but, given the choice between failure and compromise, agreement should always win out. The fact that postpassage bargaining failure is ever observed is a theoretical puzzle, especially for large, complicated, or important legislation where the chambers have strong incentives to reach a compromise. But one of the central puzzles noncooperative bargaining models are able to address is why compromise sometimes does not occur, despite both actors' incentives to reach an agreement.

Noncooperative Bargaining Theory and Postpassage Resolution in Congress

To answer these important questions about policy outcomes and failure, I develop a noncooperative bargaining theory of the House-Senate resolution process. The theory, like all explanations of empirical phenomena, is a simplification of the real world, but it incorporates many of the possible factors that affect interchamber negotiations. It also develops explicit assumptions and, most importantly, creates a tractable, encompassing theoretical framework through which to study postpassage bargaining, allowing for an evaluation of the important factors that affect policy outcomes, while developing clear implications for empirical testing.

The two relevant players of the bargaining game are the majority coalitions in each chamber. In the modern Congress, the majority coalitions are usually party based, where members of the majority constitute a stable, durable coalition, and where the party leadership coordinates members, solves collective action problems, and passes legislation that benefits the party (Aldrich 1995; Rohde 1991), though, notably, assuming that parties have independent effects on member behavior is not a necessary condition for the theory. Instead, the theory requires only that the members who support and pass the first version of the bill within a chamber also engage in bargaining over the bill. This is true in Congress due to the institutional rules that allow the legislative majority to appoint conferees and manage the bill on the floor during amendment trading. The theory assumes that each chamber seeks to protect its own preferences and works to resolve differences with the other chamber rather than intentionally sabotaging the bill. Rather than conceiving of the bargaining players as the entire coalition, the relevant players may also be conceptualized as the pivotal actor in each chamber (i.e., the House median and Senate median or filibuster pivot) or some nonpivotal actor like the party median or party leadership (Ryan 2014). In any case, each coalition attempts to garner a larger share of the total benefits available from the bargain.[2]

The bargaining theory also requires a characterization of the level of information each bargainer has about the other's preference. Returning to the car buying example, both the buyer and the dealer have incentives to misrepresent their actual preference, and each bargainer is uncertain what exact offer the other will accept. The dealer may be willing to sell the car for $10,000 but, wishing to sell it for more, may claim $12,000 is the lowest acceptable offer. A similar condition exists in most bargaining situations, including House-Senate negotiations. Neither knows exactly what the other coalition will accept, so each tries to make a specific demand. If the House, for example, sets its demand too low, the Senate will accept, but the House could have done better had it asked for more concessions. On the other hand, if the House sets its demand too high, it may not be able to reach agreement with the Senate, and neither will receive the benefits of the compromise. Therefore, I characterize the House and Senate as negotiating with uncertainty, where one coalition has incomplete information about the other's preferences, making each unsure as to the exact policy the other will accept.

Defining Bargaining Situations

As explained above, the theoretical framework applies only to situations in which both bargainers are mutually better off when agreement is reached consistent with the House-Senate resolution process after each chamber has passed its own version of a bill. Both agree, by entering into the bargaining process, that a policy exists that will leave each coalition better off than they are with the status quo; each, however, also wants the final bill to more closely resemble its own preferences and, so, attempts to reach an agreement that provides it a larger share of the benefits.[3]

Chamber majorities sometimes pass bills with the intent of making a political statement or position taking rather than engaging in bargaining. For a prominent example, consider that after the passage of the Affordable Care Act Republican majorities in the House and then later in the Senate (beginning with the 114th Congress) took dozens of votes to repeal the law, despite knowing that President Obama would veto any repeal bill.[4] Addressing this type of behavior is an empirical rather than theoretical problem as it requires sorting out the passage of symbolic bills from bills the coalitions actually want to resolve. Fortunately, in nearly all cases of purely symbolic passage, the second-acting chamber will simply ignore the bill (as is the case for a large number of bills every congress). Bargaining requires resources, and the members in each chamber will be reluctant to waste precious floor time and energy passing legislation that has little chance of being sent to the president or signed into law (Ryan 2018). If the House knows the Senate will never agree to the provisions in the bill, it may pass the bill to score political points, but the Senate will not take up the legislation.[5]

Furthermore, ample evidence exists that individual members and the winning coalitions go into the postpassage bargaining process with the intention of reaching agreement on the bill (Longley and Oleszek 1989). That is, most postpassage bargaining, especially when conferences are used, are legitimate attempts to find an acceptable compromise. Almost all legislation passed in different forms by *both* chambers has some postpassage action taken on it—bills are usually either sent to a conference committee or amended at least once using the amendment trading or ping-ponging process. These actions require an even greater cost to the coalitions, investments that would be meaningless were there no realistic hope of reconciling differences. Bargaining situations are limited to those instances in which coalitions act, in good faith, to enact policy change by cooperating with the other chamber. As described below, members of the winning coalitions must receive some benefit from passing legislation, which is added to the utility each receives from the status quo. Empirically, as described in chapter 4, I define bargaining situations as those in which both chambers pass some version of the same bill with the intention of resolving their differences.

Disagreement Benefits

The fundamental insights generated by the noncooperative bargaining model are that the winning coalitions in each chamber receive benefits both from reaching agreement and from disagreement and that the process of resolving differences is costly. Because a mutually beneficial compromise exists in any bargaining situation, compromise is always *possible*, but it may not be reached because the costs of finding an agreement outweigh the benefits that would be received. As a result, the winning coalitions in the House and Senate weigh each of these competing factors when deciding whether to accept or reject an offer.

The measurement of disagreement benefits is described in subsequent chapters, but these are conceptualized as electoral payoffs to members for not supporting a bill; payoffs might come from position taking (i.e., members can claim to their constituents to have stood their ground), increased campaign support from an interest group opposed to the legislation, or some other shared resource. Given that members of Congress seek reelection as a primary goal (Mayhew 1974), most members experience a tension between pursuing collective action in the form of policymaking and satisfying constituent demands. This is certainly not true for all members all of the time, but there is substantial evidence that senators and representatives seek to strike a balance between partisan or collective action and individual concerns (Arnold 1990). There is a trade-off between the two in that more ideologically extreme members see reduced vote shares (Arnold 1990) and moderate members are more likely to vote against their party or be cross-pressured, receiving conflicting signals from different constituent groups. As a result, moderate types derive benefits from opposing bills supported by the majority or even switching their vote as the bill changes from passage to the compromise version developed in the postpassage bargaining process. Previous research also shows that these members are more likely to have diverse constituencies and moderate their voting behavior or partisanship or risk losing constituent support (Ansolabehere and Jones 2010; Canes-Wrone, Brady, and Cogan 2002; Carson et al. 2010; Kirkland 2014). There is also evidence, for example, that cross-pressured members take significantly fewer positions on roll-call votes than other members (Jones 2003). On the whole, winning coalitions with higher benefits from disagreement are *resolute* and more likely to reject an offer, while winning coalitions with lower benefits from disagreement are *irresolute* and more likely to accept an offer.

Allowing the winning coalitions to receive benefits from disagreement serves two purposes. First, it puts an important constraint on offers made by one coalition during the bargaining process. As I will discuss in more detail, if members in the winning coalition receive low benefits from disagreement, the coalition will offer a more modest proposal in order to induce acceptance by the other coalition. If it receives high benefits from disagreement, it can make a more aggressive offer because it still receives substantial benefits even if the other coalition rejects the offer and the two chambers do not agree on policy change. In this way, unreasonable offers are punished, providing an incentive for the offering chamber to act in good faith and make a reasonable proposal that might be accepted by the other chamber. Receiving a benefit from disagreement also ensures that the choice between accepting or rejecting a policy offer by the other coalition is nontrivial. If disagreement yielded no benefit, then any policy offered by one chamber would be accepted by the other; there would be no real risk of failure, and any amount of benefits greater than zero would produce immediate acceptance by a coalition.

The Costs of Bargaining

Besides benefits from disagreement, the costliness of the postpassage bargaining process reduces the relative value of the benefits from agreement or disagreement, which creates specific incentives for each of the negotiating chambers. As explained below, the theory suggests that one coalition makes a policy offer to the other at the passage stage. Because the chambers incur costs if they do not agree at initial passage, the offering chamber must make a reasonable proposal or pay costs associated with resolving differences and risk disagreement during the postpassage bargaining process. The chamber that receives the policy offer must carefully consider accepting or rejecting this policy; rejection may allow it to receive a larger share of the benefits during postpassage bargaining, but it is also costly to engage in additional bargaining, which negatively affects the overall gains from enactment.

If a chamber majority were able to reject an initial offer without incurring costs in the future, the coalition considering the offer would always be willing to forgo the first offer in the hopes of receiving something better in the subsequent round. The costliness of conferencing or amendment trading makes postpassage bargaining inefficient and presents a substantive dilemma for coalitions that is present in many bargaining situations: accept the current offer and end the bargaining process or reject it and expend more time and energy negotiating for a better deal. Postpassage bargaining is inefficient ex post; chambers engage in postpassage bargaining as means to an end, not an end itself, and they prefer to reach a deal sooner rather than later (Fearon 1995; Powell 1996, 1999).

Costs are conceptualized as arising from two distinct mechanisms. The first is the opportunity cost associated with additional action on a bill. For both conferencing and amendment trading the winning coalitions are required to set aside additional floor time and must devote attention and energy to the bill, which limits the collective resources devoted to other bills (Adler and Wilkerson 2007; Cox 2000, 2006; Cox, Kousser, and McCubbins 2010; Den Hartog and Monroe 2011; Wawro and Schickler 2004, 2006). These costs are especially acute in the Senate (Koger 2010; Smith and Flathman 1989), where the majority attempts to use procedures to speed up action and decrease opportunities for obstruction (Smith, Ostrander, and Pope 2013), and may be exacerbated when differences between the chambers are large and they are highly committed to their legislative preferences. Additional bargaining on legislation also requires party leaders to lobby and cajole recalcitrant members to support the legislation in question (Lebo, McGlynn, and Koger 2007). Some conference committees take weeks or months to resolve issues, while others are unable to reach agreement at all. Amendment trading involves significant effort to ensure passage on the floor and can require numerous votes on motions, amendments, and passage.

The second source of costs in the resolution process is the expenditure of inducements or goods by the majority party or winning coalition to keep members in line, such as promises of particularized benefits to a member's district or PAC money (Cann 2008; Jenkins and Monroe 2012; Snyder and Groseclose 2000). These payments are costly to the leadership, however, and each subsequent round of bargaining requires the distribution of additional benefits. Some compromises may result in the defection of certain members unless paid off by the leadership.[6]

The specific costs of amendment trading and conferencing differ. While conferencing does not take up much floor time because the bargaining is delegated to a set of conferees, it requires the actors in each chamber to pay procedural or monitoring costs. Conferees have the ability to propose a take-it-or-leave-it offer to the chamber, a powerful tool that may result in agency loss to the parent chamber (Krehbiel, Shepsle, and Weingast 1987; Shepsle and Weingast 1987, 1989). This loss may encourage the use of amendment trading as a way of circumventing uncooperative conferees by denying them the power to exercise an ex post veto (Krehbiel, Shepsle, and Weingast 1987). Using a conference is also more procedurally difficult than using amendment trading, especially in the Senate. Indeed, this claim seems to be supported by the Senate rules changes made in 2013 that reduced the number of necessary motions from three to one, which the Senate majority hoped would produce more conferences. Jeff Merkley, a Democrat from Oregon, emphasized this point when he said, "It should be easy to get to conference. Filibustering the path to conference is just a pure, pointless form of paralysis."[7]

When amendment trading is used as the reconciliation venue, the winning coalitions must allocate floor time to resolve their differences and lack the power to make take-it-or-leave-it offers to the members. During this process, each chamber sequentially passes amendments designed to bring the bill closer to the other chamber's version. It is usually coordinated by committee members or the party leadership, but the rules generally follow regular procedures, as amendments can be offered, and any amendment can itself be amended, which allows members to introduce "poison pill" amendments, making the process substantially more difficult and time consuming (Jenkins and Munger 2003; Wilkerson 1999).

These costs affect the overall utility that coalitions receive from agreement or disagreement and can make coalitions more or less resolute. Simply by using postpassage bargaining, the two chamber majorities must consider the ratio of costs to benefits from reaching agreement and from the additional resources required and opportunity costs imposed. If a coalition has very high costs of postpassage bargaining, it will prefer to avoid both venues and strike a deal as quickly and easily as possible or to make a very accommodating offer that will be accepted by the other coalition, avoiding postpassage bargaining altogether.

I conceptualize disagreement values and the costs of agreement as independent of how each coalition values the status quo. By definition a bargaining situation must contain some outcome that makes both parties better off; thus, the status quo alone can never drive bargaining failure. The theory developed here and the empirical methods employed to test it focus on the costs of resolution, the benefits received from disagreement (separate from the status quo), and the benefits received from agreement. If one coalition receives more benefits from the status quo as compared to the proposed policy, the coalition will reject the compromise as it offers no mutually beneficial division of benefits. By assuming that a mutually beneficial agreement exists, the theory and the empirics focus on disagreement benefits as a function of the costs of bargaining instead of the value that each coalitions receives from the status quo, which is unchanged by how difficult it is for the chambers to resolve their differences.

The Postpassage Bargaining Sequence

The postpassage bargaining process takes place between two actors, defined here as chambers 1 and 2, which dispute the division of benefits accrued from agreeing on legislation.[8] The total amount of the benefits can arbitrarily be defined as worth *one*, and, though both chambers are better off by any division of the benefits, the larger the share one chamber receives, the smaller the other receives, consistent with the give-and-take of negotiations. For example, if the final bill reflects the Senate's policy preferences, then the benefits the majority coalition in the Senate receives are greater, while the share the House receives is smaller.[9] Note, however, that bargaining is not zero-sum in that both chambers must receive some share of the benefits.

In the first stage of bargaining, chamber 1 proposes a division of the total benefits available, b, to chamber 2. Chamber 1 can pass legislation that exactly matches its preferences so it receives the entire share of the benefits (one); it can pass a legislative compromise that exactly matches what chamber 2 wants, such that chamber 1 receives zero; or it can pass a bill that divides b between zero and one. Once the division is proposed through passage in chamber 1, chamber 2 can accept the offer and receive benefits equal to $1 - b$, or chamber 2 can reject the offer and allow chamber 1 to select a bargaining venue. Substantively, if chamber 2 accepts the legislative offer, the bill is passed by that chamber—as is and without amendment— and is sent directly to the president. Of course, chamber 2 can reject the initial offer, engage in postpassage bargaining, and hope to receive a better outcome, but the share of the total benefits will decline because the chambers pay costs associated with postpassage bargaining.

According to the theory, the use of postpassage bargaining is an explicit choice made by the House and Senate. Sometimes a majority prefers to pass a bill without changes even if it believes a more favorable policy would emerge from postpassage bargaining because of the costliness of conferencing or amendment trading. For example, in 2009, there was significant resistance to the House-passed version of the Cash for Clunkers Bill, but the Senate passed the legislation without amendment because the leadership believed that any changes were likely to draw out the bargaining process and risk failure of the bill when the politically popular program was about to expire. Other examples of bills deemed important but on which no postpassage action was taken include the Civil Rights Act of 1991 and the Intergovernmental Emergency Assistance Act of 1975, which provided a $2.3 billion short-term loan to New York City.[10]

The Choice between Amendment Trading and Conferencing

The decision about whether to use a conference committee or amendment trading is made after the rejection of the first offer by chamber 2. At this stage, the chambers coordinate on the choice because both are fully informed about which postpassage bargaining venue will be used, and the chambers share common expectations about the process in each.[11] In the modern Congress, conferencing is the preferred method, but either chamber may be unwilling or unable to use a conference, necessitating amendment trading. As a result, each chamber seems to retain the ability to "veto" a conference, requiring both to mutually agree that it is a preferable venue.

Conferencing and amendment trading offer two different choices for the chambers because of the different institutional structures of each venue. In a conference committee with a take-it-or-leave-it offer, the conferees determine the division of benefits, while in amendment trading, chamber 1, which originally made the offer to chamber 2 by passing a bill, makes a second legislative offer. In conferencing, it is possible the conferees are unable to develop a compromise, or they propose a bill that at least one chamber rejects, resulting in bill failure. Therefore, the offer made by the conferees is unknown to both chambers a priori, though the winning coalitions in each chamber have prior beliefs about the likelihood of an acceptable offer and the components of the offer.

Bargaining Using Amendment Trading

If chamber 2 rejects the initial offer and the chambers agree to use amendment trading, the next stage of the game is a second offer, in the form of a revised bill, made by chamber 1. Chamber 2 can reject this offer and make its own offer, and the chambers can trade offers repeatedly. It is unnecessary to model each iteration of amendment trading given that that the coalitions are constrained by time and opportunity and that, at some point, a final offer by a coalition must be made to the other. It must also be the case that the offering coalition does not know the other coalition's benefits from rejection, because if it did the first-moving coalition would make an offer that maximizes the division of benefits for itself while still inducing acceptance in the other chamber. When the second-acting coalition receives the final offer, it faces a decision about whether to accept or reject based on its benefits from each action, though the costs of engaging in postpassage bargaining must be borne if the chamber chooses to reject. If the offer is accepted, each chamber receives the share of the benefits from acceptance, while, if it is rejected, each receives its disagreement value. For each coalition, the disagreement value allows it to benefit from rejection and, as explained above, ensures that an offer is substantive. Otherwise, the second-acting coalition would accept any division of the benefits greater than zero. At this last stage, once an offer is accepted or rejected, the postpassage bargaining process ends.

Bargaining Using a Conference Committee

The process differs in conference committees due to congressional rules. In this venue, each coalition delegates negotiations to a group of legislators, usually selected from the standing committees that marked up the bill and who possess substantial autonomy to develop the final version of the legislation. While conferees, according to the rules of each chamber, must be in agreement with the bill after initial passage (Longley and Oleszek 1989; Oleszek 2007), there is some chance the bill sent back to each chamber will be unacceptable to at least one coalition and rejected.

Crucial to the development of the conference committee is the congressional norm that, though the leadership has the power to appoint members, and majorities in each chamber have control over whether to accept the bill

TABLE 3.1 **Sequence of the bargaining game**

First stage	Chamber 1 passes a bill and offers a division of the benefits worth b and $1 - b$, which chamber 2 accepts as is or rejects by passing its own version of the legislation.
Second stage	If chamber 2 rejects, the chambers agree to use a conference if the probability of an acceptable offer and the benefits each chamber expects to receive are sufficiently high. If not, the chambers choose amendment trading.
Third stage	*Conference:* In a conference, the conferees offer a division of the benefits, which is accepted by both chambers with some probability. *Amendment trading:* In amendment trading, the chambers exchange offers that propose a division of the benefits, resulting in eventual acceptance or rejection. *Both:* In both conferencing and amendment trading, the chambers incur costs of bargaining, making postpassage bargaining inefficient.
Fourth stage	The new policy is accepted or rejected, and benefits are distributed to chambers 1 and 2.

negotiated by the conference committee, conferees have jurisdictional authority over the legislation and are not necessarily loyal agents of the party or the chamber (Lazarus and Monroe 2007; McQuillan and Ortega 1992). Therefore, though the majorities have prior beliefs about the chances an acceptable offer will be made and the contents of the legislation, there is some probability the offer received from the conference committee will be unacceptable. For chambers choosing to use a conference after rejection in the first round, the expected utility of a conference is the possible division of benefits, which is realized with some unknown probability. If the conferees cannot reach agreement or if they make an unacceptable offer, both chambers receive their disagreement benefits. Table 3.1 summarizes the key stages of interchamber bargaining.[12]

Drawing Implications from the Bargaining Game

I have claimed that interchamber negotiations are best viewed as a noncooperative bargaining situation in which one winning coalition makes a policy offer to the other by passing legislation. If, however, the second winning coalition does not agree to this version of the bill and prefers to engage in further bargaining, the coalitions choose which bargaining venue to use. In amendment trading, another offer is made, as in the first stage of the model, but, importantly, the process is costly, and each coalition must consider its own benefits from disagreement when deciding on an offer. If the coalitions choose the other postpassage bargaining venue, a conference committee, they delegate responsibility for the legislation to a set of conferees and accrue benefits from the conference's division of benefits, though at the time of delegation, they are uncertain about the probability of success. The costs associated with rejecting the initial offer are included in the theory because bargaining is not frictionless. Indeed, if it were, there would be no incentive for the House and Senate to reach a deal in the first round and no incentive for chamber 1 to make reasonable offers that seek agreement. Substantively, this structure mirrors the actions of the House and Senate, whose members seek to minimize the time and energy they expend reaching agreement.[13] These costs punish the coalitions for not reaching agreement immediately, and they are expansive enough to include the costs that come from legislating and expending resources on specific bills, which reduces the benefits available to the chambers should they be unable to reach a compromise. The coalitions receive benefits from rejecting an offer, which ensures that reasonable offers must be made to induce acceptance. The total utility available to the chambers declines as bargaining becomes more costly.

One of the primary advantages of using the noncooperative bargaining framework is that it mirrors the congressional process while maintaining logical consistency and elucidating the various factors that affect policy outcomes. The theory sets up a risk-return trade-off for the coalitions in each chamber when they make their first legislative request: should the majority reduce its demand in the first stage of the game and accept a less favorable deal (from its perspective), or should it make an aggressive offer that increases the risk of using an inefficient bargaining venue? On the one hand, an aggressive offer may be accepted, in which case Congress will pass legislation much closer to the preferences of the offering coalition, giving its members a greater share of the benefits than they would have otherwise received and without having to expend additional resources on bargaining. On the other hand, an aggressive offer makes it more likely rejection will occur, forcing the chamber majorities to spend time and energy resolving their differences through postpassage bargaining. Likewise, for the coalition that receives an offer, it is faced with the dilemma of accepting a less favorable initial offer or taking its chances in conference or with amendment trading.

There is uncertainty for both winning coalitions associated with engaging in bargaining, especially when a conference committee is used. Though conferencing allows the chambers to avoid the costs associated with amendment trading, each coalition must be sufficiently confident an acceptable offer will be made by the conferees. In general, with both bargaining venues, if a coalition believes it will do well in postpassage bargaining, it is more likely to make an aggressive demand of the other and accept the associated risk of an initial rejection. It also must accept some risk that bargaining in amendment trading will eventually fail or the conferees will propose an unacceptable compromise. Both scenarios result in the status quo and impose costs on both coalitions.

The Initial Offer and Venue Selection

When initially passing a bill, both coalitions are punished for the use of an inefficient postpassage bargaining venue, forcing chamber 1 to make an offer that balances its payoff in the present period with its beliefs about chamber 2's resoluteness and the payoff it might receive in the next round of bargaining. Chamber 2 will reject the offer if it thinks it can do better in the subsequent round, even though continuing the bargaining process is costly. Chamber 1's strategy at passage is to maximize its benefits by allocating the largest possible share to itself while also maximizing the chances chamber 2 accepts the offer. Chamber 1, regardless of the bargaining venue to be used, must also consider the reduction in future benefits because of the costs of using a postpassage bargaining venue, though it does not know exactly how to allocate the benefits to ensure acceptance by chamber 2.

As the offering coalition's benefits from disagreement decrease as a result of increasing costs, it must be more conciliatory to the other coalition, and as a result it makes a more generous offer on initial passage, which leads to acceptance by chamber 2. From chamber 1's perspective, if the first offer is rejected, and the chambers reach agreement by amendment trading, the size of the benefits chamber 1 receives may be substantially reduced due to the costs it must pay to achieve agreement on the floor through the amendment trading process. As a result, chamber 2 is likely to receive a much better offer as chamber 1 seeks to avoid this outcome. Likewise, chamber 2's decision to accept an offer at initial passage is based on its own benefits from disagreement. When it receives more benefits from disagreement in the second round and has lower costs of bargaining, it is more willing to reject an initial offer and risk that it will receive a better offer because, even if it does not, rejection remains an attractive option. Said differently, as costs for a chamber increase, its benefits from disagreement are less important, and it becomes more willing to accept the first version of a bill.

Combining the implications for both chambers, large benefits from disagreement encourage one coalition to make more aggressive offers and the second coalition to reject those offers because its high disagreement benefits allow it to demand a better offer. Small benefits from disagreement for both chambers encourage compromise; one chamber has little incentive to demand a lot of the other, and the other chamber has little incentive to reject an offer. The result is counterintuitive: when the chambers are unwilling to reject and resolution is likely to be very costly, they have incentives to make more conciliatory offers and to accept those offers in the first round. This inference is generalizable to the broad political conditions in Congress. When resolving differences are more difficult, both winning coalitions want to avoid postpassage bargaining altogether. Two very divergent chambers will have a difficult time reaching resolution, making the process costly and reducing the overall size of the benefits available to the chambers. In these situations, it may not be worth it for the chambers to use a resolution mechanism to extract slightly more benefits, because these benefits will be more than outweighed by the costs of coming to agreement. Besides coalition stability and strength, I also use ideological differences within and between the chambers to measure the political costs of resolution. Again, as these increase, the use of a postpassage bargaining venue should be less frequent.

The Choice between Amendment Trading and Conference Committees

After a rejection in the first stage, the chambers must choose between amendment trading and conferencing. The theory suggests that the chambers coordinate on a bargaining venue with amendment trading the fallback option if one chamber prefers not to use conferencing or is unable to. The decision between the venues depends on the division of the benefits each chamber believes it will receive from the conferees, the disagreement values the chambers receive from rejection in either venue, and the costs of using each venue. The first implication drawn from the model is that the cost of using a venue decreases the willingness of the chambers to choose that venue. If amendment trading is costly, perhaps due to the difficulty in organizing supporters of the legislation and time constraints on floor action, then conferencing will be preferred, and as a result an increase in costs, or a decrease in a chamber's overall utility after completion of the process, always makes the other venue more likely. Even if the coalitions may have low confidence that a conference will be successful, they may use it rather than risk realizing high costs from amendment trading.

This claim provides a crucial insight into the use of conferencing: coalitions prefer them because they are easier to use and more efficient (less costly) than amendment trading. The costliness of amendment trading vis-á-vis conference committees depends on how difficult it is for each chamber to go to conference. The House is a majoritarian institution; thus, if the majority coalition size is small, it should prefer conferencing because it will be less costly than amendment trading. In the Senate, however, going to conference can be difficult given the necessity of attracting support from sixty members. The willingness of those opposed to the bill to filibuster conferences as a way of forcing amendment trading is due to their view that amendment trading is more difficult and extracts more resources from the majority coalition, decreasing the benefits the winning coalition receives from either agreement or disagreement. Thus, conferencing should become more likely as more lawmakers support the bill. Finally, the costs of amendment trading increase as the chambers are forced to spend a lot of time and energy changing the bill and shuttling amendments back and forth. These costs are related to the degree of differences among the chambers, suggesting that larger interchamber differences make conferencing more likely as it requires much less of the chamber majorities. (This insight, and subsequent ones, are summarized in table 3.2.)

Interestingly, the value of the status quo, independent of benefits each coalition receives from a compromise or disagreement, has no bearing on which venue is chosen. In either case, both chambers receive some benefit from the status quo if they do not reach agreement, but that value is the same regardless of the venue. Chambers prefer to reach agreement, and they will choose the venue that maximizes the chances of compromise, contingent on the share of the benefits they receive and the costs of using either venue. A chamber that values the status quo more because its preferences are closer to the current policy will not prefer one venue over the other, nor will the other chamber prefer conferencing if its utility for the status quo is low. Empirically, this explains why the use of conferences does not depend on party control of the chambers or unified (divided) government. In situations in which two different parties control each chamber and bargain over legislation, one party will prefer the status quo more than the other, but neither will prefer a particular bargaining venue aside from the costs of using that venue. Consequently, venue selection is not based on utility from the status quo as compared to the alternative policy but is instead based on the costs the chambers expect to bear and the benefits they expect to receive.

Resolution and Failure in Conference

Unlike amendment trading, when the coalitions choose to use a conference committee, a second offer is not made by one of the winning coalitions. Instead, the conferees propose an acceptable offer to both chambers with some unknown probability. When considering an offer from the conferees, a winning coalition accepts the legislative proposal if it receives more benefits from the legislation than from the disagreement value.

The factors that lead a coalition to accept the conferees' offer include, first, an increase in the benefits a chamber receives from the conferees. Because the benefits are divided between the chambers, the same must be true for the other coalition. That is, if one coalition receives a large share of the surplus, it will accept, but the other chamber will receive a small share of the surplus and may reject. Thus, the conferees must, all else equal, create policy that lies somewhere between the chambers' preferences, though the disagreement costs for each chamber change their willingness to reject the proposal.

The theory allows for some easily developed insights regarding conferee discretion, assuming the conferees prefer their compromise version of the bill be accepted by the chambers when it is returned from the conference committee.[14] While the conference committee members are free to change the legislation as they see fit, their level of discretion will vary with the willingness of each chamber to reject the offer, which is a function of the benefits of rejection, suggesting that the less beneficial rejection becomes the more freedom the conferees have to change the bill.

The total benefits from the compromise are divided up between the coalitions, meaning as one receives more benefits the other receives less (though by definition neither chamber is strictly worse off than it would be under the status quo). If both coalitions have high disagreement values, it will be difficult to find a compromise that allocates enough of the benefits to each coalition, giving the conferees low discretion and constraining the division of the benefits. The same logic applies when only one chamber has a high disagreement value because the relevant binding constraint is for the coalition most willing to reject the conference bill; both chambers accept a conference report independently, and each has a veto over the bill. The conferees must satisfy the coalition more willing to reject the report, and aggressive attempts to change policy from the preferences of the constrained chamber will lead to rejection by that coalition. Thus, coalitions that are more willing to reject the conference bill constrain the conferees more. Empirically, I show in chapter 5 that these types of coalitions are made up of moderate members, as they are more likely to prefer rejection under some circumstances due to their cross-pressured nature. Small coalition sizes also increase the risk of failure, as even a few defections might doom the bill. The empirical results suggest that more moderate coalitions produce more constraint for the conferees, conditional on small coalition size, while larger, more extreme coalitions give the conferees greater freedom to change the bill because they are relatively unwilling to reject the conference proposal.

A similar logic exists with respect to bill failure. Low discretion, by itself, cannot explain bill failure because, regardless of how much discretion the conferees are granted, there is, by definition, an outcome that makes both chambers better off than they would be by rejecting the conference bill. Why, then, is failure sometimes observed? Conferee discretion is defined as the ability to change the bill while still ensuring the benefits to each chamber from acceptance are greater than the benefits from disagreement. Rejection only occurs because the conferees change the bill in such a way that at least one chamber receives more benefits from rejecting than from accepting. The conferees, however, seek to find a compromise, so the cause of rejection must be conferee uncertainty about exactly what each winning coalition in the House and Senate will accept. When uncertainty is high and discretion is low, the conferees risk changing the bill in a way one chamber finds objectionable. Uncertainty on the part of the conferees will result from greater ideological heterogeneity within a winning coalition, making it more difficult for the conferees to locate an appropriate proposal that attracts a majority (or supermajority) of coalition members. Again, failure is conditional on having a small coalition, which gives the conferees a low margin for error.

This key implication, that the conferees mistakenly make a bad proposal because of uncertainty about what the chambers will accept, explains bill failure at the conferences stage in a way distributive and median voter theories cannot. If benefits accrue from logrolling, support should increase at the conference stage according to distributive theory, while if the conferees ensure policies are median oriented, coalition sizes will become larger not smaller. Partisan theory can explain bill failure, but, as I will show, there is little empirical support that bill outcomes become more partisan as a result of conferences.

The typical claim by political scientists is that conferees have virtually unlimited autonomy, within the rules, to change policy or even to rewrite legislation entirely. And, according to previous work, even if serious disagreements do arise between the conferees and the chamber majorities, members have little enforcement power over the conferees as long as the bill improves upon the status quo (Shepsle 1989), making rejection an idiosyncratic occurrence, rather than an outcome that can be theoretically explained. But the theory here demonstrates that even the *threat* of rejection is enough to constrain conferees under most circumstances. That the legislation can be rejected (and occasionally is) speaks to the content of the conferees' proposal and how willing the chambers are to reject.

Policy Change Resulting from Conferencing

When the conferees begin constructing a compromise, the extent to which they adhere to one coalition's version of the bill reflects the willingness of that coalition to vote against the bill given its disagreement value. If, as suggested above, more moderate coalitions are more willing to reject, this implies that the more moderate coalition in either the House or the Senate "wins" during the conference process. In short, the conferees must make the more moderate coalition a better offer by giving it more of its preferred policy. This does not mean that the more moderate coalition receives exactly what it wants from the conferees, because the structure of the conference process prevents it. The chamber with a higher disagreement value must receive a larger share of benefits to induce acceptance, but this is not equal to what the coalition might receive if the conferees had full information or, as in amendment trading, the chambers engaged in repeated bargaining. The disagreement value of both chambers is unknown to the conferees, so, though an offer may strictly satisfy both coalitions because their benefits are larger than their disagreement values, the more moderate (and, hence, constraining) coalition might receive less than if the conferees had full information, while the more extreme chamber might receive more from the conferees. That is, there are a range of outcomes that satisfy a coalition when deciding between acceptance and rejection, and the more moderate chamber may receive an offer that causes it to accept but is not the best possible offer it could receive.

Because the more moderate chamber or coalition is the relevant constraint on the conferees, the coalition could demand a better deal, where it receives more of the benefits and the more extreme coalition receives fewer. As long as the share of benefits for the more extreme chamber is greater than its disagreement value, it will continue to accept increasingly unfavorable offers. Why then, does the coalition more willing to reject not receive its exact preference at the conference stage? Though the more moderate chamber might want a better bargain, the institutional rules of conferencing prevent it. Unlike amendment trading, there is no way for the coalitions to amend or change the offer. The result is that offers may not be as favorable to the more moderate coalition as they might be if the coalition were able to modify the offer. Thus, postpassage bargaining in conference ensures the more moderate chamber is favored because it is more likely to reject a proposal from the conferees, but it is not able to change offers to match its exact preference. The other chamber receives some of its preferred policy because it must receive a share of the benefits, and the conferees may overestimate that share, given their uncertainty. The conferees will seek to overestimate the benefits necessary to both coalitions so as to ensure acceptance, but if the moderate, constraining coalition had the ability to amend its offer, it could push the irresolute chamber to the very edge of what it would accept, maximizing benefits for itself.

Resolution and Failure Using Amendment Trading

By contrast, the institutional rules of amendment trading produce a somewhat different outcome. As the theory demonstrates, a coalition with low disagreement benefits that is irresolute will never reject in the first stage in order to receive a better offer in the second stage because it does not want to bear the additional costs of using a postpassage bargaining venue. Additionally, once a bill is rejected, the offering chamber will never increase its demand, making a more extreme offer during amendment trading, because it knows an irresolute chamber would never reject the first offer (given that postpassage bargaining is costly). Even with uncertainty about what each coalition will accept, offers made at the initial stage and subsequently in amendment trading separate more resolute coalitions from more irresolute ones, where irresolute chambers accept an offer in the first round of the game, while more resolute chambers reject the first offer and accept the second. The offering chamber, having screened out the most irresolute types in the first round, makes a second offer, which moves policy a little closer to the other chamber, though it still reserves some share of the benefits for itself. Extremely resolute chamber types, with very high benefits from disagreement, will reject the last offer and prefer the status quo. This seems to substantively match the process in Congress where the House and Senate move toward each other over repeated amendment trading iterations rather than becoming more aggressive with each subsequent bargaining round.

As the costs of amendment trading increase, the overall gains from the process decrease so that when the winning coalitions get to the amendment trading stage they have observed the rejection of the first offer and know they are bargaining with a resolute chamber. The further exchange of offers reveals information about the level of benefits each chamber must receive to accept the offer. No single amendment exchange between the chambers requires outright acceptance or rejection and, as a result, this iterative process favors the more constrained coalition because it can make a series of offers that moves policy closer to its own preferences. If a proposed bill is passed by the other winning coalition, the more moderate coalition can change the legislation again to determine whether the more irresolute chamber is willing to reject the bill. Unlike conferencing, where a nonamendable offer is made, amendment trading allows the coalition with a higher disagreement value to update its beliefs about the resoluteness of the other chamber and receive policy closer to its exact preference because the other coalition will be willing to accept that version of the bill.

The result is that policy should lie very close to the preferences of the constraining chamber. Contrary to the common complaint that amendment trading empowers parties or the leadership, the iterative amendment trading process favors a winning coalition more willing to reject the bill, which I claim is the more moderate coalition. Any proposal that is not close to what the coalition with the higher disagreement value wants will converge to that point because the coalition has the ability to amend the bill and bring it closer to its preferences, while the other winning coalition is unwilling to reject, given its low disagreement values. That is, amendment trading grants the constraining coalition full amendment and proposal rights in the two-chamber context, forcing acceptance from the other, more extreme coalition.

Bill failure also occurs in amendment trading though its explanation is

TABLE 3.2 **Summary of theoretical claims and empirical implications**

Theoretical claim	Empirical implications
Higher costs of bargaining for one or both chambers reduce the incentives to engage in postpassage bargaining.	1. Small coalition sizes, lower majority party member support in the House, and lower overall support in the Senate reduce the probability of postpassage bargaining. 2. An increase in ideological heterogeneity within a chamber reduces the probability of postpassage bargaining.
The bargaining venue that is less costly will be preferred by the winning coalitions.	1. Greater majority support in the House decreases the probability of conferencing. 2. Greater interchamber differences on the bill increase the probability of conferencing. 3. An increase in ideological heterogeneity within a chamber increases the probability of conferencing.
Winning coalitions that receive higher disagreement values constrain conferees more than winning coalitions with low disagreement values, conditional on coalition size.	1. The more moderate the coalition in a chamber, and the smaller the coalition, the more similar the conference bill will be to that coalition's original bill.
Greater uncertainty and low discretion on the part of the conferees make rejection of the conference bill more likely.	1. The smaller and more ideologically heterogeneous the winning coalition, the higher the likelihood the conference bill will be rejected.
Conference bills favor the more moderate winning coalition but are not located at its ideal point.	1. Ideologically extreme winning coalitions will become moderate at the conference stage as policy moves toward the other chamber. 2. Ideologically moderate winning coalitions will become more extreme at the conference stage as policy moves toward the other chamber. 3. The change in extremity at the conference stage is conditional on whether the chamber coalition is more or less extreme than the other chamber's winning coalition.
Failure in amendment trading occurs due to increased costliness when resolving differences.	1. Ideological distance between the chambers combined with bills that have smaller winning coalitions makes failure in amendment trading more likely. 2. Ideological distance between the chambers combined with increased bill importance makes failure in amendment trading more likely.
The iterative process of amendment trading favors the more moderate coalition.	1. Winning coalition extremity will decrease for the more extreme coalition and will not change for the more moderate coalition.

based on the increasing costs of negotiating. If the coalitions can exchange offers repeatedly, moving closer to a resolution as the theory suggests, failure should be rare. And, because of the iterative nature of amendment trading, uncertainty about what each coalition will accept should not produce failure in the same way it does in a conference committee when the conferees propose an unacceptable offer. Instead, failure must be driven by an increase in anticipated costs as the coalitions progress through the amendment trading process. The repeated exchange of amendments allows the chambers to find a mutually agreeable solution, but eventually the coalitions may abandon the process if they anticipate it becoming too costly. Costs expended in the past are sunk and have no bearing on future benefits, but the coalitions may realize that any future benefits derived from resolution success will be significantly reduced by the costs of reaching those benefits, such that benefits from disagreement are expected to become larger than anticipated benefits from resolution. This results in the coalitions abandoning amendment trading and rejecting an offer, even though additional iterations of bargaining are possible. More ideologically distant coalitions and the level of support for the bill are expected to increase the costs of amendment trading. Therefore, I expect that when the chambers are ideologically distinct *and* a bill has relatively low support in the chambers it will be more costly to resolve because maintaining a winning coalition is more difficult, ultimately making the bill more likely to fail. Table 3.2 summarizes the major theoretical claims and empirical implications drawn from the bargaining game.

Comparisons to Existing Theories

The theory is based on the idea of noncooperative bargaining in the context of interchamber disagreement. Broadly, it suggests that the benefits the coalitions receive from agreement or disagreement, along with the costs of bargaining, result in the acceptance or rejection of offers, the venue used, the chances of failure, and the eventual policy outcome. The model differs substantially from partisan theory in that it is ambivalent about the role of partisanship and polarization, two common explanations for recent changes in postpassage bargaining. These factors have an indirect role to play in that polarization, for example, may increase the costs of bargaining or the willingness of the chambers to reject an offer. And certainly the breakdown of norms, especially in the Senate, where filibustering conference motions increases the costs of using that venue, is an important determinant of postpassage action. In the bargaining model, however, the causal mechanism occurs through agreement and disagreement values and the costs of action not partisanship itself. It is not strengthening parties, the breakdown of norms, or polarization that causes different postpassage bargaining outcomes. In fact, holding those factors constant, the same relationship should exist between costs, benefits, and bargaining outcomes. Further, the noncooperative bargaining framework is a general theory of how the chambers negotiate with each other and does not depend on party coordination or different levels of interchamber agreement. Throughout the book, when I test the theory using empirical models, I conduct additional tests that examine whether the results can be explained by party strength, polarization, or other unobserved factors (such as the breakdown of norms) *independent* of the measures of agreement and disagreement values. I find virtually no evidence that parties are the key causal factor behind the postpassage bargaining process. Instead, they play an indirect role in changing disagreement benefits and changing the conditions under which conferees have agency.

Distributive theory suggests that committees control the process through the conference committee, with legislative outcomes reflecting the preferences of outlying committee members. Unlike distributive theory, the bargaining theory accounts for the use of both conferencing and amendment trading and provides a larger role for the winning coalitions, demonstrating how they might control outcomes and constrain conferees. Further, distributive theory does not address legislative failure, which sometimes occurs, while the bargaining theory provides an explanation of how and why both conference committees and amendment trading occasionally fail.

The noncooperative bargaining theory resembles median voter theory in that the moderate chamber controls policy outcomes because moderation increases the disagreement value of a chamber, making it more willing to reject an offer. This is in contrast to both partisan and distributive theories, which suggest policies will be outlying in nature. Amendment trading, because of the iterative nature of the process, is predicted to produce policy very close to the preferences of the more moderate chamber, as that winning coalition can repeatedly move policy closer to its preferences as the more extreme chamber is unwilling to reject. Conferencing is predicted to produce near-median policies, but the take-it-or-leave-it nature of the process means that the more moderate chamber has no mechanism to enforce its preferences. Unlike median voter theory, the noncooperative bargaining model claims that acceptance or rejection is driven by benefits received from disagreement, even when a compromise preferable to the status quo is possible. Median voter theory simply posits that any policy will be accepted if it is preferred to the status quo by the median. In non-cooperative bargaining theory, a preferred policy exists but is not necessarily accepted, leading to failure even when a compromise is possible.

CHAPTER FOUR

Bargaining Frequency and the Use of Conference Committees or Amendment Trading

I now turn to testing the empirical implications developed in the theoretical framework, beginning with the selection of the interchamber resolution venue. Specifically, why are some bills, even seemingly important ones, agreed to immediately in the chambers without the use of a postpassage bargaining venue? In addition, what explains the choice to use a conference for some bills but amendment trading for others? In answering these questions, I highlight the ways in which limited lawmaking resources and the procedural rules in each chamber affect the bargaining venue choice.

Chapter 3 highlighted a number of bills that were passed immediately by the second-acting chamber but were also deemed important legislation, including NAFTA, a reauthorization of the Civil Rights Act, and the Cash for Clunkers Bill in 2010, which was part of a larger appropriations package. As the discussion of the Republican Obamacare repeal bill in 2017 notes, had the Senate successfully passed the bill, it too was at risk of being passed by the House without changes. A number of other significant bills in recent years were bargained on by the winning coalitions after initial passage but only through the amendment trading process. The Obamacare passage bill is the most obvious, but there are numerous other examples. The 96th Congress passed the Comprehensive Environmental Response, Compensation, and Liability Act of 1980, more commonly known as Superfund, using only one round of amendment trading, in which the House accepted the Senate's amendments to its own bill. The Family and Medical Leave Act, passed in 1993 and an important legislative goal of the new Democratic Congress and the Clinton administration, was agreed to when the House accepted the Senate's amendments after initial passage without the use of a conference committee. An appropriations bill, H.R. 2206, passed by the new Democratic majority in Congress in 2007 included funding for Hurricane Katrina relief and, more controversially, additional funding for the Iraq War. The bill was passed after a similar measure that included a timetable for the withdrawal of troops from Iraq was vetoed by President Bush, though the new measure included "benchmarks" for the Iraqi government to meet. Negotiations over the bill were difficult, and the carefully crafted compromise was bounced between the House and Senate three times before agreement was reached. Other important bills resolved using amendment trading include the Children's Health Act of 2000, the Government Securities Act Amendments of 1993, and a number of recent appropriations bills. While conference committees have received nearly all the popular and scholarly attention, as these examples show, they are by no means the only way the chambers reach agreement. And the decision Congress makes about whether to use a conference committee is an important one. As theorized in the previous chapter and explored empirically in greater detail in subsequent chapters, the policy implications of using a conference, as compared to amendment trading, are significant.

Understanding *why* different bills go to different bargaining venues is a necessary first step in understanding policy outcomes, as theories of congressional organization suggest conferences produce certain types of legislation. If the standing committee exercises an ex post veto (Shepsle and Weingast 1987), that implies amendment trading or skipping post-passage bargaining preserves the preferences of the chamber (Krehbiel, Shepsle, and Weingast 1987). Shepsle and Weingast (1987) dismiss the use of amendment trading, saying that nearly all important bills go to conference. Using *Congressional Quarterly* Key Votes in the 98th Congress, Shepsle and Weingast note that "nearly seven of every eight 'important' bills require a resolution of differences by conference" (940). As I have shown, however, a nontrivial number of important bills are not reconciled in conference, contra their claims. (See figures 2.3 and 2.4, which show that, for a particular congress, somewhere between 10 percent and 50 percent of important laws are reconciled in conference.) Party-based theories of Congress make a different claim: that conferencing promotes more moderate outcomes while amendment trading creates more partisan bills due to the ability of parties to control the agenda and distribute benefits to members in exchange for votes (Sinclair 2012; Wolfensberger 2008).

This chapter develops empirical predictions from the postpassage bargaining model, constructs measures of the important concepts, predicts whether a bill will go to postpassage bargaining and, if so, whether resolution occurs through a conference committee or amendment trading. The empirical tests are based on bill initial passage votes as a measure of the potential costs of bargaining in each venue, the type of bill, and the ideological differences within and between the chambers. The results show that an increase in costs (a decrease in the disagreement value available to the chambers) has important effects on the likelihood of postpassage bargaining and the venue used. Majority party votes in the House and total votes in the Senate in favor of a bill, conditional on having a filibuster-proof majority, encourage postpassage bargaining. Among the subset of bills that are negotiated after initial passage, fewer majority party votes in the House increase the chances of a conference committee, while the same is not true in the Senate. In that chamber, ideological variation and larger coalitions, conditional on larger interchamber differences, encourage conferencing but only if the Senate can overcome a possible filibuster. Another measure of the costliness of negotiations—whether or not the bill makes appropriations—also influences the use of a conference. The different results for the House and Senate are due to the different institutional rules in the chambers, especially the Senate procedures required to go to conference.

Some interesting and counterintuitive insights on the postpassage bargaining process emerge from the empirics. Bills with less support in the chambers are more likely to skip the postpassage bargaining process for a simple reason: they are too costly to resolve, and there is too much uncertainty associated with their passage. The second important insight is that House and Senate action are not driven by the same mechanisms when it comes to using a conference. Nearly all bills in the Senate with roll-call votes are passed with a supermajority, but amendment trading is more costly than conferencing. If the Senate is able to use a conference, it always seems to prefer one. There is evidence that, if the Senate is not able to use a conference because the bill has less than sixty votes, the minority tries to force the chamber to use amendment trading. The House, on the other hand, will use amendment trading or a conference depending on the relative costs of negotiating the bill on the floor of the chamber.

Ideological disagreement within the chambers has an indirect effect on postpassage bargaining. By increasing costs, it changes the incentives of the chambers to accept an initial offer and changes the ability of the Senate to use a conference. There is no evidence these effects have increased over time concurrent with stronger party power as conditional party government theory predicts.

Empirical Predictions of Postpassage Bargaining

The venue choice is modeled as one in which a winning coalition is first faced with a decision of accepting or rejecting the initial offer made by the other coalition. Acceptance of this initial offer corresponds to one coalition accepting the other's bill and obviating the need for postpassage bargaining. If the coalition rejects the other's initial offer, then the offering chamber picks a postpassage bargaining venue—conferencing or amendment trading—and the process continues. Allowing one chamber to pick a venue is a modeling convenience, but in reality the coalitions coordinate on a venue based on their own preferences. Conferencing seems to be the preferred venue, but if either the House or Senate does not agree, amendment trading is used.

The likelihood of postpassage bargaining and conferencing varies based on the costliness of negotiating. These costs, as outlined in the previous chapter, include the coalition-building and member-buying resources that must be distributed to members and the time and energy required to push the bill, develop legislative strategies, and whip members. These "consideration costs" may be especially acute in the Senate, due to the inability of a simple majority to call the previous question or limit debate (Den Hartog and Monroe 2011), but the larger the coalition in favor of the bill, the lower these costs are likely to be. First, fewer members have the potential to be pivotal on the vote and therefore cannot demand as large a share of the resources available to the leadership to distribute (Groseclose 1996; Groseclose and Snyder 1996); second, it is simply less time consuming and less difficult for a majority to pass a bill over the objections of a small, marginalized minority than over those of a large coalition of opposing members, consistent with what is regularly observed in Congress.

Therefore, I expect that as the number of votes in favor of a bill on passage increases, the more likely it is the bill will be reconciled using postpassage bargaining. High levels of support in both chambers make postpassage bargaining a more attractive option because the costs of engaging in further negotiations are likely to be low, making the possibility of additional concessions from the other chamber worth the extra effort. The chamber or party leadership need not spend as much time or energy whipping members or cajoling reluctant voters when support for the legislation is broad. Even if agreement is not reached, the majority coalitions will have had a relatively easy time of bargaining, allowing them to realize benefits from disagreement without paying the high costs of bargaining. More specifically, in the House the costs of passage are tied to support by majority party members. Whether or not parties are able to create nonmedian outcomes, members of the same party have similar ideological beliefs, which translates into lower costs when passing legislation, resulting in a higher probability of postpassage bargaining as the number of majority party votes increases. As a result, it is much cheaper to buy off party members than members of the other party (Aldrich 1995), maximizing the efficiency of coalition building (Lee 2000).

House Majority Support Hypothesis: In the House, an increase in majority party support for the bill increases the probability of postpassage bargaining.

I expect the effect of majority party votes to be less important in the Senate because of that chamber's rules. In the House, with sufficient party cohesion, legislative action can be accomplished entirely with support from members of the majority. This is almost never the case in the Senate as most action requires sixty votes, and the Senate majority rarely has this level of partisan advantage. In the sample, the Senate majority party had sixty votes during only the 94th, 95th, and for about half of the 111th Congress.[1] Though an increase in majority party votes should decrease legislative costs in the Senate, I predict there will be no independent effect of majority party votes accounting for the percentage of the chamber in favor of passage because of the necessity of incorporating minority party members into a winning coalition. Instead, in the Senate, I investigate the effect of overall support on the probability of postpassage bargaining; when more members of both parties are in the winning coalition, the less able minority members who oppose the bill can slow down or prevent legislative action. The rules of the Senate also require that the winning coalition overcome a potential filibuster for any postpassage bargaining to occur. For example, Kaiser (2013) relates how during negotiations over the Dodd-Frank Financial Reform Bill members involved in the negotiations assumed the bill would require sixty votes, which shaped their strategy. Thus, not only does an increase in coalition size make bargaining more likely but having a filibuster-proof majority should enhance the relationship between coalition size and the probability of postpassage bargaining.

Senate Overall Support Hypothesis: In the Senate, an increase in the size of the coalition supporting the bill increases the probability of postpassage bargaining.

Senate Conditional Filibuster Hypothesis: In the Senate, an increase in the size of the coalition supporting the bill conditional on having a filibuster-proof majority increases the probability of postpassage bargaining.

It is also easier for the winning coalition to buy off or organize members around the compromise bill when there is greater agreement on the legislation. Intrachamber differences increase the difficulty of bargaining because it becomes more difficult for the chamber or party leadership to rally their members and ensure passage of the compromise bill. Greater disagreement within chambers make the coalitions less likely to want to bargain because costs increase, as does the uncertainty that the eventual compromise bill will be approved by members of the winning coalition. I use measures of ideological heterogeneity within both chambers as a proxy for disagreement on a particular bill and expect that more disagreement makes a chamber less willing to bargain and more likely to simply accept the other chamber's offer.[2]

Intrachamber Disagreement Hypothesis: In both chambers, an increase in ideological variation increases the costliness of bargaining and decreases its likelihood.

Empirical Predictions on the Use of Conference Committees

The use of conference committees and amendment trading presents different forms of costs to the chambers. Amendment trading, which involves the shuttling of different versions of the bill back and forth between the chambers, poses similar challenges to those of initial passage. The bill must be repassed in different forms on the floor of each chamber, perhaps multiple times. This process uses up more floor time and requires the distribution of additional resources to members if support for the amended version of the bill wavers.

Conferencing is a more efficient process from the coalitions' perspectives because it avoids the costly consideration problems by delegating to a small group of members who resolve the bill outside the normal legislative process. Still, the conferees' offer to the chambers must be acceptable, and the chambers must have sufficiently high belief that the conferees will not make an offer that leads to rejection. Unfortunately, as discussed above, measuring the chambers' level of confidence in the conferees is difficult. But the chambers' confidence decreases as the costs of amendment trading increase, so that a very costly amendment trading process will lead the chambers to prefer conferencing even if they have relatively low confidence in the committee. Thus, for the House, the same measure of majority party support within the chamber predicts amendment trading.

House Amendment Trading Hypothesis: *In the House, an increase in majority party support for the bill increases the probability of amendment trading.*

Unlike the House, the unique institutional rules of the Senate empower a minority of virtually any size to substantially increase the costs of reconciling legislation on the floor. That is, the costs of amendment trading in the Senate are likely to always be high, short of unanimous or near unanimous support. The necessary coalition size for legislative approval in the Senate is sixty votes (beginning in 1975), but even small minorities, with sufficient incentives to slow down action on bills, can object to unanimous consent agreements, force the majority to invoke cloture, or extend debate through talking filibusters.[3] These rules seem to encourage conferencing regardless of the number of votes in favor of the bill because, though *both* require a filibuster-proof majority, in amendment trading coalitions might have to overcome minority obstruction multiple times. The ability of the Senate to overcome the minority largely depends on its coalition size and its ability to move the bill to conference. Determined minorities, understanding that amendment trading is harder, will seek to force the majority to use that venue in order to slow down the process and offer amendments that may make the bill more palatable.

Suppose though that the differences in preferences between the chambers is small and the Senate has a small winning coalition; in these cases, the Senate might be willing to quickly resolve differences using amendment trading because it is less costly than creating a conference to deal with minor differences. The converse should also be true in that greater interchamber differences on the bill make amendment trading much more costly. The theory suggests that conferencing is an efficient resolution mechanism because it moves legislation off the floor and delegates the negotiation process to a small committee. As a result, the more the chambers disagree, the more they prefer that bills be resolved in conference rather than through the amendment trading process. But large, determined minorities might make it difficult to use a conference, forcing small Senate majorities to use amendment trading. The larger the Senate coalition, the more likely it is to overcome this obstacle and use a conference but only when interchamber differences are high. Unfortunately, it is difficult to measure the extent to which the House and Senate versions of an individual bill differ. In lieu of measuring differences on particular legislative items, I use the overall ideological distance between the chambers as measured by "common space" DW-NOMINATE scores, with an increase in differences leading to a higher chance of conferencing if the Senate can overcome potential obstruction by the minority.

Interchamber Conditional Disagreement Hypothesis: *As interchamber disagreement increases, so does the likelihood that a conference is used to resolve differences given a large Senate coalition.*

Other Measures of Resolution Costs

In addition to the percentage of members voting in favor of passage in the House and Senate, other variables included in the empirical models are intended to capture the effects of costs on the likelihood of bargaining and conferencing. Among these is the count of *CQA* lines taken from the Policy Agendas Project. This variable, as explained in chapter 2, captures the importance of legislation, with more important bills receiving greater coverage in the *Congressional Quarterly Almanac*. Though other variables measuring legislative importance exist (e.g., Mayhew's landmark laws [Mayhew 1991] and Clinton-Lapinski scores [Clinton and Lapinski 2006]), the *CQA* lines variable has some notable advantages: it is measured for all bills, not just those that became law, and it extends through nearly the entire study period (through the 111th Congress). More important bills are more salient—meaningful to members, the media, and the general public. It is expected that the chambers will be more willing to spend time resolving these bills in postpassage bargaining, but, because opposition is likely to be higher for these bills, they are more likely to be resolved in conference. Legislative importance likely correlates with divisiveness, so accounting for importance is a critical test for the theory. The vast majority of bills receive no coverage, while a few bills receive thousands of lines. To account for the skewed nature of the variable, I dichotomize it, assigning a value of 1 to bills that received at least one line of *CQA* coverage.[4]

Appropriations bills are identified in the data and are expected to have a higher probability of postpassage bargaining and amendment trading. Appropriations are universalistic in nature in that they distribute goods to a large number of members, and, as a result, historically they have a reputation for being more bipartisan, which is less true in the modern Congress (Crespin and Rohde 2010). Still, in most cases individual members have little incentive to object to or delay appropriations spending because logrolling distributes benefits across the entire winning coalition (Kiewiet and McCubbins 1991). Thus, their passage in the chambers has tended to be relatively noncontroversial, resulting in low costs, despite the low disagreement value the chambers receive if they are unable to agree on an appropriations bill. Whether or not appropriations bills are more likely to go to conference is a source of debate within the congressional literature. Distributive theory suggests they are, as conferencing offers a final opportunity for the standing committee to shape the legislation to its preferences. The theory developed here, in the context of postpassage bargaining, claims appropriations are actually less likely to go to conference than other bills due to their low-cost nature.

Congress-Level Predictors of Postpassage Bargaining Type

Differences in ideological agreement within and across the House and Senate must be taken into account. The most common claim about conferencing is that an increase in polarization has made it far less common than in previous congresses, but my theoretical claims differ somewhat. The ease or difficulty with which the chambers resolve their differences drives the decision to engage in postpassage bargaining and the decision of whether to use a conference. First, polarization will increase the costs of legislative action within a chamber by making floor action more difficult. Counterintuitively, the more polarized each chamber becomes, the less frequent postpassage bargaining between the chambers becomes, leading to more acceptances of an offer by one chamber. Ideological differences within a chamber make it harder to construct winning coalitions and promote immediate interchamber agreement, at least prior to postpassage bargaining. The theory makes no strong theoretical claim as to whether interchamber differences make postpassage bargaining more or less likely. On one hand, greater differences should encourage the chambers to reconcile their competing bills more frequently; on the other hand, it is likely more difficult, giving the winning coalitions incentives to avoid bargaining. With respect to conference committees, the theory predicts that within-chamber differences encourage them because conferencing avoids the numerous votes and amendments that occur during the amendment trading process. According to the passage costs framework, more ideological polarization should promote more conferencing, as it is the cheaper resolution mechanism if floor action is difficult or protracted.

Theories of polarization suggest that the ways in which Congress operates have fundamentally changed (Sinclair 1997). The difficulty in getting anything done requires majorities to use legislative procedures and processes in unconventional ways as a means of circumventing minority obstruction. In the Senate, where increased majority power is of little help in overcoming a more unified minority (short of having sixty votes), passing legislation has become even more difficult. Claims of partisan power suggest that the increase in polarization has caused a decline in norms, greater power vested in the leadership, and an unwillingness to vote against party lines on procedural votes (Theriault 2008). While I expect ideological disagreement to increase the costs of bargaining, I also test whether the relationship between ideological disagreement and conferencing has changed over time. If there is a role for increased party power in postpassage bargaining, it should be observable across the study period.

Sample Selection and Data Considerations

For all empirical analyses, I define the universe of bills as those passed in some form by both chambers. Only bills on which both chambers agree to change the status quo are eligible for bargaining, and, though there is no direct way to measure whether the chambers agree to change the status quo in the same way (i.e., whether a set of possible policies exists that improves upon the status quo for both chambers), I take passage by both the House and Senate as an indicator that the chambers believe compromise is possible. Bills passed by only one chamber are not eligible for postpassage bargaining and indicate that the chambers' unobservable ideal points may preclude agreement or that the bill was passed for symbolic purposes only. Why include all bills in the sample, even ones that did not go to conferencing or amendment trading after passage by both chambers or that failed to become law? As discussed in chapter 3, excluding these bills introduces selection bias into the sample because these bills, though they were not bargained on, had the *opportunity* to be resolved by the

chambers through a conference or amendment trading. By studying only
those bills that actually went to a conference or through the amendment
trading process, the sample would be censored and exclude some values
of the dependent variable, potentially biasing the results (King, Keohane,
and Verba 1994).

The Library of Congress maintains a publicly available database of all
bills introduced beginning with the 93rd Congress at Congress.gov. Using these data, the sample consists of all public, noncommemorative bills
passed by both chambers between the 93rd and 113th Congresses.[5] The
Library of Congress also codes "major" actions taken on each bill, allowing me to determine whether any postpassage bargaining occurred and
whether the bill was resolved using amendment trading or a conference.
Data from the Library of Congress were scraped by software, with each
bill passed by both chambers given a code for amendment trading, conferencing, or both. As noted previously, some bills, notably appropriation bills, are subject to both amendment trading and a conference because conferees file a "partial conference report," where items disagreed
on in conference are subject to amendment trading (Oleszek 2007). I
treat bills that were bargained on in both chambers as having gone to a
conference, given the greater importance and prevalence of that venue in
the process.[6]

The resulting data contain 7,377 total bills passed by both chambers
between the 93rd and 113th Congresses. However, the vast majority of
these bills were passed without a recorded roll-call vote in one or both
chambers. Only 749 bills received a roll-call vote in *both* the House and
Senate during the study period. These tend to the most important bills,
a fact that is reflected in the two measures of importance, *CQA* coverage
and the Clinton-Lapinski measure of bill importance. For bills that received roll-call votes in both chambers, the average number of *CQA* lines
written about the bills is 997, substantially higher than the overall average of 157 lines. The median importance on the Clinton-Lapinski scale
is −0.313 for these bills, compared to the overall average of −1.45 for all
bills (93rd through 103rd Congresses only, where larger numbers indicate
greater importance).

Those bills that did not receive a roll-call vote and were passed by unanimous consent or voice vote in one or both chambers are excluded from
the following empirical models. The vast majority of these bills are trivial,
and while it is the case that some are bargained on usually this involves
one round of amendment trading that makes small, technical corrections

to one chamber's version of the bill.[7] These bills are simply not what most people think of when they conceive of the postpassage resolution process. Further, with these types of bills, the chambers anticipate that the costs of postpassage bargaining will be close to zero, which significantly reduces variation on a key measure. If these bills are included, unanimous consent bills must be treated as passed with 100 percent support in both chambers and, as a result, because of the number of these observations relative to substantive bills, these bills overwhelm all other results. This is especially true in the Senate, where passing bills by unanimous consent is far more common than it is in the House. Given the chamber rules, many of the bills passed by unanimous consent may be more substantive in nature, at least as compared to those passed by unanimous consent in the House.[8]

Variables Used in the Analysis

The primary independent variable used to predict postpassage bargaining is coalition support in favor of the bill on the passage vote. Rather than using the raw number of votes, I use the number of yes votes divided by the total number of votes cast for a measure, consistent with previous research, of the percentage of voting members supportive of the bill (e.g., Krehbiel 1998, McGrath, Rogowski, and Ryan 2015). Vote totals are taken from roll-call voting data on Voteview.com, and from the Library of Congress. For majority party support, I use the number of votes from majority members divided by the total number of majority party voters. When the number of majority party defections increases, the variable will take on lower values, while complete support from the majority party equals one.

To account for other possible causes of postpassage bargaining and the selection of a bargaining venue, I also use a variety of bill-level, chamber-level, and institution-level variables. Some of these additional variables capture different types of bargaining costs, while others are meant to control for other political or institutional factors that may affect which bills are bargained on and whether or not a conference is used instead of amendment trading. Bill-level variables include the bill's importance as measured by the number of article lines written about the bill in *Congressional Quarterly*, whether or not the bill became a public law, and a dichotomous variable equal to one for appropriations bills.

The theory is meant to speak to all types of bills, important and insignificant, and it is the case that more important bills tend to be bargained over more frequently than unimportant bills for a simple reason: Senators and Representatives, like the public, simply do not care enough about unimportant legislation to spend a lot of time dealing with them. As the theory explains, the higher rate of postpassage bargaining for more important bills is due, at least in part, to factors associated with importance like divisiveness. The purpose of the *CQA* lines variable is to control for bill importance, independent of other factors that affect bargaining.

Likewise, public laws are likely to be different than those bills that fail during the postpassage bargaining process. The postpassage bargaining theory offers explanations of why bills fail, which are explored in more detail in the next chapter, but controlling for whether or not a bill became law controls for unobservable characteristics that may be correlated with postpassage bargaining, such as party or committee support or whether the bill was introduced and passed within a chamber for position-taking purposes only. Finally, appropriations bills have a special role in Congress and are frequently subject to different congressional procedures. Because of their role in funding the government, appropriations bills are must-pass legislation but have traditionally been bipartisan, which likely results in low bargaining costs. Despite recent controversies over appropriations bills, they are usually successfully enacted and offer opportunities for logrolling and the distribution of particularized benefits across a wide coalition. The theory predicts then that, despite the apparently low disagreement value due to their mandatory nature, appropriations bills should be relatively easy to pass and therefore more likely to be reconciled in postpassage bargaining using amendment trading. Appropriations bills are identified by searching the short titles and short descriptions created for all laws by the Congressional Research Service using forms of the keywords *appropriation* or *appropriating* (e.g., emergency appropriations, supplemental appropriations, additional appropriations, etc.) (Minkoff and Ryan 2012).

Congress-Level Measures

Chamber and institution-level variables are measured by year or congress rather than by bill. These factors explain broader political phenomena, and some may account for a higher baseline probability of bargaining or conferencing across congresses. I include variables that measure the distance between the chamber medians using common-space DW-NOMINATE scores because greater ideological distance indicates that bills passed by the House and Senate are likely to be very different in terms of policy, indicating a greater need to engage in postpassage resolution. Also included are two chamber-level costs of bargaining. The first is the standard deviation of all House members' ideology as measured by DW-NOMINATE scores. Greater ideological diversity reduces the ability of the majority to build coalitions and maintain support for the bill. In the Senate, I use the distance between the Senate median and the sixtieth member or filibuster pivot as measured by DW-NOMINATE scores. Again, this variable represents the difficulty in creating and unifying a majority to allow for the passage of a bill. Both measures are commonly used to capture the difficulty of legislative action in the House and Senate. It should also be noted that, although DW-NOMINATE scores capture a member's ideology in the primary left-right dimension that divides American politics, they cannot speak to a member's policy or ideological position on an individual bill. This is a significant limitation, but there is no better measure of ideological preferences for all members in Congress across time.

Descriptive Statistics

I begin by describing the average level of support bills received on initial passage in both chambers. It is important to keep in mind that the sample of bills used here were passed by roll-call vote in both chambers and thus were eligible for postpassage bargaining. Table 4.1 shows the average importance of these bills within the Congress, the average House passage percentage, the average Senate passage percentage, and, for reference, whether or not the conditions of divided government or divided chambers existed during the congressional term.

The average importance of bills changes some, with the 104th and 106th Congresses being outliers, but, generally, average bill importance across most congresses is within one standard deviation of the mean (the standard deviation of *CQA* lines is 1,274.11). Both the House and the Senate tend to pass bills with large majorities, with the Senate having slightly larger majorities than the House, consistent with long-standing findings that most bills are passed with oversize coalitions (Fenno 1966, 1973; Ferejohn 1974; Manley 1970). One might expect that coalition sizes would increase during periods of divided government or divided chambers; any legislation that passes will need significant support from both parties. T-tests of House passage percentages support this claim, though Senate passage

TABLE 4.1 **Summary statistics for postpassage bargaining bills by congress**

Congress	No. of bills	CQA line avg.	House pass %	Senate pass %	Div. gov.	Div. cham.
93	73	715.96	87.2	90.7	Yes	No
94	77	830.18	80.1	84.1	Yes	No
95	66	917.88	80.7	86.9	No	No
96	48	913.15	77.3	83.0	No	No
97	21	869.95	83.3	87.8	Yes	Yes
98	26	871.65	78.0	86.7	Yes	Yes
99	16	982.69	79.5	84.7	Yes	Yes
100	52	1030.06	80.8	87.9	Yes	No
101	30	1239.2	78.5	85.8	Yes	No
102	34	1115.79	80.0	85.5	Yes	No
103	39	1185.64	70.5	80.7	Yes	No
104	39	2076.26	75.2	84.1	No	No
105	20	1416.9	80.9	91.0	Yes	No
106	26	2617.39	81.2	88.8	Yes	No
107	26	338.04	82.0	88.3	Yes	Yes
108	28	523.21	83.3	90.1	No	No
109	31	549.29	81.5	88.4	No	No
110	32	788.81	73.8	85.8	Yes	Yes
111	32	574.94	71.9	78.9	No	No
112	20	—	75.8	84.7	Yes	No
113	13	—	68.6	79.0	Yes	No
Total/avg.	749	996.71	79.3	86.1		

Note: Entries for article size and number of votes are averages for all bills passed by both chambers with a roll-call vote taken in each chamber for each congress. *CQA* article lines data are not available for the 112th and 113th Congresses.

percentages during periods of divided chambers and divided government are not statistically different from the percentages under unified government. It makes sense that the House, but not the Senate, has larger coalition sizes during divided chambers and divided government, as the House median and Senate filibuster pivot must approve of the proposed legislation, which the pivotal politics model and other institutional-rules-based theories predict (Krehbiel 1998; Wawro and Schickler 2006). There is also a significant difference in the number of bills passed by both chambers during periods of divided chambers, though not divided government. In short, fewer bills deemed important enough for roll-call votes are passed during congresses with divided chambers. Interestingly, bill importance, as measured by *CQA* lines, is not different during divided chambers or divided government. It is not the case that divided chambers produce fewer *and* less important bills.

Comparing the average level of support in the House and Senate for bills that went to a conference, conditional on divided government and divided chambers, dramatically changes the results. As shown in table 4.2, for bills that went to conference, the House passage percentage and the Senate passage percentage are statistically indistinguishable from each other. Many more bills go to conference during unified chambers, as one would expect, but they receive the same amount of support in both chambers as do those bills that go to conference during periods of divided chambers (the same is true for divided government). These results seems to imply a selection effect for those bills that go to conference. Fewer conferences occur because there are fewer bills with sufficient support in the chambers for a conference and because fewer overall bills are passed. The bills that do go to conference during periods of divided chambers, however, are about as important as those that go to conference during periods of unified government.[9]

To understand what causes conferencing, it is important to understand why some bills go to either postpassage bargaining venue and then why some bills go to conference. A second conclusion drawn for these

TABLE 4.2 **Difference-of-means test for conference bills during periods of divided chambers**

	Divided chamber		
	Yes	No	Combined
House passage %			
(N)	58	260	318
Mean passage %	79.5	79.0	79.1
SD	(15.5)	(15.3)	(15.3)
Mean difference	-0.2		
t-statistic	-0.21		
p-value	0.83		
Senate passage %			
(N)	58	260	318
Mean passage %	86.8	86.5	86.5
SD	(13.5)	(13.7)	(13.7)
Mean difference	-0.3		
t-statistic	-0.14		
p-value	0.892		
***CQA* lines coverage**			
(N)	58	260	320
Lines category (1 = received coverage)	0.89	0.91	0.91
SD	(0.31)	(0.28)	(0.29)
Mean difference	0.02		
t-statistic	0.44		
p-value	0.33		

descriptive statistics is that a bill-level explanation for conferencing is needed. The conditions of divided government and divided chambers do not offer specific empirical predictions about why conferencing occurs, only that fewer bills are likely when the chambers agree on fewer policy items. This result offers prima facie evidence for the theory that the chambers only pass bills that have widespread agreement (i.e., those that the majorities in both chambers believe will be successfully reconciled in postpassage bargaining) and for the claim that the chambers are not passing bills with the expectation that they will fail.

Which Bills Go to Postpassage Bargaining?

The hypotheses developed above claim postpassage bargaining is more likely when bargaining is relatively costless (as measured by coalition size) within the chamber (Senate) and the majority party (House) because of each chamber's institutional rules. To estimate the relationship between coalition size on passage and postpassage bargaining, I begin with logit models using the 716 bills with a recorded vote and passed by both chambers in the 93rd through the 111th Congresses,[10] where the dependent variable equals one if the bill went to postpassage bargaining. In the sample, 118 bills or about 16 percent of all bills passed did not go to either postpassage bargaining venue. Of these 118 bills, 109 became law, meaning they were accepted without modification by one chamber. The nine bills that did not become law and were not bargained on represent about 8 percent of the total number of bills in the sample that did not become law (108 bills out of 749).

Table 4.3 shows the results of logit models predicting postpassage bargaining for bills that received a roll-call vote in both the House and Senate and were passed in both chambers.[11] The key independent variables in the models are the percentages of yea votes received on passage in each chamber. The theory predicts, somewhat counterintuitively, that, holding bill importance constant, postpassage bargaining is more likely for the bills that receive more support in the chamber, not less. The first model in table 4.3 includes all bill-level and chamber-specific variables. Model 1 includes continuous variables for overall percentage in support of the bill in both the House and the Senate. Though both variables are positive, only the Senate coefficient is significant, providing support for the claim that an increase in overall support in the Senate makes postpassage bargaining more likely by

TABLE 4.3 **Effect of voting support on the probability of postpassage bargaining**

Independent variables	(1)	(2)	(3)
Public law	−1.50**	−1.35**	−1.36**
	(0.33)	(0.37)	(0.39)
CQA article lines coverage	1.08**	1.09**	1.07**
	(0.24)	(0.25)	(0.25)
House total yea %	0.18	−0.68	1.14
	(0.99)	(1.09)	(1.60)
Senate total yea %	2.11**	1.58	2.66*
	(0.94)	(1.11)	(1.55)
House majority yea %		1.73	
		(1.68)	
Senate majority yea %		1.09	
		(1.69)	
Appropriations bill	2.45**	2.46**	2.47**
	(0.47)	(0.46)	(0.46)
House chamber SD	−4.88**	−6.42**	−6.38**
	(1.31)	(1.91)	(1.94)
Senate median-filibuster distance	−2.85*	−2.46	−2.52
	(1.52)	(1.73)	(1.70)
Distance between chamber medians	3.89	5.05*	4.95*
	(2.47)	(2.87)	(2.86)
House majority yea % share			1.11
			(1.08)
Senate majority yea % share			0.58
			(1.08)
Constant	2.05**	0.94	−0.76
	(0.68)	(1.10)	(2.31)
AIC	484.27	481.83	481.92
N	716	716	716

Note: The dependent variable is whether a bill with a roll-call vote, on passage in both chambers, went to postpassage bargaining, 93rd–111th Congresses. Entries are logit coefficients with clustered standard errors by congress in parentheses. Ideological extremity and distance variables are measured using common-space DW-NOMINATE scores. *$p < 0.1$; **$p < 0.05$.

about 7.2 percent (95 percent CI: .31 percent to 51 percent) for each percentage point increase in support (Senate overall support hypothesis). The theory also suggests majority party support is an important predictor of postpassage bargaining in the House because action can be (and is) largely dictated by the majority, in contrast to the Senate. In model 2, variables are also included for total majority party support in both chambers. These results demonstrate that neither greater majority party support in the House or Senate affects the probability of postpassage bargaining, contrary to the House majority support hypothesis. The final model in table 4.3 reinforces these two findings. Model 3 excludes the majority party vote share variables and instead includes a variable that measures the percentage of the winning coalition made up of members from the majority party.[12] In both the House and Senate, a winning coalition dominated by members of the majority has no additional effect on postpassage bargaining, but in the Senate overall support remains positive and statistically significant (at the .1 level).

A number of other results consistent across the three models are also worth noting. Most notably, for both the House and Senate, the intracham-ber disagreement hypothesis is supported. The more difficult it becomes to find a compromise acceptable to a winning coalition, the less likely the chambers are to engage in postpassage bargaining. In model 1, the effect of a one standard deviation increase in the variation in House ideology, as measured by the standard deviation of all members' DW-NOMINATE score, results in a 35 percent lower chance of postpassage bargaining (95 per-cent CI: −17.8 percent to −100 percent). The results are less robust for the Senate as the variable is only significant at the .1 level in model 1.

Bills that eventually become public law, according to model 2, are about 78 percent less likely to go to postpassage bargaining (95 percent CI: −54 per-cent to −90 percent). More important bills, as expected, are more likely to go to postpassage bargaining. For bills that received coverage in *CQA*, the substantive effect is an increase in the probability of bargaining of 195 percent (95 percent CI: 68.5 percent to 414 percent). Appropriations bills are also about twelve times more likely to go to postpassage bargaining than other types of bills (95 percent CI: 5.28 to 31 times more likely). This result is consistent with the theory given the history of appropriations as nonpartisan and nearly universally supported by members. Finally, mod-els 2 and 3 suggest that an increase in the distance between chamber me-dians increases the probability of postpassage bargaining.

Two other findings are of note. First, interacting majority party votes in the House with whether the majority party was "rolled"—that is, whether a majority party made up less than half of the yea votes—has no effect on the probability of postpassage bargaining. I conclude that, holding con-stant coalition support in the Senate, little evidence exists that coalition support in the House affects postpassage bargaining. Perhaps this is be-cause the House, as a strong majoritarian institution, has low costs of nego-tiating regardless of how small its coalition is. The Senate, rather than the House, seems to be the key to postpassage bargaining. The House seems always willing to bear the additional costs of negotiating for a better bill, while the Senate must be cognizant of the difficulty it will have in ensur-ing a winning coalition exists for any compromise legislation that might emerge from bargaining. Second, no relationship exists between House majority votes and Senate votes. That is, postpassage bargaining does not become more likely as both increase simultaneously, as measured by an interaction term between the two. The chambers, while sharing an agenda and a preference to work on bills likely to pass (Ryan 2018), make their own decisions about whether to use postpassage bargaining based on their own anticipated share of the surplus and their own benefits from disagreement.

Which Bills Go to Conference?

The same reduction in the costs of legislating that promote postpassage bargaining should also promote the use of amendment trading. Amending and sending bills back and forth between the chambers requires the same floor procedures as the normal passage process, where members are allowed to debate and amend the bill. When only considering legislative costs, conferencing should be more common when the costs of floor action are high. As detailed in the theory, however, this argument obscures a crucial fact about Senate action: a supermajority of votes is necessary to pass the bill and to use a conference. Thus, virtually any bill with postpassage bargaining in the Senate should already have a substantial amount of support and, perhaps, given the venue preference of the chamber, ceteris paribus, mitigate the relationship between overall chamber support and the use of a conference.

I estimate Heckman selection probit models to better understand when conferences are most likely. The choice of a conference is a candidate for selection models because not all bills are eligible for a conference if they skip postpassage bargaining altogether. By only considering whether a bill went to conference, the models would censor those bills that did not go to postpassage bargaining, and selection bias might be introduced into the empirical models (Heckman 1976). To estimate the factors that affect both postpassage bargaining and conferencing, Heckman selection models are used, which are composed of a selection equation (whether or not a bill went to postpassage bargaining) and an outcome equation (whether the bill went to conferencing or amendment trading). When the dependent variable in the outcome equation is dichotomous, as it is here, probit models are the preferred method of estimation.

In table 4.4 I estimate three selection models with interactions in the

TABLE 4.4 **Heckman probit selection models of conferencing—Senate support and a filibuster-proof majority**

Independent variables	(1)	(2)	(3)
Probit outcome model, conference = 1			
Public law	0.15	0.14	0.14
	(0.25)	(0.25)	(0.25)
CQA article lines coverage	0.01	0.01	0.01
	(0.18)	(0.18)	(0.18)
Filibuster-proof majority	0.15	0.18	0.17
	(0.29)	(0.29)	(0.29)
Senate total yea %	−0.07	−0.97	−0.06
	(0.66)	(−0.68)	(0.65)
House majority yea %	−1.30**	−1.36**	−1.78**
	(0.62)	(0.60)	(0.87)
Appropriations bill	−0.80**	−0.80**	−0.80**
	(0.25)	(0.24)	(0.25)
Senate median-filibuster distance	3.29**	3.40**	3.32**
	(1.41)	(1.39)	(1.45)
Distance between chamber medians	−1.40	−15.10**	−6.63
	(1.12)	(4.21)	(8.17)
House chamber SD	1.29	1.151	1.32
	(1.13)	(1.13)	(1.11)
Senate total yea % × distance between medians		15.78**	
		(5.36)	
House majority yea % × distance between medians			5.83
			(9.94)
Constant	0.45	1.29*	0.84
	(0.70)	(0.67)	(0.70)
Probit selection model, postpassage bargaining = 1			
Public law	−0.71**	−0.71**	−0.71**
	(0.19)	(0.19)	(0.19)
CQA article lines coverage	0.61**	0.60**	0.61**
	(0.15)	(0.15)	(0.15)
House majority yea %	1.21	1.15	1.18
	(0.88)	(0.87)	(0.90)
House total yea %	−0.59	−0.54	−0.55
	(0.63)	(0.62)	(0.63)
Appropriations bill	1.44**	1.43**	1.44**
	(0.23)	(0.23)	(0.23)
Senate median-filibuster distance	−1.21	−1.17	−1.21
	(0.94)	(0.94)	(0.94)
Distance between chamber medians	2.17**	2.29**	2.22**
	(1.09)	(1.08)	(1.09)
House chamber SD	−4.86**	−4.87**	−4.85**
	(0.90)	(0.90)	(0.90)
Senate total yea %	−3.28	−3.36	−3.24
	(2.12)	(2.21)	(2.15)

TABLE 4.4 *(continued)*

Filibuster-proof majority	−3.24*	−3.33*	−3.21*
	(1.77)	(1.80)	(1.78)
Senate total yea % × filibuster-proof	4.77*	4.90*	4.71*
majority	(2.54)	(2.61)	(2.57)
Constant	4.19**	4.27**	4.16**
	(1.32)	(1.36)	(1.33)
Wald test; p-value	163; 0.20	0.08; 0.77	1.09; 0.30
AIC	1261.611	1254.647	1259.242
N	716	716	716

Note: Entries are Heckman probit coefficients where the selection model is whether or not bargaining occurred (bargaining = 1), and the outcome equation is if bargaining occurred, was conferencing or amendment trading used (conference = 1), 93rd–111th Congresses. Standard errors are clustered by congress. Ideological extremity and distance variables are measured using common-space DW-NOMINATE scores. The Wald χ^2 statistic and p-value test whether the joint likelihood of an independent probit model for both the selection and outcome equations is equivalent to the Heckman selection model. The null that independent tests are the same as the Heckman cannot be rejected for each model. *$p < 0.1$; **$p < 0.05$.

selection stage to further investigate what causes bills to go to postpassage bargaining and, conditional on postpassage bargaining occurring, what causes bills to be reconciled in conference or through amendment trading. The variables included in the outcome models are the percentage of the Senate that support the bill and the percentage of the House majority that support the bill as those two variables are the most theoretically important in determining whether postpassage bargaining is used; they are also expected to affect whether a conference is used. The *CQA* lines variable is included as a measure of importance, to capture whether more important bills go to conference more frequently. Both the public law and appropriations bill indicators are also included, with appropriations bills expected to be less likely to go to conference. Because of the importance in overcoming a filibuster to use a conference, a dichotomous variable indicating whether the bill had sixty votes on passage is included as are variables measuring within-chamber ideological variation for the House and Senate and the ideological distance between the chambers.

Before examining the outcome model, I estimate three models that include a dichotomous variable for a sixty-vote majority in the Senate then interact that with the total percentage of Senate votes in support of the bill. The previous logit models showed positive results for overall Senate support, but I also hypothesize that postpassage bargaining is conditional on having a filibuster-proof majority (Senate conditional filibuster hypothesis). In each of the three models, the interaction between sixty votes and an increase in

Senate support is positive and significant (at the .06 level in models 1 and 2 and the .07 level in model 3). That is, as Senate support increases when there are at least sixty votes in the Senate, postpassage bargaining becomes more likely. This result suggests not only that larger Senate coalitions make post-passage bargaining more likely but also that having enough votes to over-come a filibuster makes it conditionally even more probable. Despite the ability of sixty members to invoke cloture, passing and debating a bill can still be a very time-consuming and costly process. But, given the precondi-tion of a filibuster-proof majority, more Senate support makes postpassage bargaining more likely. Substantively, when only 60 percent of the Senate is in favor of the bill on passage, the likelihood of postpassage bargaining is about 63 percent (95 percent CI: 45 percent to 80 percent), but, when 90 per-cent of the Senate is in favor of the bill, the likelihood increases to 76 percent (95 percent CI: 71 percent to 82 percent).[13]

An increase in ideological divergence within the House also decreases the probability of bargaining, as demonstrated by the negative coefficients for the standard deviation of ideology in the House. Taken with the pre-vious results, these coefficients provide strong evidence for the theory: when bargaining is relatively low cost in the House, it becomes more likely. Low costs in the House are driven by a unified coalition, though not necessarily a large one, while low costs in the Senate are driven by over-all support conditional on a filibuster-proof majority. In all three models, public laws are less likely to be bargained on, probably because most bills are resolved quickly and are not salient or worth fighting over. Appro-priations bills, consistent with the logit results, are also more likely to go to postpassage bargaining. Alternatively, when the ideological differ-ences between the chambers are large, they must resolve their differences using postpassage bargaining. The coefficient is positive and significant in each of the three selection models, though the effect is substantively small: about a 1 percent decrease in the likelihood of bargaining moving from the minimum to mean of interchamber differences.

Turning to the outcome model, the theory broadly predicts that a de-crease in the costs of legislative activity on the floor should increase the chances of amendment trading (a negative coefficient in table 4.4). All three models show just such a relationship for majority party support in the House (House amendment trading hypothesis). As the percentage of the majority party supporting the bill increases, the likelihood of a conference decreases, conditional on a bill going to postpassage bargaining. In model 1, the House majority support variable is significant, and the substantive effect is large.

When 51 percent of the House majority supports the bill on passage, the probability of going to conference is .80 (95 percent CI: .71 to .89), while at 95 percent of majority support, the probability of going to conference is only .73 (95 percent CI: .65 to .81). There is no similar relationship for overall Senate support, however, as the variable is not close to the level of statistical significance. More ideological heterogeneity within the Senate promotes conferencing because, large coalitions are necessary to overcome the procedural hurdles. According to model 1, at the minimum observed median to filibuster ideological distance, the probability of conferencing is .55 (95 percent CI: .43 to .67), while at the maximum distance the probability of conferencing is .92 (95 percent CI: .78 to 1). Appropriations bills, consistent with their nonideological nature, are easy to resolve and much more likely to go to amendment trading than other types of bills. The likelihood of conferencing given an appropriations bill is .35 (95 percent CI: .13 to .57), while the probability of conferencing for other bills, holding other variables at the mean and public law at 1, is .65 (95 percent CI: .49 to .80).

Overall Senate support is not related to conferencing, nor is the distance between the chamber medians. The Senate seems to always prefer conferencing given the ability of the minority to obstruct or delay amendment trading, but it also almost always has a sixty-vote majority. In the sample, only 60 bills out of 749 were not passed with at least sixty votes, and of those only 33 went to amendment trading. Although overall support is not related to conferencing, more divergence between the chambers should encourage the Senate to use a conference, even if the coalition size is large. That is, at low interchamber differences, larger Senate coalitions will have no effect on conferencing (because the Senate prefers that venue, all else equal), but, at high interchamber difference, the Senate will be more likely to conference. At the same time, small Senate coalitions may be unable to force a conference and may have to settle for amendment trading if a strong minority coalition is able to block a conference. The interchamber conditional disagreement hypothesis suggests that the Senate prefers to use conferences when interchamber disagreement is high but that conferencing becomes more likely as coalition size increases because it becomes easier for the majority to overcome a minority that seeks to force amendment trading.

The results in model 2 of table 4.4 include an interaction term that captures this relationship, between the size of the Senate coalition and the distance between the chamber medians. Though neither component term is significant in model 1, here the interaction term is positive and statistically significant. To better illustrate the substantive implications of the interaction term, figure 4.1 shows how an increase in coalition size, conditional on interchamber distance, affects conferencing in Congress. When interchamber distance is low, the probability of conferencing is relatively high and does not depend, to a significant extent, on the proportion of the Senate voting in favor of the bill on passage. In these situations the Senate prefers to use a conference, as it always does, but resolution is expected to be fairly easy, and there is perhaps less of an incentive for

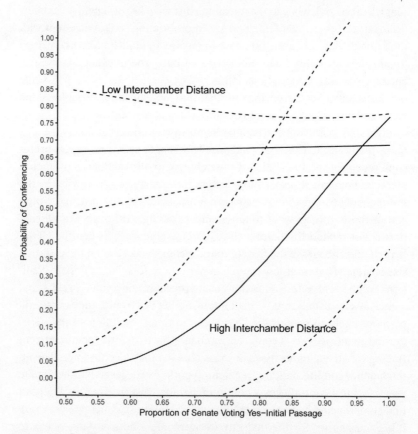

FIGURE 4.1. Predicted probabilities of conferencing varying interchamber distance and Senate coalition size. Dashed lines indicate predicted probabilities from model 2 in table 4.4 with 95 percent confidence interval. The slightly upward-sloping line indicates the relationship between an increase in the proportion of the Senate voting in favor of initial passage and low interchamber ideological distance as measured by common-space DW-NOMINATE scores. The sharply upward-sloping line indicates the relationship when there is high interchamber ideological distance. All other variables held at their means except for appropriations, which is held at 0, and public law, held at 1.

the minority to force amendment trading by attempting to block the conference committee. When interchamber distance is high, the situation becomes more difficult. The Senate prefers to use conferencing because amendment trading would be quite costly. This increases the incentives of the minority to force the majority to use amendment trading because of the time and energy it will extract from the majority coalition. As the size of the Senate majority increases, so does its ability to overcome an obstructionist minority. Consider that, when coalitions are small and interchamber distance is high, the probability of conferencing is very low, less than .25. As the coalition size grows and approaches the mean of around 86 percent in favor, the probability of using a conference increases dramatically, to about .5. This suggests that the minority seeks to block conferences but only when amendment trading is likely to be costly. The winning coalition can use a conference but only if it has enough support to overcome a minority; tenuous or smaller majority coalitions may be forced to use amendment trading, a much costlier process, when negotiations are likely to be difficult. For comparison, model 3 of table 4.4 interacts House majority party support with interchamber distance and finds no significant relationship. Larger coalitions in the House encourage conferencing, but interchamber distance is irrelevant to the House. The majority's ability to dictate the agenda and limit minority obstruction simply mean that smaller coalitions prefer conferencing under nearly all circumstance.

The Indirect Effect of Congressional Polarization

The evidence here strongly supports the notion of conferences as a risky but efficient method of resolving differences with the other chamber. In the House, the risk is sometimes worth it, if support for the bill is tenuous, but the Senate seems almost never to prefer amendment trading. When resolution is most difficult, during periods of high interchamber disagreement, the minority attempts to force amendment trading, while strong majorities attempt to overcome minority obstruction and use a conference. It is also the case that internal divisions in both chambers make them less likely to want to use postpassage bargaining and less likely to engage in it. Importantly, conferences are more likely when the Senate is able to muster sufficient support in the face of minority obstruction given a difficult resolution process. The reduction in the number of observed conferences in recent years seems to be the result of two factors. First, fewer substantively important bills are being passed. Second, in a bid to reduce the costs of postpassage bargaining, majorities in the Senate seek to use a conference in order to avoid amendment trading. However, as chamber support for the bill shrinks, it becomes more difficult to use a conference, and the minority will try to force amendment trading. Congressional polarization contributes to the decline in conferencing by reducing overall support for the bill.

While increased ideological heterogeneity increases the costs of bargaining and lowers chambers' disagreement values, parties do not directly drive the bargaining process. There is no evidence that recent congresses are more willing to violate the norm of allowing a majority to use a conference committee; close partisan divides within the chamber simply make it easier to prevent them. There is also no evidence that the majority party leadership is using amendment trading to exert more control over the process. Bargaining costs may be increasing as a function of polarization, but various tests have yielded no evidence to support the claim that strong parties have an independent effect on bargaining. For example, interaction terms between the pre- and post-103rd congresses, when many scholars believe polarization really took flight with a corresponding decline in norms and chamber comity (Aldrich and Rohde 1997; Theriault and Rohde 2011), and measures of chamber and institution-level ideology (Senate median-filibuster distance, distance between chambers) are insignificant. Interactions between divided government and divided chambers and the post-103rd congresses are negative and significant, suggesting that conferencing is less likely during the recent period if divided government or divided chambers exist. This simply seems to be a function, however, of the fact that far fewer bills are passed and bargained on during this time period. Likewise, a time variable for Congress interacted with the measures of ideology should show significant effects if there were a real decline in informal cooperation or another unobservable party-driven factor, but it does not. Postpassage bargaining occurs because, despite the costs, the chambers believe the legislation in question and their potential benefits from compromise are worth fighting for.

CHAPTER FIVE

Conferee Discretion and Bill Failure in Conference Committees

Conferences have long been seen as the most important way for the House and Senate to resolve their differences, but, before investigating the ways in which they change policy, this chapter explores *when* the conferees exercise their policymaking power free from constraints placed on them by the majority coalition in their chamber. While the conferees are empowered to change policy on many of the most important bills passed by Congress, they must do so with an eye toward their respective chambers, despite the fact that reaching agreement always requires the conferees to change at least one chamber's version of the legislation. In most cases, the new legislation sent back to the chambers for final passage differs from what both winning coalitions originally passed and represents a compromise that matches neither of the coalitions' original bills. Sometimes the new legislation reflects more of one chamber's policy preferences than the other's, and sometimes the bill appears to be an attempt to split the difference between each chamber's policy preferences. And, while chamber rules govern the types of changes that can be made by conferees, these rules seem to impose little practical constraint on the conference committee.

Using the bargaining model, I develop theoretical expectations about the conditions that allow for conferee discretion and the creation of bills that significantly differ from the legislation originally passed by both chambers. Generally, the theory predicts that the more moderate winning coalition of the two chambers is more willing to reject the proposed conference bill, resulting in a higher level of conferee constraint and a reduction in conferee discretion. The rejection of the conference report, though rare, is the institutional mechanism through which parent chambers control their conference representatives. These failures occur, according to the theoretical model, when the conferees use their discretion to move the legislation so far from a chamber's preferred outcome that rejection of a bill by a majority coalition results in a larger payoff than acceptance. Conference failures can be thought of, according to the theory, as an exercise of too much discretion. Contrast this perspective with most existing literature, which focuses on the tension between the changes made by conferees to promote certain policy goals (their own or that of some other actor, like the party or committee), and the preferences of the majority or median of the chamber. While this tension is apparent in the theory developed here, the strategic interaction between the chambers and the conferees has been neglected in prior research, despite the ability of a single chamber to derail the resolution process through rejection of a proposed compromise bill. Broadly, the model claims that conference committees are not always free to make drastic policy changes, even if the conferees want to, and that the institutional rules that empower the majority coalitions to reject the proposed bill must be taken seriously. When the chambers have high disagreement values, the conferees are not able to exercise discretion because the chambers are very willing to reject the bill.

To understand the policy changes made by the conferees, from the first bills passed by each house to the final legislative compromise agreed on by both, I use vote switching by members as an indication of policy change. If a senator or representative opposes a bill on initial passage then subsequently votes for the bill after going to conference, I infer that the bill moved closer to the member's ideal point (and vice versa if a member switches from a yes to a no vote). By aggregating the total amount of vote switching, the "quantity" of policy change for any bill can be measured. Conference failures are identified as those bills that were passed by both chambers and were taken up, at least nominally, by a conference committee. Moderating coalitions increase the probability of failure, but the conferees must be uncertain about what the chambers will accept for failure to occur. Without sufficient uncertainty on the part of the conferees, even low levels of discretion can be successfully managed by the conferees. In addition to conferee uncertainty about the preferences of the coalition voting on the bill, the winning coalition must also be sufficiently small. Defections in smaller coalitions are much more damaging to the bill's prospects because vote switching by even a few members can produce a majority opposed to passage.

The Importance of Conferee Discretion

A basic premise of interchamber bargaining is that the majority coalition, as a whole, prefers the passed bill to any other possible outcome. Individual members may prefer a different bill, and different bills may generate smaller or larger coalitions with different membership. But the bill passed by the chamber represents the winning coalition's collective optimal outcome, and any change to the bill creates a different coalition, reducing the collective benefits (see Baron and Ferejohn 1989; Groseclose and Snyder 1996; Riker 1962; and Shepsle 1974 on the size of winning coalitions). For individual members within the majority coalitions, the legislation produced by Congress has direct effects on members' ability to represent their constituents and on members' reelection prospects (Mayhew 1974). For example, when a compromise bill more closely reflects the House majority's policy preferences, members of the House can claim credit and receive the benefits from enacting legislation that matches their preferences.[1] To summarize, the two chambers can be thought of as engaging in a competition over potential policy, and the majority coalition in each chamber attempts to protect their own policy preferences from the other (Diermeier and Myerson 1999).

Possible Uses of Discretion

The competition for policy happens in the bargaining venues the chambers use to construct compromises. While postpassage bargaining involves more than conferencing, the influence of conference committees on policy outcomes has received a relatively high amount of scholarly attention, due to their unique institutional role as an antimajoritarian feature of the overall passage process. A conference committee is made up of a small group of members, usually chosen from the relevant standing committee, who have preferences that may differ from those of the winning coalition and who also have the power to modify legislation as they see fit with no chance for a majority (or even a supermajority) to amend the conferees' bill. The power of conferees to change policy and then submit those changes as a take-it-or-leave-it offer back to the chambers suggests that standing committees can use the conference as an ex post veto over legislative changes made on the floor (Shepsle and Weingast 1987).

Distributive theory largely rests on the claim that high-demanding members who self-select onto standing committees and whose preferences do not reflect the preferences of the chamber median have the last word on legislation creation in the conference (Oleszek 2007; Sinclair 1983; Shepsle and Weingast 1987; Smith 1988; Smith 1989). The theory claims that all members are better off receiving outsize benefits within their policy area, but to ensure collective benefits an enforcement mechanism is required. The standing committee system offers just such a mechanism because members are able to create their preferred policy while other members surrender their preferences in that policy area in exchange for legislative freedom in their own preferred jurisdiction (Shepsle and Weingast 1981, 1987, 1994). The "gains from exchange" are achieved when members across jurisdictions logroll to support each other's policy (Weingast and Marshall 1988). According to this theory, conference committees offer a bulwark against changes made to the bill at the floor passage stage.

The two primary competing theories claim that conferences are tools of the chamber median or tools of the party. Information theory suggests that conferees are in fact constrained by the chamber, which could reject the bill, but also exerts control through the appointment process and the chamber's ability to circumvent conferences if needed (Krehbiel, Shepsle, and Weingast 1987). While distributive theory predicts conference outcomes should resemble the preferences of the outlying and homogeneous standing committee, information theory predicts conference outcomes close to the chamber median, better reflecting the preferences of the median and near-median members.

As a result of the increase in attention to the role of parties and their leadership, their role in the conference process is being taken seriously. The leadership has substantial discretion to appoint conferees, and conferences have been shown to be stacked with party loyalists (Lazarus and Monroe 2007). There is some evidence that majority party control over the conference shifts outcomes toward the majority party and away from the median (Ryan 2014; Vander Wielen 2010; Vander Wielen and Smith 2011). This may allow the party to ensure bills disproportionately benefits members of the majority, allowing the party and its members to build its brand and claim legislative successes (Cox and McCubbins 1993, 2005).

Conferee discretion may be used in any of these ways, and in the next chapter I investigate whether policy outcomes move closer toward the

Senate or House policy preferences, speaking to theories of legislative organization. I first establish that conferees are constrained and that the quantity of changes made to the bill by the conferees varies significantly depending on the characteristics of the bills and winning coalitions. While all of the theories discussed above offer implications for conference membership and the types of legislative outcomes that occur, none of them make specific predictions about the extent to which conferees can change legislation or, more importantly, the conditions or situations that allow the conferees to make large-scale changes to the bill passed by the chamber majority. To date, there has been little research on legislative outcomes produced by the conference as compared to those produced by the chambers themselves, and the ways in which policy outcomes change at this final, important stage of the legislative process are not well understood.

Explaining Conference Committee Discretion

The current literature emphasizes ex ante control of the conference committee through the appointment process with influence being brought to bear by the standing committee, the party, or the median, but the postpassage bargaining model developed in chapter 3 emphasizes the roles of uncertainty, disagreement benefits, and negotiating costs as the key drivers of bargaining strength and legislative outcomes rather than party power or ideological disagreements. Though the chamber leadership or majority seek to constrain conferees before the conference committee ever meets, the chambers are empowered to reject a conference report if it diverges too much from their preferences. The strategic nature of the bargaining game shows that this institutional tool—conference rejection—shapes legislative outcomes even if rejection is not frequently observed.[2]

For each of the chambers, the relationship between winning coalition characteristics and conferee discretion is straightforward: as a chamber's disagreement value increases, the more willing it is to reject the proposed bill and the less discretion the conferees have. If the conference report strays too far from the preferences of the chamber, the benefits to the majority coalition for acceptance decline, making disagreement more valuable, potentially leading to rejection and the status quo prevailing. If one chamber has low disagreement benefits and one chamber has high disagreement benefits, the conferees must ensure the chamber more willing to reject is satisfied, allowing that chamber to constrain the conferees.

Therefore, as one coalition's disagreement benefits increase relative to the other's, that coalition begins to exert more of an effect on conferee discretion.

Based on the logic of rejection and disagreement benefits received, more moderate winning coalitions should have higher disagreement values. There is overwhelming evidence that moderate members tend to engage in less consistent behavior in their vote choices and other legislative activities. This work suggests that moderate members are more likely to vote against their party or be cross-pressured, resulting in a higher latent probability of voting yes or no on a given bill than more extreme members. Waffling—when a member cosponsors a bill but votes against it—is also strongly associated with ideological moderation (Krehbiel 1995). I connect the willingness of moderates to impose constraints on conferees to the composition of the winning coalition on initial passage. Coalitions that are moderate will constrain the conferees more, conditional on the extremity of the other winning coalition. This also implies the more extreme chamber will "lose" in the conference process because it has no credible way of limiting conferee discretion given its unwillingness to reject the bill, a claim that is tested in the subsequent chapter. Thus, I predict that the more moderate coalition relative to the other increases the constraints placed on the conferees and substantially reduces discretion, as measured by the percentage of members who switch their votes.

Coalition Relative Extremity Hypothesis: *The more moderate chamber coalition, relative to the other chamber coalition, will constrain conferee discretion and produce less vote switching within that chamber.*

This theory is consistent with observed negotiations over bills. Returning to the 2014 Farm Bill example, the House gave in to the Senate on SNAP (food stamp) spending and commodity regulations because the conferees knew the House's position would never get through the Senate (Bosso 2017). As a result, the House conferees were forced to accept the Senate's position on these two critical issues, despite claiming for months that the House would not budge on its own position.

The size of the winning coalition is also predicted to condition the relationship between coalition moderation and conferee discretion. Even moderate coalitions may not constrain conferees if the winning coalition within a chamber is very large. The conference committee observes the size of the winning coalition and may be willing to risk the loss of support from some members, especially if the conferees have a lot of votes to work with. Therefore, conferee discretion will be limited by the number of members in support of a bill, conditional on a chamber's willingness to reject the offer. If the majority in a chamber is small and also relatively willing to reject the proposed bill, even a small change to the bill made by the conferees may induce enough vote switching within the chamber to cause failure, a situation the conferees wish to avoid. The empirical implication is that small, moderate coalitions offer the least amount of discretion for the conferees, a proposition that is tested using coalition size on passage and the moderation of the winning coalition.

   Coalition Extremity and Size Hypothesis: *Greater coalition extremity conditional on larger coalition size produces greater conferee discretion and more switching within a chamber.*

Conferee Discretion and Bill Failure

The bargaining model conceives of bill failure at the conference stage as caused by the conferees exercising too much discretion, resulting in a majority in at least one chamber opposing the bill. This occurs despite the theoretical existence of a possible compromise as the noncooperative bargaining model assumes there exists some mutually agreeable policy that makes both chambers better off; failure occurs not because there is no possible compromise but because the conferees are unable to locate that compromise. Recall that the coalitions reject only if the bill proposed generates a smaller share of benefits than the chambers' disagreement value. But if a compromise exists, the question then becomes why the conferees would ever propose a bill that leads to rejection by at least one chamber? As evidence of how unlikely rejection is, consider that only about 10 percent of bills fail at the conference stage, suggesting that even constrained conferees usually propose a bill that both chambers accept. Moderation constrains the conferees but cannot by itself, cause rejection. Only by incorporating the uncertainty of the conferees with respect to each chamber's disagreement value can an unsatisfactory offer from the conferees be explained. As with limitations on conferee discretion, rejection becomes more likely as the winning coalitions in each chamber become more ideologically disparate, making it difficult for the conferees to find an appropriate compromise.

   Ideological heterogeneity within a chamber has been shown to matter in many lawmaking contexts because it increases the difficulty of coordinating and organizing a majority (Brady and Epstein 1997; Brady, Brody, and Epstein 1989). Ideological heterogeneity within the majority party is a key component of conditional party government theory and suggests that members delegate to the majority when agreement is widespread and roll-call voting by members becomes more predictable (Aldrich 1995; Aldrich and Rohde 1998; Fleisher and Bond 2004; Rohde 1991). Sarah Binder (2003) finds that ideological homogeneity is strongly associated with more active lawmaking, suggesting that more coherent coalitions are able to achieve more legislative success. Individual member voting may also be more predictable when the majority coalition is more homogeneous, as there is evidence that individual members frequently look to the leadership and committee members for guidance on how to vote (Box-Steffensmeier, Ryan, and Sokhey 2015). In short, greater ideological heterogeneity within a chamber makes it more difficult for the conferees to coordinate with their winning coalition and produce a bill that will be accepted.

Interchamber heterogeneity, in addition to intrachamber heterogeneity, is predicted to have a similar effect in that it increases uncertainty among the conferees about the policies each chamber will accept. Constrained chambers, though they are limited in how much they can change the bill, still must make changes, and when the chambers are far apart the conferees will have a harder time finding a bargain that makes both chambers happy. This requires the conferees be precise about the compromise they develop, and, because each chamber has an incentive to misrepresent what it will accept from the conference, the conferees have little guidance in terms of how to structure a compromise.

Though most bills are passed with oversize coalitions (even those that fail), I also test whether smaller coalitions combined with uncertainty are more likely to produce failure. Smaller winning coalitions, conditional on greater levels of ideological heterogeneity, which promote conferee uncertainty, are predicted to increase the probability of conference failure.

Bill Failure Hypothesis: *Greater coalition ideological diversity conditional on smaller coalition size produces a higher probability of bill failure at the conference stage.*

Measuring Conferee Discretion

Policy changes from initial to final passage occur as a result of the bicameral bargaining process, but they have proven difficult to empirically capture. The dominant approach in previous research was to select legislation with quantifiable policy outcomes, such as appropriations bills, as a way to measure change from the chamber-passed bill to the conference bill. By examining the difference between these bills, researchers could determine by how much a bill changed, and whether the final bill more closely matched the House's or Senate's preferences. There are two problems with this strategy. First, using only spending bills limits the possible cases that can be examined, potentially missing important variation or introducing bias into the inferences made. Second, this approach neglects the strategic aspect of an initial offer; if the request originally passed does not represent the true disagreement value of the winning coalition, then it might appear that one side lost when its proposal successfully moved the bill toward a more favorable outcome. During the Farm Bill negotiations, a House Republican conferee said that the proposed $39 billion in SNAP cuts was "never real" (Bosso 2017, 146).

I measure changes to the bill by comparing individual members' votes on initial passage to their votes on the conference bill. Members' roll-call votes are largely treated as an expression of their true preference, especially on final passage (Poole and Rosenthal 1997).[3] Consider a legislator voting on the bill at the initial passage stage. The legislator votes for the bill when preferred to the status quo and against it when it is not. Collectively, the members voting for the bill compose the winning coalition, and, all else equal, if the bill did not change after conference, these exact same members would vote for the bill again. If we take voting as an expression of a member's true preference, consistent with other research, then the members who opposed the bill initially will also oppose it when it returns from conference if the conferees have not sufficiently modified the bill. Thus, identical bills at both stages should produce no vote switching within the chamber. If the bill is changed slightly, then a few additional members may support the bill after having opposed it initially, while a few other members may move from support to opposition. If the conferees make substantial changes to the bill, a significant number of members will switch their votes. A similar strategy has been used in previous research to compare the ideological placement of a bill before and after conference by examining the NOMINATE score of members who vote for the bill at each stage (Vander Wielen 2010).

A few caveats about the vote switching measure are warranted. In a one-dimensional policy space, changes made to the bill should produce vote switching in a consistent direction, where more moderate members on one side of the bill switch their votes as the proposed policy moves away from their ideal point, and members on the other side of the ideological spectrum switch in the opposite direction. Understanding these changes requires assumptions about the direction of policy movement, but these additional assumptions are not necessary for empirical tests of conferee discretion. Here it is assumed that more vote switching signals a larger change in the legislation from chamber passage to conference, without accounting for direction. The subsequent chapter focuses in greater detail on *how* the conferees move policy (i.e., toward more moderate or extreme outcomes).

It is also important to note that vote switching measures legislative change and is not a direct measure of conferee discretion. It is possible that conferee discretion exists and is not used (though the reverse is not true), but, in the absence of any action by the conferees, discretion is unobservable. If conferees are always free to move policy during a conference committee with virtually no limitations, the only circumstance in which conferee discretion is available but unused is when the bill reflects the preferences of the chamber median, and the chamber median is also the conference committee median, an unlikely situation when one considers the composition of conference committees. Still, even if the conferees sometimes have discretion but choose not to use it, observed changes to legislation across a large number of bills are likely to capture conferee discretion in most circumstances. Thus, while actual legislative change between passage and conference is an indirect measure of conferee discretion, conferees must have discretion if legislation is to change, and the measure of change—vote switching—is observable for every bill.

To adjust for the number of members voting for a bill, the vote switching measure is calculated as the percentage of members voting on initial passage who switched their vote on conference passage. In chapter 4, only bills with a roll-call vote were included in the analysis, but here, because I have the ability to compare two votes directly, I include all bills that received a roll-call vote at either the passage or conference stage. This strategy also allows the inclusion of bills that may have been passed by unanimous consent originally but were changed in a such a way as to make the bill more controversial, resulting in a roll-call vote at the conference stage (or vice versa when a bill became less controversial). Unanimous consent votes are treated as if every member voted yea; the dependent variable is the percentage of members switching their votes for every conference bill receiving a roll-call vote at either stage and considered by both chambers.

As table 5.1 shows, vote switching by representatives and senators is quite common, with about 15 percent of House members switching their

TABLE 5.1 **Summary statistics for percentage of vote switching—initial passage to conference**

House vote switching (%)	
All conference bills	
Mean	15.26
SD	(15.39)
N	1006
Coalition < .75 on passage	
Mean	21.77
SD	(15.68)
N	252
Senate vote switching (%)	
All conference bills	
Mean	10.16
SD	(11.14)
N	789
Coalition < .75 on passage	
Mean	16.63
SD	(15.68)
N	252

Note: 93rd–113th Congresses. Only bills with a roll-call vote at either the passage or conference approval stage in both chambers are included. For those bills with a roll-call vote in one but not the other, the unanimous consent vote is coded as all members voting yes.

vote from passage to the conference vote, and about 10 percent of senators switching. The table also shows the amount of vote switching that occurs on more controversial bills, those that received less than 75 percent support in the chamber on initial passage. A higher percentage of members switch on these bills, suggesting that greater changes are made to them by the conferees, as one would expect given their greater salience within Congress. The table demonstrates that conferee discretion exists, as measured by vote switching, and that substantive changes are made to the bills at the conference stage. These changes are so large, even on controversial bills, that on average nearly ninety-five members of the House switch their vote when the bills come back from conference. In the Senate, fewer members switch their vote on regular bills than in the House, but on important bills the conferees produce enough change to induce nearly seventeen senators to change their vote.

One of the bills with the greatest percentage of vote switching in the study is H.R. 2346, a supplemental appropriations bill enacted in 2009, which included funding for the wars in Iraq and Afghanistan; nearly 42 percent of members switched their vote from passage to the conference version. The bill originally passed the House with the support of 368 members, including 200 Democrats and 168 Republicans. This suggests the conferees had substantial discretion, which they used, to change the bill so that it reflected the Senate's preferences. The conference bill received the votes of only five Republicans, while twenty-one more Democrats supported the bill after conference; in the Senate more senators supported the conference version than the original version.

Measuring Bill Failure

The second dependent variable used to explore conferee discretion is whether or not a bill failed during the conference stage. Those bills in the data set identified as going to a conference but not sent to the president are considered to have failed. These include bills in which the chambers agreed to hold a conference but no bill emerged from the conference or a formal conference was never held despite the chambers procedurally moving for a conference. Interestingly, outright rejection of the conference report on a roll-call vote is exceedingly rare; the data set includes only nine such bills rejected by the House and two by the Senate (93rd through 113th Congresses). Usually, the conference bill is never brought for a vote, or the conferees opt not to refer the report to the chambers rather than see it fail on the floor.

The vast majority of bills that fail and never receive a vote in the chambers are observationally equivalent to those that fail due to disagreement among the conferees. I assume that the failure to resolve a bill by the conference is driven by constraints created by the chamber and that, if the conferees were free to create a bill of their choosing, failure in the conference would occur much less frequently (or not at all). Though the chambers almost never vote to reject a conference report, the failure of the conferees to reach agreement is a manifestation of the conferees' inability to craft a compromise they believe will be acceptable to their respective winning coalitions. The sample for bill failure is limited to those bills that received a roll-call vote in a chamber, where a unanimous vote in the other chamber is assumed as all members voting yea.

For a sense of the characteristics of these bills, table 5.2 shows the vote percentage they received on passage in both chambers as compared to successful bills (those resolved by the conference committee and sent to the president), and their importance as measured by the CQA lines variable. As the table shows, successful bills received more support than failed bills

TABLE 5.2 **Difference-of-means test on winning coalition size for failed conference bills**

	Successful bills		Failed bills
Mean House vote %	84.98		81.25
SD	(15.18)		(16.08)
N	989		112
Mean difference		3.73	
t-statistic		2.45	
p-value		0.01	
Mean Senate vote %	91.54		91.37
SD	(11.87)		(12.05)
N	989		112
Mean difference		0.17	
t-statistic		0.14	
p-value		0.89	
CQA article lines	1110.75		775.46
SD	(1486.82)		(1023.84)
N	979		112
Mean difference		664.71	
t-statistic		2.32	
p-value		0.02	

Note: 93rd–113th Congresses (through 111th for CQA article lines). Only bills with a roll-call vote on passage in either the House or Senate are included. For those bills that received a vote in one chamber but not the other, the unanimous consent vote is coded as all members voting yes.

in the House but not in the Senate. Clearly, bill failure is not the result of tenuous support within the chamber, as on average these bills received support from more than 80 percent of each chamber. Nor is the cloture requirement in the Senate driving failure. Only 5 of the 112 bills that went to conference and failed had fewer than sixty votes on initial passage in that chamber. Finally, bills that failed were less important than those that succeeded in Congress, as shown by the significance of the difference-of-means test for CQA lines.

Majority Coalition Moderation and Other Variables

To test whether the ideological characteristics of coalitions constrain conferees I use the average absolute value of the common-space DW-NOMINATE score of the winning coalition. These scores are measured on a −1 to 1 scale, where −1 and 1 represent extreme liberalness and extreme conservatism, respectively. I take the average DW-NOMINATE score of members in each winning coalition and then take the absolute value, resulting in a scale that ranges from 0 to 1, where 0 represents the most moderate coalitions, and 1 represents the most ideologically extreme coalitions.

NOMINATE scores measure a member's overall ideology and are not specific to a particular bill; it is possible an ideologically moderate member is an extremist on a particular legislative item. Much of the problem measuring preferences on individual bills stems from an inability by scholars to identify status quo points within an ideological space and compare that position to the proposed bill (Peress 2013). The zero point, identified as the most moderate coalition score possible, has no inherent meaning for a particular bill for the same reasons. Still, for most bills, as Poole and Rosenthal show, voting behavior conforms to a single-dimensional ideological space, so, over a large enough sample of bills, NOMINATE scores should reflect a member's ideological position relative to other members and the status quo.

To measure conferee uncertainty on where to locate the legislative compromise, I use the standard deviation of DW-NOMINATE scores of members in the winning coalition for each bill. These are relative NOMINATE scores rather than absolute scores so that, as the standard deviation increases, what I call ideological diversity also increases. More ideological diversity in the winning coalition creates more conferee uncertainty about the coalition's disagreement value and how much of the benefits to allocate to it. Other variables are included in the models to control for confounding factors. These measures—the standard deviation of ideology in the House, the distance from the Senate median to the filibuster pivot, and the distance between the chamber medians—capture the variation in preferences within and between each chamber. Also included are bill-level measures, including one for bill importance, the *CQA* lines variable, a variable identifying the bill as making appropriations, and, finally, the size of the winning coalition on the bill.

Predicting Conferee Discretion

Results predicting the percentage of members who switch their votes from the initial passage vote to the conference report vote are shown in table 5.3 for all bills that received at least one roll-call vote; vote switching captures the amount of change made by conferees exercising their discretion. The theory predicts that a decrease in coalition moderation will increase

TABLE 5.3 **Effect of coalition moderation on vote switching**

Independent variables	House vote switching (1)	Senate vote switching (2)
House coalition extremity	1.56**	0.90**
	(0.20)	(0.15)
Senate coalition extremity	1.97**	1.26**
	(0.30)	(0.22)
CQA article lines coverage	−0.02	−0.002
	(0.02)	(0.01)
Appropriations bill	−0.01	−0.01
	(0.01)	(0.01)
House chamber SD	0.24*	0.06
	(0.14)	(0.11)
Senate median-filibuster distance	−0.34**	0.05
	(0.12)	(0.09)
Distance between chamber medians	−0.10	−0.01
	(0.11)	(0.08)
House extremity × Senate extremity	−17.18**	−8.03**
	(2.31)	(1.71)
Constant	0.001	−0.04
	(0.05)	(0.03)
Adj. R^2	0.10	0.08
N	700	700

Note: The dependent variable is the percentage of members who switched their vote from initial passage to conference passage for any bill that received a roll-call vote at either the passage or conference stage in both chambers and was sent to the president, 93rd–111th Congresses. Entries are regression coefficients with clustered standard errors by congress in parentheses. Ideological extremity and distance variables are measured using common-space DW-NOMINATE scores. $*p < 0.1; **p < 0.05$.

the percentage of members who change their vote, because more extreme coalitions have smaller disagreement values, while less ideological coalitions are more resolute and more willing to reject the conference report, thus reducing conferee discretion. The theory also predicts that when both chambers are simultaneously willing to reject the report, conferees exercise less discretion and must minimize the amount they change the bill. The two models predict vote switching in the House (model 1) and Senate (model 2), with interactions between the extremity of the winning coalition in the House and Senate, where higher values indicate a higher (more extreme) average absolute DW-NOMINATE score. The interaction terms capture how the effect of coalition extremity in one chamber changes conditional on extremity in the other chamber.

Each of the coalition extremity component terms can be interpreted as the effect of increasing extremity on vote switching when coalition extremity in the other chamber is equal to 0 (or absolute moderation). Thus, in model 1, when the Senate is moderate, an increase in House extremity from the minimum to the maximum increases vote switching in the House by about 41 percent (95 percent CI: 30.5 percent to 51.4 percent). The same is true for the effect in the Senate; an increase from minimum Senate coalition extremity to maximum increases vote switching by 25.6 percent (95 percent CI: 16.7 percent to 34.5 percent). These component term effects support the theory in that vote switching increases in a chamber when the other coalition is moderate and its own coalition extremity increases. Interestingly, the component terms for the other chamber are also positive and significant, indicating that vote switching increases as the other chamber becomes more extreme. Senate extremity increases vote switching in the House, while House extremity increases vote switching in the Senate. It should be noted, however, that, though absolute moderation is possible, it never occurs in the data, meaning the component term coefficients are theoretically suggestive but require the interpretation of the interaction terms to fully understand the theoretical relationship.

To identify how *relative* extremity influences vote switching, the interaction terms in both models between House and Senate extremity test the theoretical claim that conferee discretion is limited by the chamber most willing to reject the conference bill. As one chamber becomes more (less) ideological, discretion for the conferees will increase (decrease), producing more (less) vote switching in that chamber. And, as one chamber becomes more extreme, the other chamber is empowered in the bargaining process, making it the binding constraint and reducing vote switching. For example, in the House, an increasingly extreme Senate should make the House the binding constraint and reduce vote switching as the House, rather than the Senate, limits conferee discretion. In other words, the more extreme one chamber is relative to the other, the less important that chamber's own extremity will be on vote switching as a measure of conferee discretion.

The interaction term shows that, as the Senate becomes more extreme, it reduces the effect of House extremity on vote switching. The relationship also exists for Senate vote switching: as the House becomes more extreme, the marginal effect of Senate extremity on vote switching is reduced. The predicted values of each chamber's quantity of vote switching given each chamber's extremity and conditional on the other chamber's extremity are shown in figure 5.1. For each panel, the x axis shows how an increase in the other chamber's extremity causes a change in the predicted value of vote switching for each chamber. Solid lines with confidence intervals are shown for each chamber at the maximum value of its own coalition extremity.

As the top panel of figure 5.1 shows, when the winning coalition in the Senate is very moderate and the House coalition is very extreme, there is a much higher rate of vote switching from passage to conference in the House, indicating that the Senate constrains discretion. As the Senate coalition becomes more extreme, the quantity of vote switching in a very extreme House coalition declines as it becomes more likely that the Senate is no longer the binding constraint on the conferees. At maximum House extremity and low Senate extremity, about 41.3 percent of House members are expected to switch their vote, indicating high conferee discretion with respect to the House. As the Senate also becomes more extreme, predicted House vote switching declines, to about 13 percent, when Senate extremity is at the third quartile. Because the other chamber's component term has a positive effect on vote switching, as House extremity declines, the negative effect of Senate extremity on vote switching also moderates. For example, when the House coalition is of average extremity, there is a much lower baseline level of vote switching, with only about 14 percent of members predicted to switch at minimum Senate extremity, as is expected. As Senate coalition extremity increases, the conferees have more discretion and vote switching increases slightly, even in the House. At the maximum value of Senate extremity, predicted House vote switching when its coalition is of average extremity is 23 percent. This relationship shows that, when neither chamber is very moderate, the conferees have more discretion to change the bill resulting in more vote switching without much constraint from the coalitions.

The pattern is very similar in the Senate, though notably there is greater variation in House coalition extremity than in Senate extremity. Again, when the Senate winning coalition is very extreme, about 24 percent of senators switch their vote when the House is at its most moderate. When the House is at its median extremity, about 18 percent of senators are predicted to switch their votes, and, when both the Senate and House are very extreme, only about 5 percent of senators are predicted to vote switch, as the Senate becomes the binding constraint on the conferees. The relationship is different when the Senate is more moderate. As with the House, there is a lower baseline level of vote switching when the House is at its most moderate and the Senate coalition is at its mean level of moderation, with zero vote switching in the Senate predicted by the model. Compare this to the 14 percent of House members expected to change their votes when the Senate is very moderate and the House coalition is somewhat moderate, suggesting that the Senate, in general,

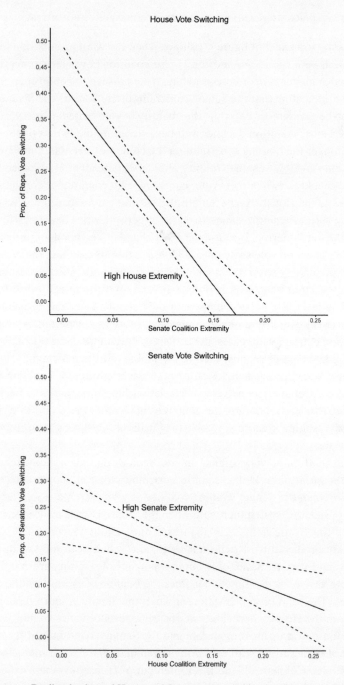

FIGURE 5.1. Predicted values of House and Senate vote switching conditional on chamber extremity. Dashed lines indicate predicted values from models 1 and 2 in table 5.3 with 95 percent confidence interval. All other variables held at their means except for appropriations, which is held at 0.

constrains conferees more. As House extremity increases, vote switching in the Senate also increases. At average Senate extremity and high House extremity, about 22 percent of senators are predicted to switch their vote from passage to conference. This is a situation in which neither chamber significantly constrains the conferees and they have a large amount of discretion to change the bill, though the Senate is likely the binding constraint given that it typically has a more moderate membership and, as a result, a more moderate winning coalition. These results confirm key predictions of the theory but also suggest that the results are stronger for relatively high values of extremity from both chambers. More extreme chambers grant more discretion to conferees and, as a result, more vote switching from passage to conference occurs, though, as the small effects at mean values of extremity show, the negative effect exists only once the winning coalition reaches an extremity threshold. Discretion is a function of both chambers' relative ideological positions, so, as one chamber becomes more extreme relative to the other chamber, vote switching decreases in the more moderate chamber. The effects of extremity and vote switching are more pronounced in the Senate than in the House, but the overall results support the coalition relative extremity hypothesis.

There is no evidence for a linear, additive relationship of House and Senate ideology. Models that use the sum of average House and Senate coalition extremity as a variable do not produce the expected results, suggesting that vote switching in a chamber is largely due to that coalition's extremity relative to the other winning coalition. That is, there is no clear effect when looking at each chamber individually. It is only when coalition extremity is conditioned on the other winning coalition's ideological extremity that vote switching changes. Another important result from the models shows that, on average, House winning coalitions are slightly more ideologically extreme than Senate coalitions, and there is more variation in House extremity, including a higher maximum extremity score than the Senate. When the same relationships are examined for only the 104th through 111th Congresses, when polarization is much higher compared to previous years, there are positive, unconditional effects of House and Senate extremity on vote switching (results not shown). Since the 104th Congress, both winning coalitions have become more ideologically extreme and, as a result, both chambers may be more sensitive to an increase in the other's extremity. Other significant variables in table 5.3 are also broadly supportive of the theory. The distance between the Senate median and filibuster pivot reduces vote switching in the House, though not in the

Senate. As this variable increases, there is more variation in Senate ideology, which may constrain discretion, especially if the House is more extreme. In the House, the measure of overall ideological variation—the standard deviation of NOMINATE scores—is the only other significant variable in the models (at the .1 level). That is, when there is greater ideological diversity in the House, there is more vote switching, as expected.

The Effect of Coalition Moderation and Coalition Size on Conferee Discretion

In addition to the interactive effect of winning coalition ideology in each chamber, the theory also suggests that coalition size will affect conferee discretion. Though more moderate chambers are more willing to reject the conference report, the conferees can afford to lose votes if the winning coalition is very large. When coalitions are small, however, the conferees must be careful about exercising too much discretion and risking rejection. In table 5.4, I test whether coalition size conditions the relationship between coalition extremity and vote switching in the House and Senate. The models interact the ideological extremity of the winning coalitions in each chamber with the size of the winning coalition and include controls for the other chamber's extremity and winning coalition size.

The first two models both use the percentage of voters who switch in the House, while the last two models examine vote switching in the Senate. Each model includes an interaction term where coalition extremity is multiplied by the percentage of the chamber voting in favor of the bill on passage (models 1 and 3) or the relative extremity of the chamber coalition is multiplied by the percentage of the chamber voting in favor (models 2 and 4). The relative extremity variable is constructed such that larger values indicate that the chamber coalition is more extreme than the other coalition (i.e., in the House models an increase in the relative extremity variable indicates the House winning coalition becomes more extreme than the Senate). This interaction determines whether smaller coalition sizes condition the relationship between chamber extremity (relative to the other chamber) and vote switching, combining the insights from the previous models.

Looking first at models 1 and 3 for the House and Senate, the interaction term between overall extremity and the percentage of the chamber voting yes on the bill at passage is not statistically significant in the House, but it is positive and significant in the Senate. As the Senate coalition becomes more extreme, it increases the effect of Senate coalition size on

TABLE 5.4 **Effect of chamber yea votes and coalition moderation on vote switching**

Independent variables	House vote switching		Senate vote switching	
	(1)	(2)	(3)	(4)
House total yea %	−0.29**	−0.22**	−0.27**	−0.23**
	(0.10)	(0.05)	(0.04)	(0.04)
Senate total yea %	−0.04	0.004	−0.49**	−0.24**
	(0.06)	(0.05)	(0.08)	(0.04)
CQA article lines coverage	−0.05**	−0.04**	−0.02**	−0.02*
	(0.02)	(0.02)	(0.01)	(0.01)
Appropriations bill	−0.002	0.002	−0.001	0.01
	(0.01)	(0.01)	(0.01)	(0.01)
House chamber SD	0.01	−0.02	0.03	−0.03
	(0.15)	(0.14)	(0.10)	(0.10)
Senate median-filibuster distance	−0.31**	−0.34**	0.05	0.04
	(0.12)	(0.12)	(0.08)	(0.08)
Distance between chamber medians	−0.20*	−0.13	−0.11	−0.06
	(0.11)	(0.11)	(0.08)	(0.07)
House coalition extremity	0.05		−0.26**	
	(0.65)		(0.10)	
Senate coalition extremity	0.02		−2.27**	
	(0.18)		(0.59)	
House extremity × House yea %	−0.50			
	(0.83)			
House extremity relative to Senate		2.54**		
		(0.51)		
Relative extremity × House yea %		−3.62**		
		(0.65)		
Senate extremity × Senate yea %			2.82**	
			(0.72)	
Senate extremity relative to House				1.68**
				(0.46)
Relative extremity × Senate yea %				−1.76**
				(0.51)
Constant	0.57**	0.44**	0.78**	0.53**
	(0.10)	(0.06)	(0.07)	(0.04)
Adj. R^2	0.10	0.13	0.22	0.21
N	700	700	700	700

Note: The dependent variable is the percentage of members who switched their vote from initial to conference passage for any bill that received a roll-call vote at either the passage or conference stage in both chambers and was sent to the president, 93rd–111th Congresses. Entries are regression coefficients with clustered standard errors by congress in parentheses. Ideological extremity and distance variables are measured using common-space DW-NOMINATE scores. $*p < 0.1$; $**p < 0.05$.

vote switching. Predicted probabilities show that, when Senate coalition size is held at its mean and coalition extremity is at its minimum, the percentage of senators expected to switch their vote is 8.87 percent (95 percent CI: 6.77 percent to 10.97 percent). When coalition extremity reaches its maximum, the percentage of senators expected to switch their vote is

13.96 percent (95 percent CI: 10.27 percent to 17.65 percent), demonstrating how the conferees have more discretion as coalition size and coalition extremity increase, even accounting for the overall extremity of the chamber. This result strongly supports the coalition extremity and size hypothesis. I investigate the relationship between House and Senate relative extremity and coalition size in models 2 and 4 in table 5.4.

These models include a variable measuring the relative extremity of each chamber's winning coalition interacted with coalition size (recall that, as the relative extremity variable increases, the chamber coalition is more extreme compared to the other chamber). In the House the interaction term is positive and statistically significant, and predicted probabilities reveal that as the House coalition size grows, there is more vote switching, conditional on coalition extremity. Again, this supports the claim that conferees have more discretion when a chamber coalition is both extreme and large. In the Senate the interaction term is also positive and statistically significant, indicating the same relationship between extremity, coalition size, and vote switching. But predicted probabilities demonstrate that there is a very small effect on vote switching unless the Senate is very ideologically extreme. At the Senate's average coalition size, an increase from minimum relative extremity to maximum extremity increases predicted vote switching from 7 percent (95 percent CI: 2.93 percent to 11.08 percent) of the chamber to 11.4 percent of the chamber. Though this relationship follows the expected direction, the substantive effect reveals that conferee discretion is relatively insensitive to changes in Senate coalition extremity and coalition size. This is additional evidence that the conferees seem to adhere more closely to the preferences of the Senate, regardless of what its coalition looks like. If the conferees are usually worried about losing support from the Senate coalition, it may not matter how much support there is in the House.

In all the models, the measure of importance is negative and statistically significant, consistent with previous results and suggesting that more important bills produce less vote switching. Substantively, for bills that received *CQA* coverage, vote switching decreases by about 5 percent in model 1 (95 percent CI: −1.86 percent to −8.58 percent). In both models 1 and 2, greater ideological diversity in the Senate reduces House vote switching, as indicated by the Senate median-filibuster distance variable. This may be an indication of the Senate's overall moderation or the overall size of the Senate coalition. In either case, House vote switching is reduced when the Senate is more ideologically diverse by about 15 percent in model 2

(95 percent CI: −3.44 percent to −27.3 percent), offering additional evidence that the Senate seems to be the driver of conferee discretion.

Explaining Bill Failure

I now turn to examining the causes of bill failure at the conference stage. The sample consists of any bill that received a roll-call vote on passage in the chamber. Bills that failed are those that the chambers attempted to resolve in a conference committee but were never sent to the president for approval, either because the conferees could not agree on a compromise bill or because the chambers received a compromise bill and a majority voted against it.[4] The previous analyses interacted each chamber's ideology to find the combined effect of increasing extremity on conferee discretion. Here I use ideological diversity within a winning coalition to capture the concept of uncertainty about the preferences of the winning coalitions. Ideological diversity is measured through the standard deviation of each winning coalition's DW-NOMINATE score. Two sets of logit results are shown in table 5.5 predicting bill failure or not (failure = 1) with the coalition ideological diversity variable included as an interaction term with the percentage of members voting for the bill on passage in models 1 (House) and 2 (Senate). A positive coefficient indicates an increased probability of a bill failing. Because these are logit coefficients and cannot be directly interpreted, I provide predicted probabilities of failure when discussing the results.

In model 1, the interaction term coefficient is negative and statistically significant, indicating that, when there is high ideological diversity *and* low support for the bill, failure is more likely.[5] The theory argues that this occurs because low support constrains the conferees (as does ideological extremity and low support), and, when the coalition is ideologically diverse, the conferees are uncertain about what type of bill to offer back to the chambers. Failure cannot occur with just a low level of support in the chamber because the conferees will know what offer to make to the chambers that preserves that support; there must be uncertainty about what the winning coalition will accept, along with low support, to cause bill failure.

The results for the Senate interaction in model 2 are very similar. To substantively interpret the effects of these variables in the House and Senate on the probability of bill failure, predicted probabilities are shown in figure 5.2 with the House in the top panel and the Senate in the bottom panel. An increase on the *x* axis corresponds to an increase in the

TABLE 5.5 **Effect of coalition moderation and ideological heterogeneity on bill failure in conference**

Independent variables	House (1)	Senate (2)
House coalition ideo. diversity	32.57**	
	(14.34)	
Senate coalition ideo. diversity		59.21**
		(22.85)
House total yea %	8.32*	−1.43
	(5.06)	(1.00)
Senate total yea %	2.37**	27.09**
	(1.05)	(7.95)
CQA article lines coverage	−0.24	−0.36
	(0.33)	(0.34)
Appropriations bill	−17.89	−17.63
	(559.80)	(603.57)
House chamber SD	5.31	4.92
	(4.05)	(4.72)
Senate median-filibuster distance	−0.35	0.12
	(3.23)	(3.84)
Distance between chamber medians	3.20	5.06**
	(1.99)	(2.43)
House diversity × House yea %	−40.43**	
	(16.85)	
Senate diversity × Senate yea %		−85.60**
		(25.76)
Constant	−12.33**	−21.10**
	(4.20)	(6.36)
AIC	494.64	394.41
N	994	827

Note: The dependent variable is whether the bill failed at the conference stage for any bill that received a roll-call vote on passage. Entries are logit coefficients with clustered standard errors by congress in parentheses. Ideological extremity and distance variables are measured using common-space DW-NOMINATE scores. $*p < 0.1; **p < 0.05$.

percentage of members voting who supported the bill on passage, while the y axis shows the probability of failure. The solid lines represent the predicted probability of bill failure when each chamber is at the maximum observed value of ideological diversity within the winning coalition, the situation in which conferee uncertainty is maximized.

As the figure shows, when there is significant ideological heterogeneity in the House and low coalition support, the probability a bill fails is quite high, at nearly .9. Small winning coalitions and high heterogeneity together produce a high likelihood of failure, but, as the coalition size increases, even high ideological diversity does not increase the chances of bill failure. When

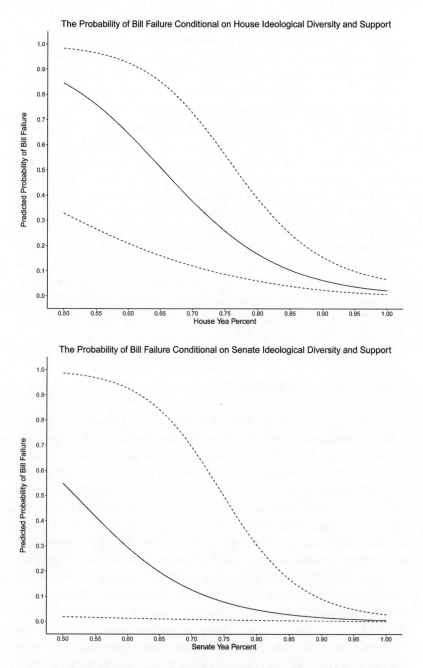

FIGURE 5.2. Predicted probability of bill failure conditional on House and Senate winning coalition size with coalition extremity held at its maximum. Dashed lines indicate predicted probabilities from models 1 and 2 in table 5.5 with 95 percent confidence interval. All other variables held at their means except for appropriations, which is held at 0.

coalition size is over 90 percent of members voting, the probability a bill fails is less than .1. The story is very similar in the Senate, with similar substantive effects, though the baseline probability of failure is lower than in the House when ideological diversity is high and coalition size is low. At high coalition diversity and low coalition size, the probability of a bill failing is about .6. The large confidence interval is itself informative as there are very few observations with a coalition size near 50 percent. The size of the confidence interval shrinks dramatically once the bill coalition size reaches about .7, and the predicted probability of failure, even for a coalition size of 75 percent of senators voting in favor, is about 9 percent. When coalition size in the Senate is over 90 percent, the probability of failure, even at the highest level of ideological diversity in the Senate, is less than 2 percent. These results validate the bill failure hypothesis and provide insight into why bill failure is exceedingly rare. By the time most bills make it to the conference stage, they have large, oversize coalitions in support. Even ideological disagreements within the coalition, which increase conferee uncertainty about where to locate a compromise, are not enough to cause the defection of a large number of members.

Implications for the Modern Congress

The formal rules of the conference process grant the conferees almost unlimited ability to change legislation. The major constraint limiting their ability to modify bills is the willingness of the chamber coalitions to reject the conference bill, an occurrence that remains rare but an important option for the House and the Senate. Notably, as the results demonstrate, the conferees must construct a compromise that satisfies both majority coalitions and anticipate the chambers' reactions to their proposal. Small coalitions limit the ability of the conferees, conditional on ideological moderation, because the loss of even a few members might produce failure, with moderates more likely than extremists to reject the bill. Additionally, conferee uncertainty, driven by high ideological diversity within the winning coalition combined with small coalition size, increases the likelihood of bill failure. These factors are distinct from party effects as conferee discretion arises out of the institutional mechanisms used to resolve interchamber differences. Ideological differences by themselves do not produce failure but create the conditions necessary for failure. I conclude that any claim about conferees changing policy to benefit themselves or their party must be circumspect. Under certain conditions the conferees are unable to change policy, even if they would like to, because meaningful change would cause at least one chamber to reject the conference bill. It is not the case that the chambers will accept any offer made—they can and do reject conference bills—even if the chamber supported the bill on passage.

The theory and results have important implications for Congress in an age of increasing ideological polarization. Counterintuitively, extremity on the part of both chambers increases conferee discretion and promotes agreement. It is the case that there are fewer bills on which a bargaining surplus exists, in that there are fewer issues on which the chambers can agree to change the status quo. But, for those bills on which they can agree, extreme coalitions and the low levels of uncertainty created by ideologically unified coalitions allow conferees to successfully propose compromise legislation. We should expect to observe more conferee discretion and fewer failures as ideological extremity increases. The results here also highlight the notion that more moderate chambers appear to be empowered during the give-and-take of conference negotiations. Despite the heated rhetoric of extreme members from ideological winning coalitions, they seem more likely to lose when faced with a moderate chamber that imposes more constraints on the conferees. This possibility is taken up in the next chapter, where I directly test whether the conference committee makes policies more centrist or more extreme, allowing for inferences on which chamber "wins" during the bargaining process.

CHAPTER SIX

Conference Committees and Policy Change after Passage

The role of conferees is unique in that their intended purpose is to make changes to the legislation in question, and their changes cannot be undone or modified, even by a majority in the chamber. While the previous chapter was concerned with *when* conferees use discretion, the focus of this chapter is *how* they use that discretion. Theories of legislative organization inform the theoretical framework developed in chapter 3, and these theories, along with the bargaining model, are used in this chapter to make specific predictions about how policy is shaped by conference committees.

Conference committees represent only one possible option for the chambers to resolve their differences, and their very use informs our understanding of policy outcomes. Congress delegates to conferees when the chambers feel there is a high likelihood of success within the conference, so failure or the misuse of discretion of by conferees must be highly unlikely. The empirical results from the last chapter bear this out: failures are rare, and they arise from uncertainty and low levels of discretion on the part of the conferees about the preferences of the winning coalitions in each chamber. Chapter 4's empirical investigation of when amendment trading or conferencing is used adds an important caveat to the claim that conferences are preferred when there is a sufficient chance of success. It seems that in the modern Congress, where legislative capacity is limited and the time demands on members are great, majorities cannot use a conference unless they have a sufficiently large coalition. If not, amendment trading becomes the preferred resolution venue because the costs of trying to push a conference over a determined, obstructionist minority are too great.

The second relevant insight from the bargaining game is that the majority coalition in each chamber must believe the compromise struck by the conferees will be sufficiently close to their policy preferences as compared to what they would receive in amendment trading, accounting for the costs of resolution through amendment trading. If one chamber believes it will not do as well in conference, but achieving compromise through chamber floor action is likely to be very difficult, it will trade off a smaller win in conference to avoid paying the substantial costs of using floor time. And, if floor time and the resources associated with passing and amending bills in both chambers are prohibitively expensive, as they have become for most majority coalitions in recent congresses, the empirical results here and in other recent work seem to suggest conference committees have even more power to change legislation in ways they see fit. That is, if amendment trading is not seen as a viable option, the conferees have a substantial degree of freedom to change bills. Scholarly interest has reflected this new reality with a significant amount of work investigating the extent to which the conferees reflect coalition preferences.

There have been two fundamental questions about how conference committees change policy. Previous work has characterized the "Who wins?" question as the most pressing issue in understanding conferencing. As detailed in chapter 2, results are inconclusive with some research finding the House wins, especially (perhaps) on appropriations, while other research suggests the Senate wins. In this chapter, I argue that "who wins" depends on the relative agreement and disagreement benefits of each winning coalition for a particular bill and the amount of discretion granted to conferees. Further, previous research on which chamber does better, in policy terms, during conferencing is almost entirely empirical in nature, and there is little existing theory to explain chamber bargaining strength or the conditions that allow one chamber to receive a greater share of the bargaining surplus.

The second commonly asked question about the relationship between conference committees and policy outcomes concerns whether conferences help the median enforce near-median policy outcomes or act as a mechanism for nonmedian members to pull policy outcomes toward their own preferences or those of other members (such as the majority party median). Though conferee discretion varies, as the last chapter showed, significant discretion exists for a large number of bills, which the conferees may use to move policy closer to their own preferences. The theorized use of the ex post veto gives the conferees substantial power because the chambers are not allowed to amend the bill, suggesting that conference committees may produce drastic change that sometimes favors one chamber over the other.

In the following sections, I use the bargaining model to develop empirical predictions of policy changes as a result of conferencing, and I compare these predictions to those generated by three theories of legislative organization. Some evidence supports distributive theory and the bargaining model. Surprisingly little evidence exists that conferences create more partisan bills. Though some bills seem to be universalistic in nature, in many cases policy outcomes seem to be located between the two chambers, as measured by changes to each winning coalition's average ideology. Importantly, bill outcomes do not move exactly to the preference of the more moderate chamber. I suggest this is because the moderate coalition has no enforcement mechanism over nonmedian outcomes due to the take-it-or-leave-it nature of the conference offer, and there is no way to move an off-median offer once it has been made by the conferees. As a result, legislation developed in conference is slightly closer to the more extreme coalition than might be the case under a more majoritarian institutional arrangement.

Competing Theoretical and Empirical Predictions of the Policy Effects of Conference Committees

As the last chapter established, it is important to be cautious about interpreting legislative changes from the passage to the conference stage because conferees can only change legislation as much as the chambers allow. But, when the conferees have discretion, how do they use it? The noncooperative bargaining model supplements those predictions made by three theories of legislative organization, each of which offers specific empirical claims about how conference committees change policy. Broadly, partisan and distributive theory predict conference committees will move policy away from the chamber median, while median voter or pivotal politics theory predicts the conference will be constrained by the median member of the more moderate winning coalition, preventing substantial policy movement away from the bill passed by that chamber and producing a near-median outcome. There are some similarities in each of the three models, especially the distributive and partisan models, which both predict nonmedian outcomes, but the empirical predictions for each of the models differ, as described below.

Universalism and Large Coalitions

Consistent with the gains-from-exchange hypothesis central to distributive theory, conferences serve as a last check on the winning coalition, modifying the legislation back to the preferences of the standing committee if the chamber removed particularistic benefits for the standing committee members. In this way, the conference acts as an enforcement mechanism, ensuring these benefits are supported by a majority of members. If a majority in the chamber strips the bill of its particularized benefits or moves policy to another actor's ideal point (e.g., that of the median or the party leadership) during the floor stage, the conferees exercise their ex post veto to ensure the bill matches their policy interests.

Distributive legislation is closely tied to the theory of universalism. If specific policy benefits are spread across members and are not zero-sum, then coalitions should be larger than minimum sized, contrary to Riker's (1962) claim that coalitions should only be as large as the minimum number of members needed to pass legislation. According to Riker, smaller coalitions allow individual members to accrue a larger share of the policy benefits, but, as has been shown here and in other literature, winning coalitions are usually oversize (Collie 1988; Fenno 1966; Ferejohn 1974; Hinckly 1972; Riker 1962). Member are incentivized to join the winning coalition because the particularized benefits they secure bolster their reelection chances and allow them to cooperate in the logroll, improving their long-term reputation and ensuring their participation in future winning coalitions. Legislation, therefore, is frequently not zero-sum, and the conference committee should seek to protect the distributive benefits preferred by the standing committee from the preferences of other actors.

Distributive theory is appealing because it explains the large coalition sizes produced by conferences, but it has one major theoretical shortcoming. The postpassage bargaining model conceives of policy change occurring along ideological dimensions rather than distributive ones and suggests that ideological moderation limits conferee discretion because of the risk of rejection. If the conferees make the policy more appealing to a larger group of members as distributive theory would suggest, resulting in

large coalition sizes, no constraints are imposed on the conferees because
there is no threat of rejection, and a bill should never fail at the conference stage. It is possible that distributive bills are a subset of all bills (Hurwitz, Moiles, and Rohde 2001) and that the theory applies to those but not
to more ideological or more partisan bills that run a risk of failure during
the conference process.

Partisan Conferees and Ideologically Extreme Bills

Contrary to distributive theory, partisan theories of conference outcomes
predict conference bills will be made more ideologically extreme as compared to the chamber version of the bill. Parties and their leadership, especially under conditions of strong party government, when party membership is ideologically homogeneous and distinct from the other chamber
(Aldrich 1995; Rohde 1991), seek to produce nonmedian outcomes that
reflect the majority party's preference. The conference committee, despite
its standing-committee-based composition, can also reflect the preferences
of the party leadership, which largely controls conference appointments.
Recent empirical work has shown that conference committees have also
included, in addition to members of the standing committee, party loyalists
(Lazarus and Monroe 2007). Similar to distributive theory, the conference
exercises discretion over the bill to produce a nonmedian outcome but one
that creates smaller, more partisan coalitions.

Making bill outcomes more partisan distributes a disproportionate
share of the benefits to party members, helping build their brand, secure
partisan reputations, and ultimately assisting with reelection. Members
of the minority party must be excluded from these benefits for the majority party to secure electoral benefits and help it expand its seat majority
within the chambers (Cox and McCubbins 2005). If conferees enforce a
partisan outcome, they move policy in a more extreme direction toward
the party median and away from the chamber median, which hurts party
members who are moderate. However, a significant body of literature examines ways in which the majority party can buy off near-median members to induce cooperation with the party's preferred policy so as to realize support from more moderate members (Jenkins and Monroe 2012).

Party theory is able to explain conference bill failure and predicts a
reduction in the size of winning coalitions from passage to conference.
If the conferees move policy away from the median member and toward
the majority party's median, the ideology of the winning coalition will become more extreme as moderates, near the chamber median, switch from

supporting the bill to opposing it. Consistent with the implications from the postpassage bargaining model, the median operates as the constraint on policy movement. The conferees can move policy toward the party's ideal only to the point where the median prefers the status quo; further movement away from the median induces rejection. Because the bill has moved toward the majority party's preference, the members of the new winning coalition postconference will be more ideologically extreme than those that voted for the bill on initial passage.

The Pivotal Voter and Moderate Bills

In a majoritarian legislature, the median must be included in any winning coalition (Black 1948; Downs 1957), while in nonmajoritarian legislatures such as the Senate where sixty votes are required for most legislative action, the sixtieth member must be included in any winning coalition, resulting in that member being pivotal (Krehbiel 1998). These pivotal actors can dictate policy outcomes because competing coalitions need their vote, and, given open proposal rights, the resulting policy will be located exactly at their ideal point. In the two-chamber context, the chamber pivot closer to the status quo will receive their preferred policy because they act as the binding constraint on the conferee. The end result is that policy will only be moved as far from the status quo as the pivotal actor in the moderate chamber closest to the status quo allows.[1]

Pivotal voter theory implies policy should become more moderate during the conference stage. The conferees, rather than enforcing a distributive outcome, instead ensure the bill reflects an outcome at the median or pivotal voter's preference. This also implies the median controls appointments to the conference committee because, if the conferees propose a nonmedian policy, the median does not have a chance to amend the bill. Like distributive theory, pivotal voter theory cannot explain conference failures. If policy collapses to the more moderate of the two chambers, the more extreme chamber will accept the bill because, according to pivotal voter theory, the new policy improves upon the status quo while the more moderate chamber receives its exact policy preference.

The Postpassage Bargaining Model and "Compromise" Bills

The postpassage bargaining theory relies on each chamber's willingness to reject the conference report because of the benefits received from disagreement. The conferees, in turn, seek to find a bargain that allocates benefits larger than each winning coalitions' disagreement value, but the conferees have imperfect information about the winning coalitions' preferences, resulting in a policy proposal that is usually acceptable to both chambers.[2] This offer, however, is likely not exactly what the more moderate chamber would prefer given uncertainty and the presence on the conference committee of members of the other chamber who seek to misrepresent their own constraints. The consequence is that both chambers are allocated benefits, with the more extreme winning coalition (the coalition less likely to reject) receiving a greater share of the benefits than might otherwise be expected. How is it that the more moderate winning coalition is not able to enforce its ideal point? Policy collapse to the median requires the ability to amend proposals or the ability of the median to propose their preferred policy. If the conference committee does not propose a bill exactly at the median's ideal point but instead proposes a bill that allocates more benefits from acceptance than rejection, the median or pivotal actor will accept a nonmedian proposal. Modifying median voter theory somewhat through the inability of the median to control conference proposals, policy will move toward the more moderate winning coalition (the coalition more likely to reject), in contrast with both distributive and partisan theory, but will not exactly reflect that coalition's preference.

In contrast to pivotal voter theory, which suggests the more median winning coalition should not change at all after conference, the bargaining model claims the more moderate coalition will become slightly more extreme. Further, median-controlled outcomes do not comport with observations about the composition of conference committees, or the occasional failure of conferences. It is also hard to reconcile this claim with the necessity of holding conferences because median-oriented outcomes imply reconciliation would be meaningless. In this scenario, the chambers would each pass their bill, and the more moderate chamber could then demand, credibly, the other chamber pass its own version of the bill. Most research views compromise bills as somewhere between what the two chambers want, and there is virtually no evidence that one of the two chambers consistently receives its exact bill after conference. Using the noncooperative bargaining model, the more moderate winning coalition will constrain policy outcomes, but it does not have the ability to enforce its preferred policy because it cannot amend the conference bill and multiple offers are not allowed. The similarities between pivotal voter theory and the bargaining model are numerous. Both see moderate actors as exerting a powerful pull on outcomes, causing policy to move toward the ideological center. Both also see postpassage bargaining as a way of enforcing these types of outcomes despite the attempts of other actors, such as committee members or party leaders, to create nonmedian policies.

Empirical Predictions from the Competing Theories

There have been only limited efforts to test how the conferees change bills from passage to conference, though each of the three established theories of legislative organization has different empirical implications.[3] Here, universalism is tested using changes in winning coalition size; partisan theory is tested using changes in the partisanship of the winning coalition, and median or pivotal voter theory is tested using changes in the ideological composition of the winning coalition.

Shepsle and Weingast (1987) describe the ex post veto as a defensive measure used by the standing committee. They say, "A committee with ex post veto power possesses the power to protect itself against welfare-reducing changes in the status quo" (94). Under some circumstances, floor action should reduce the size of the winning coalition to provide particularized goods to a smaller group of members, making the ex post veto necessary. Thus, if the conferees protect distributive preferences and encourage universalism, increases in coalition sizes from passage to conference in both chambers should be observed. An increase in the size of the coalition will not be limited by the size of the coalition in one chamber because there is no inherent limit on the quantity of benefits that can be distributed, resulting in coalition sizes in both chambers becoming larger, on average, across many conference committees. If the conferees increase coalition size from passage after a conference, the increase will not be the same across all sizes of passage coalitions. I expect the effect to be greater for smaller coalitions than for larger coalitions. Small coalitions on passage are those that are least universalistic in nature and most likely to see an increase in coalition size. Large coalitions, on the other hand, will not increase because they already encompass most members willing to support the bill, and the conferees are unable to make near unanimous coalitions larger.

Evidence of distributive theory can also be verified by examining coalition size changes for different types of legislation. Some types of bills are ideological in nature and split members into clear policy coalitions. For example, in the 1800s, tariff bills were perhaps the defining partisan or ideological issue and one on which policy benefits were zero-sum and not universalistic (Epstein and O'Halloran 1996; Madonna 2011; Schick-ler 2001). More recently, appropriations bills are commonly thought of as bipartisan and distributive in nature rather than partisan (Crespin and Rohde 2010; Fenno 1966; Kiewiet and McCubbins 1991). If any subset of bills is expected to show increasing coalition sizes and, hence, evidence of universalism, appropriations is the most obvious candidate.

In contrast, partisan theory rests on the ability of the conferees to make the bill more ideologically extreme in general but more partisan in particular. That is, if members of the parties are arrayed along a one-dimensional ideological spectrum, the bill outcome will move away from the chamber median and toward the party median. Within one chamber, the revised bill will attract fewer overall voters, but this loss of support should be dispro-portionately from members of the minority party. The revised bill will ben-efit only members of the majority party to an extent that the bill originally passed by the chamber did not. As a result, a more partisan bill should in-clude fewer members of the minority party and be composed, to a greater extent than the initial passage bill, of majority party members. I examine differences in minority party support because some members of the ma-jority may continue to support the bill even as it becomes more partisan if the party is willing to buy them off, making majority party support less sensitive to bill movement away from the median when the bill moves in the direction of the majority party. Minority party support, in contrast, is not subject to party inducements and is driven only by these members' spatial location relative to the proposed bill and the status quo. As with coalition size, the effect is not expected to be the same across all values of minority party support. Only when bills are bipartisan in nature dur-ing passage will a majority exercise its conference power and make the bill less partisan. On bills that are already fairly favorable to the majority party, the conferees are not expected to make the bill more partisan, thus reducing the expected effect size.

Partisan changes connect to universalism as well and can also be mea-sured through the size of the legislative coalition. Not only will the winning coalition become more extreme, it will also become smaller. At its smallest, it will be minimum sized, composed of 50 percent plus one of members in the House and sixty senators due to that institution's supermajority rules. Partisan theory conceives of bills as ideological rather than universalistic, and, as a result, policy is zero-sum. Thus, evidence for the conferees act-ing as party loyalists would be a reduction in coalition size as compared to passage, in addition to a more partisan coalition. This effect should be especially pronounced during periods of unified party control of the chambers because of ideological agreement between the House and Senate. I also test whether more partisan outcomes occur in unified chambers after the 104th Congress, during a period of strong party control by the leadership (Aldrich and Rohde 1997).

Pivotal voter theory makes a distinct empirical prediction, different from either distributive or partisan theory. Unlike distributive theory, pivotal voter theory is explicitly unidimensional and predicts policy will collapse to the more moderate chamber pivot. Within each chamber, policy collapses to the pivot because that member controls the conferees and the rules by which the bill is considered. Even if the bill is not moved to the pivot's ideal point at the floor passage stage, the conferees should move it there during the resolution stage. In the two-chamber context, the chamber closer to the status quo is able to dictate policy because the more extreme chamber will accept policy at the other chamber's ideal point, assuming open proposal or amending rights. If bills are moved closer to the status quo, then the ideological composition of the winning coalition should moderate relative to the winning coalition's ideology on passage. That is, more extreme winning coalitions should become more moderate, while the more moderate winning coalition should see no change in its ideology, because policy collapses to its ideal point, which is reflected in the bill passed initially by the chamber.

Pivotal voter theory requires unidimensional, zero-sum assumptions, while the noncooperative bargaining theory claims that even extreme coalitions must receive benefits from the compromise. Further, conference committees do not empower the pivotal member of the coalition to make a proposal closer to the status quo, and, once one is made by the conferees, it cannot be amended. The conferees are uncertain about what each coalition will accept, but the larger share of the surplus will be given to the more moderate coalition because it will reject too small a share. The more extreme coalition will also receive some of the benefits, and, combined with uncertainty, the results are off-median but moderate outcomes, despite the binding constraint of satisfying the more moderate coalition.[4]

As a result, conferences should produce three distinct effects. First, extreme chamber coalitions will become more moderate, as measured by the average ideological extremity of the winning coalition, as the conference committee will produce a bill closer to the preferred policy of the moderate chamber. Conversely, an increase in extremity in the other chamber will increase ideological extremity within a chamber as policy is pulled, even if slightly, toward that chamber's preferences. Finally, the average ideological extremity of a winning coalition will decrease conditional on it being the more moderate of the two winning coalitions. Each of these claims is consistent with the notion that the conferences distribute benefits to the two winning coalitions, making policy slightly more extreme than the more moderate winning coalition but less extreme than the more extreme winning coalition would prefer.

    Intrachamber Extremity Change Hypothesis: *As winning coalition extremity on passage increases, winning coalition extremity on the conference bill will decrease.*

    Opposing Chamber Extremity Change Hypothesis: *As winning coalition extremity on passage for the other chamber increases, winning coalition extremity on the conference bill will increase.*

    Moderate Chamber Conditional Extremity Change Hypothesis: *For the more moderate of the two chambers, winning coalition extremity on passage will increase winning coalition extremity on the conference bill.*

    Conferences should cause the more extreme winning coalition to moderate, which will also increase coalition size, similar to distributive theory,

TABLE 6.1 **Key empirical predictions from competing theories**

Distributive/universalism	1. Coalition size from passage to conference will increase in both chambers.
	2. Coalition size increase from passage to conference will be most pronounced for appropriations bills.
Partisan	1. Coalitions will be increasingly dominated by the majority party from passage to conference.
	2. Majority party dominance will be most pronounced during unified party control of the chambers and in more recent congresses.
Pivotal politics/median voter	1. Coalition extremity will decrease in the more extreme winning coalition from passage to conference.
	2. There will be no change to the extremity of the more moderate coalition from passage to conference as policy collapses to that chamber's ideal point.
Bargaining theory	1. Coalition extremity will decrease from passage to conference.
	2. An increase in coalition extremity in the other chamber will produce an increase in coalition extremity from passage to conference.
	3. The direction of coalition extremity change will be conditional on whether the winning coalition is the more moderate of the two.

while the more moderate coalition will become slightly more extreme, resulting in legislation somewhere between the preferences of the two chambers. This is consistent with the claim that conference bill failure results from the conferees proposing bills that are too extreme in the absence of well-understood preferences and that the other chamber must receive benefits to approve the compromise bill. Additionally, coalition sizes should increase as policy becomes more moderate; minority support should increase, and the more extreme chamber should become more ideologically moderate, while the more moderate chamber should become slightly more ideologically extreme. Table 6.1 summarizes these stylized predictions for each of the competing theoretical claims.

Measuring Changes to Coalition Sizes, Party Support, and Ideological Preferences

Ideally, one would compare the ideological position of bills to determine how partisan or median oriented they become, but it is impossible to determine the location of the status quo and the relatively extremity of a bill compared to the status quo. Instead, I use coalition size, minority party support, and coalition extremity as measured by the absolute value of the winning coalition's common-space DW-NOMINATE score. For each of these dependent variables, I take the difference in coalition values between the winning coalition at conference and the winning coalition at passage. I am interested in predicting how each of these values changes — whether, for example, coalition sizes increase or decrease from passage to conference. This concept requires a differenced measure rather than simply predicting the overall size of coalitions, majority party support, or ideological extremity. It is certainly the case that larger coalitions on passage will predict larger coalitions after a conference, but I am interested in whether or not coalition characteristics change in a positive or negative direction.

The change in coalition size is calculated as

(6.1) *change in coalition size = proportion of members supporting conference bill – proportion of members supporting bill at passage.*

Because the proportion of members supporting the bill at conference can range from 0 to 1 and at passage from .5 (or, more specifically, the minimum winning coalition size on passage is .5 + 1 additional member) the value can range from –.5 (all members supported the bill at passage but none did at conference) to .5 (only .5 of members supported the bill at passage but all members supported the bill after the conference).[5] The differenced variables are more difficult to interpret than a standard regression coefficient. A positive coefficient indicates that the change in coalition size grew from conference to passage, while a negative coefficient indicates that the difference between conference coalition size and passage size decreases as the independent variable increases but does not necessarily mean the conference coalition was smaller than the passage coalition.

Likewise, the change in minority support is

(6.2) *change in minority support = proportion of minority party members supporting conference bill – proportion of minority party members supporting bill at passage.*

This differenced variable must be interpreted with caution, as a negative coefficient does not necessarily indicate that fewer minority party members supported the bill, only that the difference between the conference passage coalition and the initial passage coalition decreased.

In the previous chapter, I took an average of the absolute value of the common-space DW-NOMINATE scores for all members of the winning coalition to measure how extreme or moderate the bill was on passage. Here I use the same variable but find the difference between coalition extremity at conference passage as compared to initial passage. As the variable increases, the greater the difference between ideological extremity for the coalition supporting the bill on conference relative to the coalition that supported it on passage.

(6.3) *change in ideological extremity = absolute value of (average DW-NOMINATE score of members in the winning coalition for the conference bill) – absolute value of (average DW-NOMINATE score of members in the winning coalition for the bill on passage).*

Difference-of-Means Tests

As a first step in evaluating the different theories of conferee discretion, I examine coalition size differences between the passage vote and the conference vote. Recall that distributive theory predicts coalition sizes will increase from passage to conference, while partisan theory suggests the winning coalition should include fewer members from the minority party. Larger coalitions are associated with less ideologically extreme coalitions and policy outcomes, as it can be shown in a one-dimensional spatial model that larger coalition sizes indicate the bill is more moderate in that it is closer to the status quo than an alternative bill (Krehbiel 1998; Snyder and Groseclose 2000; McGrath, Rogowski, and Ryan 2015). An increase in coalition sizes from passage to conference should be interpreted as evidence the bill is becoming more moderate, while smaller coalitions indicate a bill became more extreme or moved farther from the status quo after conference in relation to the passage bill.

Table 6.2 shows the mean coalition size for bills in the data set on chamber passage and then on that bill's subsequent conference version. The first set of descriptives are for all conference bills that received a roll-call vote on either passage or the conference report, while the second set limits the sample to more controversial bills, those that received less than 75 percent of members voting in favor of the bill. Results are shown for both the House and Senate. First, as has previously been noted, most bills are passed with large coalitions, but conference reports tend to have more support in each chamber than the bill initially passed. This is preliminary evidence that the conferees use their discretion to change legislation in a substantive way that makes the bill more palatable to a larger group of members. For all bills in both chambers and for the more controversial set of bills in both chambers, there is a statistically significant increase in coalition size after the bill returns from conference. This is additional evidence that conferees exercise substantial discretion in the conference committee, and it provides prima facie evidence against the party control of conferences claim; larger coalitions suggest more moderate rather than more extreme policy outcomes.

It is also relatively uncommon for the coalitions to become larger in both chambers simultaneously. There are 206 observations where this occurs, and 406 where the coalition size in one chamber increases and the other decreases, both decrease, or the coalition sizes remain the same. Of the 206 bills where the coalition size in both chambers increases, 105 (51 percent) are appropriations bills. This lends some support to the idea that appropriations bills are distributive or universalistic in nature, while other types of bills are more ideological in nature. The 2009 Supplemental Appropriations Act attracted much less support in the House, as Republicans largely voted against the bill after it came back from Congress, while at the same time it attracted more support in the Senate from the minority party (Republicans). This result is difficult to square with partisan theories

TABLE 6.2 **Difference-of-means test on winning coalition size for passage and conference votes**

	Vote type	
	Passage	Conference
House		
All conference bills		
Mean vote %	85.23	86.53
SD	(15.18)	(15.54)
N	1006	
Mean difference	−1.30	
t-statistic	−1.90	
p-value	0.06	
Coalition < .75 on passage		
Mean vote %	62.54	75.79
SD	(7.37)	(18.18)
N	252	
Mean difference	−13.25	
t-statistic	−10.68	
p-value	0.00	
Senate		
All conference bills		
Mean vote %	89.40	91.81
SD	(12.52)	(13.40)
N	789	
Mean difference	−2.41	
t-statistic	−3.69	
p-value	0.00	
Coalition < .75 on passage		
Mean vote %	64.69	78.33
SD	(6.90)	(18.24)
N	117	
Mean difference	−13.64	
t-statistic	−7.57	
p-value	0.00	

Note: 93rd–113th Congresses. Only bills with a roll-call vote at either the passage or conference approval stage are included. For those bills with a roll-call vote in one but not the other, the unanimous consent vote is coded as all members voting yes.

of conference outcomes but also suggests that bills are multidimensional and that coalitions can become larger and smaller in the two chambers at the same time.

The standard deviation for the percentage of votes cast in favor of a conference bill is much larger than that for the passage vote, suggesting there is a wider range of coalition size on conference bills and indicating the conditional nature of conferee discretion where different bills are changed in different ways. Some bills, it seems, attract a disproportionate share of support after going through the resolution process.

Majority and Minority Party Coalition Size

An increase in coalition size is difficult to reconcile with the idea that bills are moved toward the majority party median and away from the minority party. Partisan control of the conference committee also requires that winning coalitions should be composed of more majority party members and fewer minority party members as the bill is moved away from the minority party. Changes in coalition sizes, separated by the majority and minority party, are examined in table 6.3.

TABLE 6.3 **Difference-of-means test on winning coalition size for passage and conference votes separated by majority and minority party**

	Vote type			
	Majority party		Minority party	
	Passage	Conference	Passage	Conference
House				
All conference bills				
Mean vote %	92.48	92.20	75.06	78.47
SD	(10.65)	(11.58)	(29.02)	(27.69)
N		1006		1006
Mean difference		0.28		−3.41
t-statistic		0.56		−2.70
p-value		0.57		0.01
Coalition < .75 on passage				
Mean vote %	83.40	87.32	33.99	59.62
SD	(14.77)	(14.66)	(21.68)	(33.77)
N		252		252
Mean difference		−3.92		−25.63
t-statistic		−2.99		−10.14
p-value		0.00		0.00
Senate				
All conference bills				
Mean vote %	94.27	95.69	83.25	86.96
SD	(9.48)	(9.98)	(21.97)	(23.51)
N		789		789
Mean difference		−1.42		−3.72
t-statistic		−2.90		−3.24
p-value		0.04		0.00
Coalition < .75 on passage				
Mean vote %	82.38	89.61	42.99	63.84
SD	(15.08)	(14.94)	(20.96)	(32.53)
N		117		117
Mean difference		−7.23		−20.85
t-statistic		−3.68		−5.70
p-value		0.00		0.00

Note: 93rd–113th Congresses. Only bills with a roll-call vote at either the passage or conference approval stage are included. For those bills with a roll-call vote in one but not the other, the unanimous consent vote is coded as all members voting yes.

As with overall coalition size, more members of the majority and minority coalitions vote for the conference bill than vote for the bill on passage. The effect is most pronounced for the minority party. According to the table, on controversial bills (those receiving less than 75 percent of all votes on passage), only about 34 percent of the House minority party supports the bill on passage, but about 60 percent supports the bill after conference. In the Senate, minority support starts out at only 43 percent at passage, and increases to nearly 64 percent support after conference. Conferees clearly change bills in a way that attracts greater support from all members and especially members of the minority. If conferences move bills away from the chamber median and toward the majority party median, then the number of minority party members voting for the revised bill should not be substantially larger. This evidence contradicts claims that conference bills are made more partisan by the process.

An increase in coalition sizes in the chambers is consistent with both the universalism and pivotal voter theories, but the descriptive statistics above do not distinguish between the two. The creation of larger coalitions should be more evident on bills that are wholly distributive in nature,

TABLE 6.4 **Difference-of-means test on change in coalition size for passage and conference votes separated by appropriations and nonappropriations bills**

	Vote type	
	Nonappropriations	Appropriations
House, all conference bills		
Change in vote %, conference to passage	−0.20	4.1
SD	17.46	14.88
N	656	350
Mean difference	4.3	
t-statistic	3.93	
p-value	0.00	
Senate, all conference bills		
Change in vote %, conference to passage	2.46	2.32
SD	15.18	15.54
N	487	302
Mean difference	.14	
t-statistic	−0.14	
p-value	0.94	

Note: 93rd–113th Congresses. Only bills with a roll-call vote at either the passage or conference approval stage are included. For those bills with a roll-call vote in one but not the other, the unanimous consent vote is coded as all members voting yes.

operationalized here as appropriations bills. To determine whether appropriations bills are more likely to see a growth in coalition size, I use the change in coalition size to conduct a difference-of-means test between appropriations and nonappropriations bills, as shown in table 6.4. A positive value indicates the coalition size increased from passage to conference, while a negative differenced value indicates it decreased.[6]

In the House, nonappropriations bills have slightly smaller coalitions, though the size of the change is effectively zero. Appropriations bills, however, increase by about 4 percent from passage to conference. The difference between the two is statistically significant, while in the Senate both types of bills see an increase in coalition size from conference to passage, and the differences between the two increases are not significant. Still, these results provide more evidence that, at a minimum, appropriations bills conform to the predictions made by distributive theory.

Ideological Extremity Changes

The last difference-of-means test in table 6.5 examines changes in ideological extremity from passage to conference. The variable ranges from 0 to .263, where higher values indicate the coalition became more extreme either in a liberal or conservative direction, while values closer to 0 are more moderate. I test coalition differences for both the House and the Senate and for all bills and controversial bills. In both chambers, the winning coalitions become more moderate after conference. In each case, the difference is significant, even for the most controversial bills. This result is consistent with previous ones and overwhelmingly demonstrates that the coalitions that support the conference bill are larger, include more minority party members, and are more moderate than the coalitions on passage.

Evidence for Distributive Theory

The first empirical analysis examines the change in coalition size from initial passage to the vote after the conference committee for bills that received a roll-call vote at either stage in both chambers. The dependent variable is the change in the size of the winning coalition, where higher values indicate the winning coalition on the conference vote was larger than the passage vote, while smaller values indicate the winning coalition on passage was larger.[7]

TABLE 6.5 **Difference-of-means test on coalition extremity for passage and conference votes**

	Vote type	
	Passage	Conference
House		
All conference bills		
Mean coalition value	0.095	0.089
SD	(0.152)	(0.155)
N	1006	
Mean difference	0.006	
t-statistic	2.75	
p-value	0.01	
Coalition < .75 on passage		
Mean coalition value	0.145	0.108
SD	(0.074)	(0.181)
N	252	
Mean difference	0.037	
t-statistic	7.39	
p-value	0.00	
Senate		
All conference bills		
Mean coalition value	0.075	0.70
SD	(0.044)	(0.043)
N	789	
Mean difference	0.005	
t-statistic	2.33	
p-value	0.00	
Coalition < .75 on passage		
Mean coalition value	0.120	0.100
SD	(0.051)	(0.056)
N	117	
Mean difference	0.02	
t-statistic	2.96	
p-value	0.00	

Note: 93rd–113th Congresses. Only bills with a roll-call vote at either the passage or conference approval stage are included. For those bills with a roll-call vote in one but not the other, the ideological extremity of the coalition is coded as the chamber ideology.

The key independent variables are the size of the winning coalition on passage and a dichotomous variable for whether or not the coalition was small—defined as less than the mean coalition size. The interaction term is expected to be positive, where an increase in coalition size conditional on the coalition being small produces larger positive changes in coalition size in the sample. The predicted effects are that small coalitions become larger, but coalitions that are already large remain unchanged. There is a limit on possible change in that passage coalitions with near unanimity cannot be increased, resulting in a decrease in the size of the change.

In model 1 of table 6.6, the House total yea percentage component term shows that an increase in the size of the House coalition has a negative effect on the change in the conference coalition size when the coalition is large, indicating that large House coalitions actually become smaller at a statistically significant level. The dichotomous variable measuring small coalitions defines them as lower than the mean winning coalition size in the House, equal to 85 percent of the chamber voting in favor. Thus, the coefficient suggests that for every percentage increase in coalition size over 85 percent, the conference coalition will be about 1 percent smaller (95 percent CI: −.71 percent to −1.34 percent). The effect is not particularly large, but the result is that, in the House, very large coalitions become slightly smaller as coalition size increases. In the Senate, the effect is very similar. Mean winning coalition size in the Senate on passage is 89 percent in favor; for coalitions larger than that, the size of the conference coalition decreases about 1.5 percent for every additional percentage point increase in coalition size (95 percent CI: −1.16 percent to −1.83 percent).

The empirical expectation drawn from distributive theory claims that small coalition sizes will increase from passage to conference as the conferees make the bill more universalistic in nature. To account for this predicted effect, an interaction term is included in models 1 and 2 for each chamber, where the small coalition dichotomous variable is interacted with coalition size. Evidence for the theory is a positive effect of small coalition size on the change in coalition size from passage to the conference vote. The positive and significant coefficients in table 6.6 indicate just such a result. Put differently, bills with small winning coalitions are then passed with larger winning coalitions after the conferees return the bill to the chambers, consistent with the previous results. The dependent variable is *change* in the size of the winning coalition. Predicted values show that, in the House, a bill passed with only 51 percent of the chamber in support will see its winning coalition size increase by about 38 percent when the chamber passes the conference bill (95 percent CI: 23.66 percent to 52.28 percent).[8] Alternatively, a bill passed with 80 percent of representatives in support on passage produces only about an 8 percent increase in coalition size on the conference vote (95 percent CI: 2.90 percent to 1.37 percent). And, as the component term shows, once the winning coalition size reaches about 86 percent no increase in the size of the conference coalition is predicted. The same relationship exists in the Senate. In that chamber, the winning coalition for the conference bill is expected to increase by about 51 percent (95 percent CI: 37.93 percent to 63.09 percent) if the

TABLE 6.6 **Effect of passage coalition size on coalition size after conference**

Independent variables	House (1)	Senate (2)
House total yea %	−1.02**	0.20**
	(0.17)	(0.07)
Small House coalition	−0.40**	
	(0.13)	
Senate total yea %	0.38**	−1.49**
	(0.11)	(0.19)
Small Senate coalition		−0.96**
		(0.16)
House coalition extremity	0.08	0.01
	(0.13)	(0.13)
Senate coalition extremity	−0.13	−0.28
	(0.18)	(0.18)
CQA article lines coverage	0.07**	0.00
	(0.02)	(0.01)
Appropriations bill	0.01	0.03**
	(0.01)	(0.01)
House chamber SD	−0.60**	−0.35**
	(0.11)	(0.11)
Senate median-filibuster distance	0.24**	0.03
	(0.09)	(0.08)
Distance between chamber medians	0.08	−0.07
	(0.11)	(0.10)
House total yea % × small coalition	0.43**	
	(0.15)	
Senate total yea % × small coalition		1.08**
		(0.18)
Constant	0.68**	1.38**
	(0.16)	(0.19)
Adj. R^2	0.42	0.40
N	700	700

Note: The dependent variable is the difference between the winning coalition size on conference and passage for any bill that received a roll-call vote at either the passage or conference stage in both chambers and was sent to the president, 93rd–111th Congresses. Entries are regression coefficients with clustered standard errors by congress in parentheses. Ideological extremity and distance variables are measured using common-space DW-NOMINATE scores. *$p < 0.1$; **$p < 0.05$.

bill was first passed with only 60 percent support in the chamber. When 89 percent of the chamber votes in favor on passage, coalition size will increase by only about 7.15 percent (95 percent CI: 4.03 percent to 10.29 percent) at the conference stage.

Thus, coalition sizes increase up to a point when the passage coalition is small, but the conferees often change the bill so as to reduce the size of very large coalitions. The component and interaction terms show that small coalitions increase after conference, but the conferees rewrite bills in ways that reduce coalition sizes if the passage coalition was large. This finding is inconsistent with distributive theory in that large coalitions should have no effect on size changes if the conferees only ensure bills are universalistic in nature. This relationship also holds when the sample is limited to appropriations bills (results not shown). I argue this supports the case that the conferees produce off-median bills, which reduces coalition size in the more moderate chamber, a point that will be addressed in the empirical investigation for the bargaining model predictions. The other notable result from the models is the positive effect of the appropriations bill indicator in the Senate but the null result in the House. Consistent with the notion that appropriations bills are usually distributive in nature, and the conferees will change them to increase coalition size, appropriations bills produce a small increase in coalition size in the Senate, equal to an increase of about 3 percent (95 percent CI: 1.40 percent to 5.19 percent).

Evidence for Partisan Theory

I now turn to determining whether there is empirical support for the proposition that conference committees make legislative outcomes more partisan. In particular, if a bill passed by the floor has a bipartisan coalition, it should become more partisan—more majority party dominated—after the conference committee moves the bill away from the preferences of the minority party. Further, if both the House and Senate are controlled by the same party, centrist outcomes will be moved even farther from the preferences of the minority because the conference does not have to satisfy a majority from an opposing party. As before, the dependent variable is a differenced measure, capturing the change in the percentage of the minority party supporting the bill from passage to conference. An increase in the variable reflects a positive change in minority party coalition support for the bill after it comes back from conference, and a decrease reflects less support from the minority coalition postconference.

The key test of the claim that parties use conferences to make bills more partisan is an interaction between a dichotomous variable for a bipartisan bill, defined as a bill supported by a majority of the minority party, and the size of the minority party coalition. As the size of the minority party in support of the bill increases, given the condition that a majority of the minority party supports the bill, partisan conferees will move the bill farther toward their own party ideal point, creating a more partisan bill and resulting in a negative coefficient on the interaction term. I use measures of the minority party rather than the majority party because, if the bill is made more universalistic, then both majority and minority party support will increase, permitting no distinction between the two. Additionally, if the bill is very moderate, all members of the majority may support it; members will be less sensitive to changes as the bill is made more partisan, and they may be bought off by inducements from the party leadership.

There is little evidence that parties pull outcomes toward the party median and away from the chamber median, especially in the House. First, in model 1 of table 6.7, bipartisan support and the percentage of the House minority voting in favor of the bill on initial passage are included as covariates. When the bill is not supported by a majority of the minority party, there is a negative and significant reduction in minority support in the House. That is, low minority support for a bill is reduced further, by about .63 percent (95 percent CI: .37 percent to −0.89 percent) for every percentage increase in minority support below 50 percent support within the party. The effect is quite small, but more importantly the interaction term is not significant, indicating the percentage of minority party support for the bill (if it was first passed with significant minority support measured by the bipartisan bill variable) does not change from passage to conference.

Unlike the House, the Senate in model 2 shows no negative effect on minority support when the bill is not bipartisan. The coefficient for the interaction term between Senate minority support and the bipartisan bill indicator is only marginally significant ($p = .092$) and negative (the direction that would be expected if the Senate majority made the bill more partisan in the conference committee). The results are suggestive that somewhat partisan bills are made more partisan, while bipartisan bills are made even more palatable to the minority party. For example, when only 51 percent of the minority party supports the bill at passage, the conference bill receives 29 percent less minority party support (95 percent CI: 24.03 percent to −34.76 percent), but, when the bill is supported by 84 percent of the minority, there is no predicted reduction in minority support. These somewhat contradictory results imply partisan bills are made slightly more partisan, but bipartisan bills are also made more bipartisan by the conference. Partisan theories of conference committees do not explain this result, as the moderation of the bill largely depends on its partisan nature when initially passed in the Senate. The null results in the House are also not supportive of the partisan control theory.

Two other variables are significant across both models. The greater the

TABLE 6.7 **Effect of minority party support on minority support after conference**

Independent variables	House (1)	Senate (2)
House minority support %	−0.63**	
	(0.14)	
House bipartisan bill (yes = 1)	0.00	
	(0.09)	
Senate minority support %		−0.27
		(0.35)
Senate bipartisan bill		0.35**
		(0.13)
House coalition extremity	0.42	−0.80**
	(0.28)	(0.27)
Senate coalition extremity	−1.66**	0.27
	(0.28)	(0.33)
CQA article lines coverage	0.14**	−0.03
	(0.03)	(0.03)
Appropriations bill	0.05	0.08**
	(0.03)	(0.03)
House chamber SD	−1.32**	−0.93**
	(0.19)	(0.24)
Senate median-filibuster distance	0.61**	0.25**
	(0.18)	(0.13)
Distance between chamber medians	−0.03	−0.02
	(0.28)	(0.20)
House minority × bipartisan bill	0.09	
	(0.19)	
Senate minority × bipartisan bill		−0.54*
		(0.32)
Constant	0.73**	0.72**
	(0.12)	(0.25)
Adj. R^2	0.41	0.36
N	700	700

Note: The dependent variable is the difference between the percentage of the minority party that supports the bill on conference and passage for any bill that received a roll-call vote at either the passage or conference stage in both chambers and was sent to the president, 93rd–111th Congresses. Entries are regression coefficients with clustered standard errors by congress in parentheses. Ideological extremity and distance variables are measured using common-space DW-NOMINATE scores. *$p < 0.1$; **$p < 0.05$.

distance between the Senate median and the filibuster pivot, the more minority support the bill receives at the conference stage. In the House, an increase from the minimum distance to the maximum distance increases minority support by about 30 percent (95 percent CI: 10.69 percent to 49.7 percent), while in the Senate the same increase produces about 12.6 percent (95 percent CI: .25 percent to 24.8 percent) more minority support. The effect for the measure of ideological diversity is negative and significant in the House, indicating that more ideological diversity in that chamber produces less minority support at the conference stage, though the effect size is quite small, equal

TABLE 6.8 **Effect of minority party support on minority support after conference—strong party conditions**

Independent variables	Unified chamber		Unified chamber & 104th–111th Cong.	
	House (1)	Senate (2)	House (3)	Senate (4)
House minority support %	−0.68**		−0.52**	
	(0.14)		(0.24)	
House bipartisan bill	0.05		−0.26**	
(yes = 1)	(0.11)		(0.07)	
Senate minority		−0.36		−1.41**
support %		(0.41)		(0.29)
Senate bipartisan bill		0.29*		0.24
		(0.15)		(0.45)
House coalition	0.44	−0.87**	1.83**	−1.26**
extremity	(0.28)	(0.33)	(0.74)	(0.47)
Senate coalition	−1.98**	0.31	−1.27	−3.05*
extremity	(0.33)	(0.45)	(0.97)	(1.63)
CQA article lines	0.14**	−0.03	−0.06	−0.19**
coverage	(0.04)	(0.04)	(0.09)	(0.05)
Appropriations bill	0.07**	0.09**	0.22**	0.19**
	(0.04)	(0.04)	(0.07)	(0.06)
House chamber SD	−1.40**	−0.88*	−2.09**	0.93
	(0.34)	(0.46)	(0.41)	(0.60)
Senate median-filibuster	0.37	0.19	0.66**	2.02**
distance	(0.33)	(0.28)	(0.24)	(0.49)
Distance between	0.70	−0.39	−0.82**	−0.29
chamber medians	(0.54)	(0.46)	(0.29)	(0.24)
House minority ×	0.03		0.46*	
bipartisan bill	(0.20)		(0.26)	
Senate minority ×		−0.44		−0.13
bipartisan bill		(0.36)		(0.34)
Constant	0.84**	0.77**	0.95**	0.46
	(0.13)	(0.31)	(0.19)	(0.52)
R^2	0.44	0.37	0.47	0.39
N	585	585	149	149

Note: The dependent variable is the difference between the percentage of the minority party that supports the bill on conference and passage for any bill that received a roll-call vote at either the passage or conference stage in both chambers and was sent to the president. Models 1 and 2 limit the sample to congresses in which the House and Senate were controlled by the same party, 93rd–111th Congresses. Models 3 and 4 limit the sample to any post-103rd congresses in which the House and Senate were controlled by the same party. Entries are regression coefficients with clustered standard errors by congress in parentheses. Ideological extremity and distance variables are measured using common-space DW-NOMINATE scores. $*p < 0.1$; $**p < 0.05$.

to a reduction of 8.5 percent (95 percent CI: −5.53 percent to −11.4 percent) minority support in the House moving from minimum ideological dispersion to maximum and equal to a 5.94 percent (95 percent CI: −3.49 percent to −8.39 percent) decrease in the Senate. Finally, appropriations bills increase minority support in the Senate but not in the House, while more important bills generate more House minority support at conference. Increased Senate coalition extremity reduces House minority support, but there is no similar effect for House extremity on Senate support.

The majority party may only be able to exercise its influence when it has a majority in both chambers. The theory predicts that this condition will promote the most partisan outcomes because the majority does not have to account for opposing party preferences in the other chamber. I subsample the data for only those congresses with unified party control (models 1 and 2 in table 6.8) and, as an additional test, for unified party control after the 103rd Congress, when party polarization is said to have strongly increased following the Republican takeover of Congress (models 3 and 4 in table 6.8) (Aldrich 2000; Theriault and Rohde 2011).

The results are similar to those encompassing all congresses, but there is even less support for the claim that parties make legislation more partisan during the conference process. In the two models for the House and Senate, the interaction terms are not statistically significant. Like the previous results for the Senate, the percentage of the minority supporting the bill on passage (the component term) is also not significant, indicating that even when the bill has little minority support there is no change in minority support on the conference bill. In the House, similar to the previous results, the minority support component term is negative, indicating that partisan bills become more partisan but bipartisan bills do not. Models 3 and 4 limit the sample to unified chambers and the 104th through 111th Congresses, and, consistent with previous results, there is little evidence that bills returned from conference committees are more partisan. In the House, the interaction term is marginally *positive* and significant, while, in the Senate, the effect is not different from zero. I conclude that conferees are not exclusively agents of the majority party and seem to change bills in a way that attracts significant support from the minority if support is sufficiently high on passage.

Evidence for Bargaining Theory

Lastly, I test implications drawn from the bargaining theory, which claims bill outcomes will move in the direction of the bill passed by the more moderate of the two winning coalitions though not to its ideal point. The average of common-space DW-NOMINATE scores of members in each winning coalition are used to measure moderation and extremity, and, while they cannot capture individual members' ideology on a particular bill, they serve as a proxy for the moderation or extremity of a particular coalition across a large sample of different types of bills. As with the previous dependent variables, these are differenced such that a high value indicates a positive change in extremity, while a low value indicates a negative change in extremity from passage to conference. The empirical predictions are, first, that an increase in extremity on passage will be moderated by the conference; second, that an increase in extremity in the opposing chamber will increase extremity in a chamber as conference outcomes are pulled toward that chamber, and, finally, that the change in extremity will be conditioned on whether a chamber is more moderate than the opposing chamber.

To determine whether the more extreme coalition moderates after the conference stage, I include the coalition extremity variables for each chamber in the model and interact each chamber's coalition extremity with a variable measuring whether that chamber coalition is more moderate than the other (more moderate equals 1). The interaction term is interpreted as the change in ideology from passage to conference if that chamber was more moderate than the other, and the component term for the chamber's ideology can be interpreted as the change in moderation when it is the more extreme chamber. In table 6.9 two models predict ideological change from passage to conference in the House and the Senate. Looking first at model 1, which includes predictors for both House and Senate ideological extremity on passage, there is a negative effect of House coalition extremity on passage with House coalition extremity after conference. In short, more extreme House coalitions tend to become more moderate after a conference, consistent with the intrachamber extremity change hypothesis. Conversely, extreme Senate coalitions increase the extremity of the House coalition after a conference, as predicted by the opposing chamber extremity change hypothesis. The interactive result in model 1 for the House is insignificant, demonstrating that there is no ideological change for the winning coalition when the House is the more moderate of the two chambers. Further, the component term of whether or not the House is more moderate is also insignificant. These results indicate that, when the House is the more moderate of the two coalitions voting on the bill, there is no significant, independent effect on coalition ideology, accounting for the extremity of both the House and Senate.

In the Senate, the results are very similar to those in the House. In model 2, the House increases Senate extremity, while more extreme Senate coalitions tend to moderate; both results are consistent with the two unconditional hypotheses. The interaction term for Senate extremity is insignificant, while the House extremity variable is positive, and the Senate coalition extremity variable is negative.[9]

TABLE 6.9 **Effect of coalition moderation on ideological change after conference**

Independent variables	House (1)	Senate (2)
House coalition extremity	−0.55**	0.19**
	(0.08)	(0.07)
House more moderate coalition	−0.001	
	(0.01)	
Senate coalition extremity	0.30**	−0.58**
	(0.08)	(0.09)
Senate more moderate coalition		−0.01**
		(0.01)
House total yea %	0.05**	−0.002
	(0.02)	(0.02)
Senate total yea %	−0.05*	0.04
	(0.03)	(0.03)
CQA article lines coverage	−0.01	0.01
	(0.004)	(0.004)
Appropriations bill	−0.01	−0.02**
	(0.01)	(0.004)
House chamber SD	0.17**	0.14**
	(0.04)	(0.04)
Senate median-filibuster distance	−0.14**	−0.13**
	(0.03)	(0.04)
Distance between chamber medians	−0.01	−0.03
	(0.05)	(0.04)
House extremity × more moderate	−0.04	
	(0.07)	
Senate extremity × more moderate		0.08
		(0.06)
Constant	0.01	−0.03
	(0.03)	(0.03)
Adj. R^2	0.43	0.32
N	700	700

Note: The dependent variable is the difference in ideological extremity of the winning coalition on passage and conference, where higher values indicate a more extreme winning coalition, for any bill that received a roll-call vote at either the passage or conference stage in both chambers and was sent to the president. Entries are regression coefficients with clustered standard errors by congress in parentheses. Ideological extremity and distance variables are measured using common-space DW-NOMINATE scores. $*p < 0.1$; $**p < 0.05$.

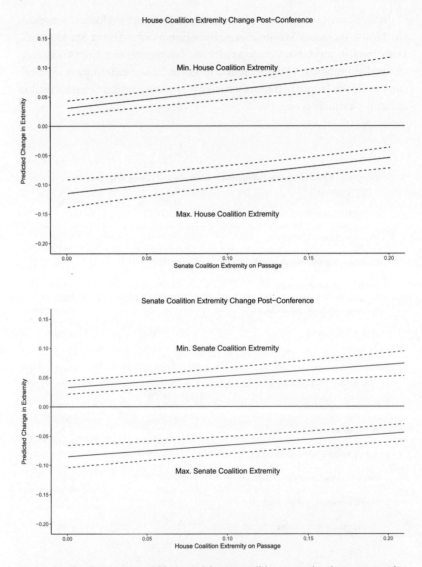

FIGURE 6.1. Predicted values of House and Senate coalition extremity change postconference based on coalition extremity preconference. Dashed lines indicate predicted values from models 1 and 2 in table 6.9 with 95 percent confidence interval. All other variables held at their means except for appropriations, which is held at 0, and the more moderate chamber indicator, also held at 0.

The empirical results support two of the three hypotheses, though whether one chamber is more moderate than the other does not seem to matter. Extreme coalitions tend to become more moderate, while moderate coalitions move toward the more extreme chamber, indicating that conferees generate bills that are located somewhere between the preferences of the two winning coalitions. For a substantive interpretation of how winning coalitions change when the conference bill is voted on, figure 6.1 displays the effect of the other chamber on ideological change at two different levels of extremity for the predicted chamber. The top panel shows how an increase in Senate extremity causes a positive change in House extremity, but the overall effect on the House is positive only when the House itself is very moderate (when predicted values are above 0). When the House is moderate, the Senate pulls the House coalition toward a more extreme outcome. But, when the House itself is already very extreme, it becomes more moderate, even at very high levels of Senate extremity. This is the result of coalition extremity on passage and its effect on postconference extremity, as the results in table 6.9 demonstrate. The predicted values for change in Senate extremity in the bottom panel demonstrate the same substantive conclusion. Coalition extremity tends to converge to a relatively moderate outcome; coalitions that are already extreme become more moderate, while coalitions that are moderate move toward a more extreme outcome if the other chamber is also extreme. Importantly, for both the House and the Senate, the change in extremity is negative for all but the most moderate House and Senate coalitions. It makes no difference as to whether one chamber coalition is more moderate than the other, but the outcomes produced by the conference lie somewhere between the preferences of the two winning coalitions.

The data were subset for only appropriations bills, and the same models were run to determine if bills that are distributive in nature are also subject to moderation. The results are nearly identical except the interaction effect for the House reaches the level of statistical significance and is positive. The sample size is small, but the result suggests that appropriations bills move toward the more extreme chamber if the House is more moderate than the Senate. This is somewhat consistent with the results above, but with respect to appropriations bills the relative ideology of the chambers matters. Perhaps the Senate exercises more power over appropriations than the House does, and, given the evidence that appropriations are most likely to be distributive in nature, the Senate may be better at achieving their goals for appropriations bills.

Conclusion

The empirical evidence presented here offers some support for distributive theory on bills that are universalistic in nature and additional support for the bargaining model on other legislation. Overall, the results suggest that the more moderate chamber generally pulls policy toward, but not to, its own preferences because the conferees are able to make a single offer, there are no proposal rights for the more moderate chamber, nor is there a mechanism that forces the conference to report back to the more moderate chamber once the proposal is made. If there were a mechanism to enforce perfectly median outcomes, the more moderate of the two chambers' bills would always prevail at the conference stage.[10] This finding complements that of the previous chapter, which found that conference rejection occurs as a result of uncertainty on the part of the conferees, resulting in a conference proposal that is too extreme for the more moderate chamber. While the reasons for these more extreme outcomes are unclear, they might be the result of bargaining internal to the conference committee and its willingness to make an offer that gives some share of the benefits to the more extreme chamber but, perhaps, most of the benefits to the moderate chamber. If the conferees were perfectly informed about each coalition's preferences, then they could offer exactly what the more moderate chamber demands, and the more extreme chamber would have no choice but to accept as long as it received a sufficient share of the benefits.

Some bills exhibit characteristics of universalism in that they become favored by a larger majority in both chambers. Appropriations bills, as expected, seem to be distributive in nature. Thus, conference outcomes are not necessarily consistent across types of bills and winning coalitions. On some bills the conference distributes benefits to a larger share of members, while on other bills the conferees split the bargaining benefits with both chambers, though the chamber more willing to reject a conference report must receive a larger share of the benefits from the conferees.

I find little evidence that bills are made more partisan by the conference committee. Minority support does wane from passage to conference only when there is very little minority support at initial passage. The comparison of coalition sizes and related *t*-tests shows that, for most bills, coalition size increases in at least one chamber, contrary to the predictions of partisan theory. Though the leadership has control over conference appointments, perhaps it is the case that the chambers delegate negotiations to a moderate group of members to expedite agreement. Failure in conference due to an extreme proposal, after all, is not a good outcome for the chambers.

Who wins in conference? More moderate chambers generally seem to do better, though extreme chambers exert some influence over the final outcome. It is probably incorrect to characterize the House or Senate as consistently winning, because it depends on the relative willingness of each chamber to reject the conference report. On the one hand, bills tend to move toward the more moderate of the two chambers, but because of the existence of a more extreme chamber, bills likely end up a bit more extreme than they would under a unicameral system with a single moderate chamber. At the same time, bills in Congress end up more moderate than they would in the presence of an extreme chamber coalition. Bicameralism, at least in the context of the conference committee, seems to produce an outcome that is located between the two chambers, with outcomes favoring the more moderate of the two.

Bill Failure and Policy Change as a Result of Amendment Trading

A mendment trading offers an alternative to conferencing but requires a different institutional process that has important implications for policy outcomes. Rather than delegating to conferees, bills are resolved on the floor of each chamber and messaged between the chambers until they agree on a final version. The rules limit the chamber to three exchanges, but they can and sometimes do violate this rule. The prominent use of amendment trading to resolve differences is a recent phenomenon, and as a result there is virtually no scholarly work on the outcomes the process produces, though, as I argue, understanding its causes and consequences is a necessary part of making claims about congressional postpassage bargaining.

Unlike conference committees, no set of members is delegated to resolve differences and propose a bill to the chambers. As a result, the winning coalition has no prior beliefs about the likelihood of resolution because it controls the process itself. Instead, amendment trading involves competing offers between chambers, and, as each chamber debates and amends the other coalition's offer, members within a chamber face voting decisions on amendments and proposals within the chamber as well. As a result, the dynamics that produce policy outcomes and bill failure are fundamentally different from the conference process.

In this chapter, I address two separate questions. First, what causes bill failure during the amendment trading process? For a sense of how little we know about amendment trading, consider that it is unclear whether amendment trading is more or less successful than conferencing in finding a compromise satisfactory to both chambers. Chapter 4 showed that conference failure was due to the misuse of discretion by the conferees, which occurs when they make an unacceptable offer based on incomplete information about the willingness of each winning coalition to accept the conference report. In amendment trading, the chambers have incomplete information about the preferences of the other chamber, but, across a series of legislative offers, members of the winning coalition can gauge the resoluteness of their counterparts in the other chamber. This should make failure in amendment trading rare (and it is), but a theoretical explanation is required to explain why it ever occurs. I show that the willingness of the chambers to reconcile their differences depends on their expected benefits from resolution. Eventually, it sometimes becomes very costly for the House and Senate to continue resolving their differences, and, when those anticipated costs become higher than their expected benefits from striking a compromise, they abandon the amendment trading process.

The second question continues the theme from the previous chapter by examining how the postpassage bargaining process affects policy outcomes relative to the bill originally passed by the winning coalitions. Competing theories of legislative organization posit different types of legislative outcomes as a result of conference, and, while these theories have not been applied to amendment trading, I test some of their claims here using the same empirical insights used in chapter 6. In short, are amendment trading outcomes distributive, partisan, median, or near-median in nature? I use the same research design and empirical models to allow for a direct comparison between conference outcomes and amendment trading outcomes.

There is no mechanism in conference committees to move policy outcomes toward the more moderate winning coalition once a conference bill has been proposed. As the results in the previous chapter demonstrated, this creates near-median outcomes, as the more moderate chamber is also more willing to reject the bill, constraining the conferees, but incomplete information and the necessity of satisfying the other, extreme coalition does not produce perfectly median legislation. The more extreme coalition also demands a share—albeit smaller than the more moderate coalition—of the benefits. In amendment trading, the ability of the chambers to make repeated offers is predicted to iterate policy outcomes toward the more moderate chamber and produce policy outcomes that are very close to the preferences of the more moderate coalition, though, again, even extreme chambers will share the benefits. The empirical results offer evidence for this claim in that coalitions become larger, minority party support increases, and the ideological extremity of the winning coalitions moderate from initial passage to amendment trading.

Bill Failure in Amendment Trading

First, I develop a theory that explains why the House and Senate are sometimes unable to reach agreement during the amendment trading process, resulting in the failure of the bill at the resolution stage. I argue that in conference committees the process is driven by constrained discretion and uncertainty, but the theoretical mechanism is different in amendment trading. Recall that conferees try to make an offer that allocates benefits to both chambers in an acceptable way, knowing that the chamber that is more willing to reject must be satisfied, though some benefits must be given to the other chamber as well, or it may also reject. In amendment trading, no unamendable offer is made by an agent of the chambers. Though both chambers are uncertain about how the other values disagreement, this is an inherent part of any bargaining process as each bargainer tries to misrepresent its position in order to achieve the best possible outcome. But each winning coalition has the ability to counteroffer with very few constraints. Any unsatisfactory offer made by one chamber can be amended and sent back to the other chamber, whereas, after a conference, an offer that is unsatisfactory to one side must be rejected by the chamber. Thus, incomplete information cannot drive bill failure because the "wrong" offer will be corrected in subsequent bargaining rounds. The ability of the chambers to engage, theoretically, in a nearly unlimited exchange of amendments should make failure extremely rare.

Despite the ability of the two winning coalitions to exchange multiple offers, it is not always the case they want to spend valuable time and energy engaging in repeated rounds of amendment trading. Each back-and-forth requires amending the bill on the floor, generating support from the relevant members, debating, and, in the case of the Senate, invoking cloture or achieving unanimous consent to proceed with the bill. The members of each winning coalition must believe that their likely benefits from the eventual agreement are outweighed by the costs of repeated bargaining on the floor. At some point, it may not be worth it for the winning coalition to engage in another iteration of amendment exchange. Why would a winning coalition quit the process if it previously expended costs to pass the bill and already engaged in a few rounds of amendment bargaining? From a theoretical perspective, the previous expenditure of bargaining costs are irrelevant because these costs are sunk and therefore have no bearing on any subsequent round of bargaining. Within the chamber, the process may become more onerous than the winning coalition initially anticipated, and, though members believe an agreement could be reached, they realize that the future costs of negotiating that agreement will be too great. Similarly, the benefits derived from agreement may be insufficient to justify the expenditure of additional costs on the agreement. Thus, the failure of amendment trading occurs due to the perceived costs of *anticipated* action necessary to reach agreement.

As I have done in previous analyses, I focus on analyzing the costs of resolution, the benefits from rejection, and the benefits from acceptance to gain empirical leverage on the conditions that promote compromise. First, the level of disagreement between the winning coalitions in each chamber makes resolving differences more difficult. Large differences require additional negotiations between party leaders and interested members, more rounds of negotiations, and, generally, the expenditure of more resources by members of the winning coalition. I predict that greater ideological differences between the House and Senate winning coalitions, as measured by average coalition ideological extremity, will increase the probability of bill failure during the amendment trading process.

Ideological Differences Bill Failure Hypothesis: *Greater interchamber differences in coalition extremity will increase the probability of bill failure.*

As with passage within the chamber, a more ideologically diverse coalition also increases the costs of passage for the majority. More diverse coalitions require a greater expenditure of resources to members and more energy and effort when developing coalitions. These factors increase the willingness of majority coalitions to abandon the amendment trading process as they anticipate the costs of resolution mounting with each successive exchange.

Coalition Extremity and Variation Hypothesis: *Greater interchamber differences conditional on greater ideological variation within a chamber will increase the probability of bill failure.*

H.R. 2660, an appropriations act introduced in the 109th Congress for the Departments of Labor, Health and Human Services, and Education, offers a good example of this dynamic. The bill originally passed the

House only very narrowly, with all Democrats and a handful of Republicans opposing it. The narrow coalition and split within the Republican
party made it likely the bill was going to fail, and in fact the House and
Senate took no action to resolve differences. Instead, a few months later,
the chambers sent a related bill and a consolidated appropriations act to
conference, where the resulting bill attracted significant Democratic support and passed with a much larger winning coalition, though thirty-eight
Republicans voted against it.

Policy Outcomes as a Result of Amendment Trading

To determine how amendment trading affects policy outcomes, I use the
same measures as those used to analyze conference outcomes: I compare
coalition sizes, minority party support, and the ideological extremity of
the winning coalition after resolution with the corresponding values following initial passage. Developing a theory of amendment trading based
on the postpassage bargaining model requires insights from theories of
legislative organization that have not been extensively applied to this process before. Amendment trading closely resembles other forms of noncooperative bargaining where offers are repeatedly exchanged between
two actors trying to reach a deal. In these situations, a number of factors
affect the bargaining strength of each actor, including the resoluteness or
willingness of one actor to reject an offer in favor of disagreement.

In the case of House-Senate bargaining, the more resolute coalition receives a larger share of the benefits from rejection because of its moderation and its willingness to accept the status quo. Moderate members might
be cross-pressured or nearly indifferent to either vote for or against the
proposed bill, and receive benefits from rejection as a result of satisfying
other constituents, interest groups, or some other set of actors.[1] A more
irresolute bargainer will accept less generous offers because it receives less
utility from rejection and prefers to receive the benefits from the bargain.
Thus, irresolute chambers are weaker bargainers and are more willing
to give up a larger share of the total benefits to the other chamber in
order to reach a deal. Generally, more extreme coalitions, which are not
composed of cross-pressured members and receive little benefit from
the status quo, are irresolute and, as a result, more willing to accept less
favorable bargains. This implies that the more moderate winning coalition should receive a greater share of the benefits, and the more extreme

winning coalition's bill should move to the policy preference of the other chamber.

When a conference committee is used, the conferees make a policy offer given the constraints placed on them by the chambers, but there is no mechanism that allows the winning coalitions to move policy toward the preferences of one chamber or the other. After conference, a more resolute chamber can accept an offer only if its benefits for acceptance are greater than its benefits for rejection, but it cannot change policy to allocate the correct amount of benefits to each chamber. Thus, conferences produce near-median outcomes in which the more resolute chamber is favored but does not receive exactly what it wants. During amendment trading, on the other hand, the ping-ponging of offers allows the more moderate winning coalition to propose a policy at or very near its ideal point. This outcome may not occur after the first exchange of offers, but, as the chambers negotiate, the relative resoluteness of each chamber is revealed, and the irresolute chamber will be forced to concede to the other winning coalition. Thus, policies should collapse to near the preferences of the more moderate chamber. While it must be the case that the more extreme chamber receives some share of the benefits, I expect the more resolute (i.e., moderate) chamber to dominate amendment trading even more so than in conferencing. The empirical expectations are, first, that more extreme passage coalitions will become more moderate when voting on the amendment trading versions of the bill and, second, that an increase in chamber moderation is conditional on being the more extreme winning coalition. I also expect the more extreme coalition to have no effect on the more moderate coalition during the amendment trading process because the rules allow the moderate coalition to demand policy close to its ideal point.

Amendment Trading Extremity Change Hypothesis: As winning coalition extremity on passage for a chamber increases, winning coalition extremity for the amendment trading versions of the bill will decrease.

Amendment Trading Conditional Extremity Hypothesis: As winning coalition extremity on passage increases for the more extreme of the two chambers, extremity will decrease for the amendment trading versions of the bill.

Most speculation on amendment trading has focused on the leadership's control of the process. The rise in amendment trading has tracked closely with an increase in polarization, and one possible reason why the process is more prominent now is because party leaders seek to avoid delegating to nearly autonomous conferees.[2] I have argued, instead, that the use of amendment trading is due to an inability by the majority to use conference committees rather than a preference of the party leadership. After all, if the majority party leadership uses amendment trading as a way of creating more partisan outcomes, why would the minority block conferencing given that it will produce, from its perspective, a more favorable policy outcome? Further, much of the push to streamline the conference process by combining the necessary motions was led by the party leadership, an action that is inconsistent with the notion that the party leadership values amendment trading.[3]

The claim that moderate chambers are resolute and hence more powerful adheres closely to the pivotal politics theory of legislative organization. Here I expect the moderate coalition to be even more dominant in pursuing its favored legislative outcomes and thus achieving median outcomes. This is contrary to partisan theories of amendment trading and inconsistent with distributive theory. As the empirical tests are the same used to examine conference outcomes, the same implications apply. Larger coalitions are consistent with distributive outcomes and moderate outcomes, while smaller, majority party coalitions are consistent with partisan theory. A change in coalition extremity from moderate to extreme suggests the resolute or moderate chamber is receiving more of what it wants—evidence for median or pivotal politics theory.

Measurement

The sample consists of only those bills that were bargained on exclusively in amendment trading. As explained in chapter 4, many bills are resolved through both conferencing and amendment trading, but most of the time, the hard work is done in the conference, and amendment trading is used only after conferencing has resolved minor discrepancies.[4] In other cases, the chambers begin the amendment trading process then quickly move to a conference without ever attempting to modify the bill on the floor, when the issues prove to be too difficult to resolve.

The sample differs slightly from that used in the previous chapter. For conferencing, I used any bill that received a vote in both chambers at either the passage or conference stage. For those bills that received one but not the other, the unanimous consent agreement was coded as a vote with all members voting in favor. Unfortunately, in amendment trading, very few bills (128) received a vote at either stage in both chambers. Frequently, bills receive an amendment trading vote in the House but not the Senate. To address this problem, I include all bills that received a vote in either chamber at the passage or amendment trading stage to allow for controversy in one chamber but not the other, as seems to happen with regularity.

As in chapter 6, for conference committees policy outcomes are measured by differences in key indicators (coalition size, minority party support, and ideology) between the initial vote and the postpassage vote. Unlike with conferences, however, amendment trading resolution takes place over a series of votes rather than one. One possible strategy to measure amendment trading voting outcomes is to examine the characteristics of the closest or most contentious vote in each chamber. The problem with this approach is that, whereas conferences force a single vote on all issues at once, amendment trading breaks up these issues into separate votes. An issue that may be contentious in the House might be voted on first, while that issue might pass easily in the Senate, and the contentious issue for the Senate might occur at the third vote. To deal with this problem, I coded winning coalition membership and characteristics for up to five votes in either chamber during the amendment trading process and averaged across the total number of votes for the bill.[5] This also includes only roll-call votes past the first vote so that unanimous consent passage at the first vote counts toward the average votes in favor, but only additional roll-call votes are included in the average. Fortunately, there are no instances where roll-call votes are interspersed with unanimous consent votes (i.e., amendment trade vote one was a roll call, vote two was advanced on unanimous consent, vote three was a roll call, etc.).

Bill failure, as with conference bills, refers to bills that had substantive amendment trading action taken on them but did not reach the president. Still, some of these bills had no vote taken after passage, so the number of observations is slightly smaller than that for the models that estimate bill change. In the next section, I explore the causes of bill failure and then take up the issue of bill change through changes in coalition size, minority party support, and ideological extremity.

Empirical Tests of Bill Failure

Table 7.1 shows three different models that predict the probability of a bill failing at the amendment trading stage. The overall results are not particularly

TABLE 7.1 **Effect of coalition support and chamber ideological diversity on bill failure at the amendment trading stage**

Independent variables	(1)	(2)	(3)
CQA article lines coverage	−0.13	−0.06	−0.15
	(0.49)	(0.44)	(0.49)
Difference in coalition extremity	−86.41**	72.17*	−6.06
	(37.41)	(39.82)	(12.55)
Average support in both chambers	−7.95**	−2.31	−2.07
	(2.77)	(3.15)	(2.73)
House chamber SD	1.07	6.09	2.28
	(3.14)	(5.03)	(3.39)
Senate median-filibuster distance	2.63	1.64	−2.14
	(2.47)	(2.62)	(2.98)
Distance between chamber medians	0.92	2.49	2.69
	(3.66)	(3.59)	(3.88)
Diff. in extremity × avg. support	116.07**		
	(39.47)		
House SD × avg. support		−129.13	
		(87.28)	
Senate median-filibuster dist. × avg. support			75.18*
			(38.76)
Constant	2.35	−4.83	−2.35
	(2.60)	(3.40)	(2.86)
AIC	194.73	201.59	201.82
N	679	679	679

Note: The dependent variable is whether a bill failed after amendment trading for any bill that was passed by both chambers and went to amendment trading, 93rd–111th Congresses. Entries are regression coefficients with clustered standard errors by congress in parentheses. Ideological extremity and distance variables are measured using common-space DW-NOMINATE scores.
*$p < 0.1$; **$p < 0.05$.

robust due to a few complicating factors. As the theory predicts, there are simply very few observed failures, comprising only 23 bills out of 726 total, or about 3.2 percent of the total (93rd to 113th Congresses). Because the chambers can trade offers and are limited only by their willingness to use additional resources to bargain, failure should occur infrequently and only under very specific conditions. These conditions, broadly, include the difficulty associated with negotiating a compromise, necessitating more time, energy, or individualized benefits directed at recalcitrant members to secure passage. As these costs increase, a chamber is more likely to abandon the resolution process, resulting in failure. These costs should be especially acute when the chambers are ideologically distant, when there is greater heterogeneity within each winning coalition, and when the coalitions are small.

Chamber support, the ideological distance between the winning coalitions, and within-chamber ideological heterogeneity measure the costs and expenditure of resources during the amendment trading process. Model 1 includes the average level of support in both chambers as a percentage of the chamber voting for the bill, a variable capturing the ideological extremity of each chamber's winning coalition, and an interaction between the two. Both component terms are statistically significant in the predicted directions, and when the two are interacted the probability of failure increases at a statistically significant rate. Thus, when bills are supported in both chambers *but* the chambers are ideologically different from each other, a bill is more likely to fail. Again, this is theorized to be the result of a bill that is difficult to resolve because of the chambers' preferences and because the costs of compromise within each chamber are likely to be high. For bills passed with an average level of support and for which the ideological difference between the chambers is 0, the probability of bill failure is .015 (95 percent CI: .007 to .032), while the probability of a bill failing is about .47 (95 percent CI: .12 to .85) when the chambers are at their maximum ideological distance. The component term measuring average support in the chambers is negative and statistically significant, demonstrating that larger coalitions in both chambers reduce the probability that a bill fails during the amendment trading process; this is consistent with expectations and accounts for the lack of ideological disagreement between the chambers. This finding is also consistent with the results for conference failure. The other component term, difference in coalition extremity, cannot be interpreted, as average support cannot equal 0.

In models 2 and 3, measures of ideological disagreement within the chambers are interacted with average support, with the expectation that lower support and greater intrachamber ideological dispersion will increase the probability of failure. In the House, the interaction term is not statistically significant, but, notably, the difference in coalition extremity variable is positive and marginally significant, lending additional support to the claim that greater differences in coalition extremity increase the probability of failure. In the Senate, there is a positive and conditional relationship between ideological variation and average support ($p = .052$). The substantive effect is somewhat small but meaningful. For example, when average support across the chambers is .6, the probability of failure is .06 (95 percent CI: .011 to .25) at the minimum Senate median-filibuster ideological distance, while it is .064 at the maximum distance

(95 percent CI: .004 to .51). In contrast, when average support increases to the mean, about .91, the probability of failure is only .031 (95 percent CI: .01 to .09) at the minimum ideological distance between the median and filibuster pivot, increasing to .33 (95 percent CI: .003 to .27) at the maximum distance. The probability of failure at this large coalition size is about half of that when average support across the chambers is 60 percent.[6] As predicted by the coalition extremity and variation hypothesis, the results support the major theoretical claim that the back-and-forth nature of amendment trading makes failure unlikely, but, when it does occur, it is generally the result of the winning coalition deciding the potential benefits of passage are outweighed by the difficulty of successfully achieving passage.

One other finding is worth noting. The appropriations indicator is not included in the results reported in table 7.1. Between the 93rd and 113th Congresses, only twenty-eight appropriations bills were resolved through amendment trading—and no appropriations bill failed to be resolved if amendment trading was used.

Amendment Trading Outcomes—Difference-of-Means Tests

By examining coalition sizes on passage and on amendment trading votes, I can determine if there are significant differences between the two, which has implications for the type of legislation passed by the chambers. As discussed previously, larger coalitions imply more moderate policy outcomes, as these coalitions include more members from both the majority and minority parties. Table 7.2 shows the differences between passage and amendment trading coalition sizes, where the amendment trading coalitions are an average of the coalition sizes for each separate amendment trading vote.

Coalition sizes in both the House and Senate become larger after amendment trading. This is true for all bills and for those bills identified as more controversial—passed with less than 75 percent support in the chamber. The differences between chamber support on passage and on amendment trading votes are also statistically significant in all cases. The average level of support for all bills is very high, as one would expect given the nature of amendment trading. Many of these bills are passed by unanimous consent in one chamber, so it is perhaps surprising that average coalition sizes increase during amendment trading despite the initially large coalition size on passage.

TABLE 7.2 **Difference-of-means test on winning coalition size for passage and conference votes**

	Vote type	
	Passage	Amendment trading
House		
All amendment trading bills		
Mean vote %	91.88	97.01
SD	(13.01)	(9.67)
N	756	
Mean difference	−5.13	
t-statistic	−8.69	
p-value	0.00	
Coalition < .75 on passage		
Mean vote %	62.48	88.86
SD	(7.68)	(17.18)
N	98	
Mean difference	−26.39	
t-statistic	−13.88	
p-value	0.00	
Senate		
All amendment trading bills		
Mean vote %	96.82	99.07
SD	(8.66)	(5.32)
N	756	
Mean difference	−2.25	
t-statistic	−6.09	
p-value	0.00	
Coalition < .75 on passage		
Mean vote %	65.64	96.26
SD	(6.53)	(11.37)
N	42	
Mean difference	−30.62	
t-statistic	−15.13	
p-value	0.00	

Note: 93rd–113th Congresses. Only bills with a roll-call vote at either the passage or amendment trading stage in either chamber are included. For those bills with a roll-call vote in one but not the other, the unanimous consent vote is coded as all members voting yes.

Further, the increase in coalition size for controversial bills is remarkable—more than 26 percent in the House and 30 percent in the Senate.

Majority and Minority Party Coalition Size

The next set of t-tests (see table 7.3) demonstrate how minority party size changes from passage to amendment trading. The increase in overall coalition size gives some indication as to how minority party support changes, but if coalition sizes convey the ideological position of the bill or its distributive nature, it seems to be the case that amendment trading, like conferencing, produces more moderate legislation. Again, it is difficult to reconcile larger coalitions supporting the bill with the notion that legislation is becoming more partisan during the amendment trading process.

TABLE 7.3 **Difference-of-means test on winning coalition size for passage and amendment trading votes separated by majority and minority party**

	Vote type			
	Majority party		Minority party	
	Passage	Amend. trading	Passage	Amend. trading
House				
All amendment trading bills				
Mean vote %	95.86	98.60	86.27	94.78
SD	(8.85)	(6.82)	(24.87)	(18.14)
N		756		756
Mean difference		2.992		−8.51
t-statistic		−6.77		−7.60
p-value		0.00		0.00
Coalition < .75 on passage				
Mean vote %	83.76	94.48	33.13	80.95
SD	(16.49)	(14.15)	(26.26)	(33.49)
N		98		98
Mean difference		−10.72		−47.82
t-statistic		−4.88		−11.12
p-value		0.00		0.00
Senate				
All amendment trading bills				
Mean vote %	98.46	99.37	94.67	98.68
SD	(6.12)	(5.64)	(16.22)	(8.38)
N		756		756
Mean difference		−0.91		−4.01
t-statistic		−2.99		−6.03
p-value		0.00		0.00
Coalition < .75 on passage				
Mean vote %	84.87	98.10	40.05	93.77
SD	(18.14)	(11.43)	(25.61)	(13.15)
N		42		42
Mean difference		−13.23		−53.72
t-statistic		−4.00		−10.68
p-value		0.00		0.00

Note: 93rd–113th Congresses. Only bills with a roll-call vote at either the passage or amendment trading stage in either chamber are included. For those bills with a roll-call vote in one but not the other, the unanimous consent vote is coded as all members voting yes.

The change in party support is positive for both the majority and minority and statistically significant in all cases. Particularly important to understanding bill changes after amendment trading is the change in minority support. In the House, minority support for all bills increases from 86 percent to 95 percent, while Senate minority support increases from 95 percent to almost 99 percent. Again, many of these bills are passed with unanimous support, especially in the Senate, so it is no surprise Senate support is very high. But, even when the bill in question is controversial, minority support increases dramatically. The increase in the percentage of minority support from passage to amendment trading is around 50 percent in both the House and Senate. This is strong evidence that amendment trading makes bills more bipartisan and less controversial in both chambers.

Ideological Extremity Changes

Finally, I investigate the difference of means in ideological extremity for the winning coalition on passage and after amendment trading. Given the previous results, which showed an unambiguous increase in coalition size and in minority party support, the ideological extremity of the coalitions should decrease from passage to amendment trading. The variable is constructed such that ideological extremity is found by taking the average of the common-space DW-NOMINATE scores of members in the winning coalition and turning it into an absolute value so that higher scores indicate the coalition was more extreme in either a liberal or conservative direction. In the case of amendment trading, if there was more than one vote, the scores were averaged together for each of the votes.

In the House, ideological extremity decreases for all bills and for more controversial bills, according to table 7.4. The decrease for controversial bills is slightly more than one standard deviation change in extremity, a large substantive effect equivalent to moving from above the third quartile to the first quartile of coalition extremity. The story is the same in the Senate; the coalition supporting the bill during amendment trading is less ideologically extreme than the coalition that supports passage for all bills reconciled in amendment trading and for more controversial bills. The size of the decrease in the Senate is slightly larger than that in the House and is about one and a half standard deviations.

The decrease in ideological extremity is consistent with larger coalition sizes and with an increase in the number of minority party members

TABLE 7.4 **Difference-of-means test on coalition extremity for passage and amendment trading votes**

	Vote type	
	Passage	Amendment trading
House		
All amendment trading bills		
Mean coalition value	0.079	0.073
SD	(0.051)	(0.042)
N	756	
Mean difference	−0.006	
t-statistic	2.58	
p-value	0.01	
Coalition < .75 on passage		
Mean coalition value	0.148	0.089
SD	(0.064)	(0.052)
N	98	
Mean difference	−0.059	
t-statistic	7.02	
p-value	0.00	
Senate		
All amendment trading bills		
Mean coalition value	0.061	0.052
SD	(0.039)	(0.029)
N	756	
Mean difference	−0.006	
t-statistic	3.19	
p-value	0.00	
Coalition < .75 on passage		
Mean coalition value	0.125	0.055
SD	(0.051)	(0.056)
N	42	
Mean difference	−0.07	
t-statistic	7.42	
p-value	0.00	

Note: 93rd–113th Congresses. Only bills with a roll-call vote at either the passage or amendment trading stage in either chamber are included. For those bills with a roll-call in one but not the other, the unanimous consent vote is coded as all members voting yes.

in the amendment trading winning coalitions. On average, the coalitions supporting the bill during the amendment trading process includes more members, more minority party members, and is less ideological. Cumulatively, these results suggest that, like conferencing, amendment trading moves policy outcomes in a moderate direction, potentially toward the median member. In the empirical tests that follow, additional variables are included to control for various bill-level and coalition-level factors and to explore the conditional nature of the relationships through interaction terms. To facilitate a direct comparison with conference outcomes, the models are exactly the same as those in chapter 6, with amendment trading bills substituted for conference bills.

Evidence for Distributive Theory

I begin the empirical tests by examining changes in coalition sizes from passage to the amendment trading process. The difference-of-means tests demonstrated that coalition sizes increase, but here I control for a variety of confounding factors and interact coalition size on passage with a dummy variable that indicates whether or not the coalition was smaller than median size on passage. A positive coefficient indicates the variable resulted in an increase in amendment trading coalition size (the dependent variable). The interaction term is included because, as coalition size increases, the positive effect of passage coalition size on amendment trading coalition size is predicted to decrease.

Models 1 and 2 in table 7.5 show the effect of increasing passage coalition sizes in the House and the Senate respectively, along with an indicator variable for a small coalition and an interaction between the two. In the House, the total yea variable is negative and significant, indicating that larger passage coalitions tend to get smaller during the amendment trading stage. For each percentage point increase in passage coalition size, the change in amendment trading coalition size gets smaller by about .95 percent (95 percent CI: −.57 percent to −1.33 percent), but, unlike the results for conference committees, the interaction term is not significant. In the Senate, neither the component variables nor the interaction term are statistically significant, indicating that passage coalition size changes have no effect on coalition sizes during amendment trading.

Predicted values show the substantive effect of passage coalition size on changes due to amendment trading. In fact, the coefficient reduces the size of the change, but it does not become negative until over 97 percent of the chamber is in support of a bill. Though small coalitions do not see a positive change relative to large coalitions, the change remains positive until coalition sizes indicate almost unanimous consent. When only 51 percent of the chamber supports the bill on passage, there is a predicted increase in coalition sizes of 45 percent (95 percent CI: 26.2 percent to 62.7 percent), but when 91 percent of the coalition supports the bill on passage, the predicted coalition size change is only about 6.4 percent (95 percent

TABLE 7.5 **Effect of passage coalition size on coalition size change after amendment trading**

Independent variables	House (1)	Senate (2)
House total yea %	−0.95**	0.03
	(0.18)	(0.02)
Small House coalition	−0.05	
	(0.20)	
Senate total yea %	0.30**	−0.37
	(0.10)	(0.78)
Small Senate coalition		0.61
		(0.79)
House coalition extremity	−0.09	−0.02
	(0.10)	(0.05)
Senate coalition extremity	0.05	−0.12*
	(0.13)	(0.07)
CQA article lines coverage	−0.02**	−0.01*
	(0.01)	(0.01)
Appropriations bill	−0.08**	−0.02
	(0.04)	(0.03)
House chamber SD	−0.48**	−0.09**
	(0.07)	(0.03)
Senate median-filibuster distance	0.24**	0.03
	(0.06)	(0.04)
Distance between chamber medians	−0.05	−0.11**
	(0.06)	(0.03)
House total yea % × small coalition	0.05	
	(0.21)	
Senate total yea % × small coalition		−0.62
		(0.79)
Constant	0.80**	0.39
	(0.22)	(0.77)
R^2	0.64	0.69
N	702	702

Note: The dependent variable is the difference between the winning coalition size on amendment trading and passage for any bill that received a roll-call vote at either the passage or amendment trading stage in both chambers and was sent to the president, 93rd–111th Congresses. Entries are regression coefficients with clustered standard errors by congress in parentheses. Ideological extremity and distance variables are measured using common-space DW-NOMINATE scores.
*$p < 0.1$; **$p < 0.05$.

CI: 3.2 percent to 9.5 percent), and the predicted change becomes negative (though overlapping with 0) at 98 percent support on passage.

This is evidence for universalism in amendment trading, as coalition sizes in the House increase at all but the very highest values of chamber passage coalition size. But coalition sizes seem to converge to near 95 percent support, which may also be the result of a bill becoming more moderate. For bills with small winning coalitions, when amendment trading may be used to increase distributive benefits, the slope is not significantly different for bills with large coalitions. Further, the appropriations variable is negative, suggesting that this type of bill actually loses support from passage to amendment trading. These bills are more contentious than regular bills; they passed with only 76 percent of members in the House on average and 90 percent of senators, which is smaller than the level of support for other types of bills. In the House, larger Senate coalitions increase the size of House coalitions, suggesting that the Senate tends to produce more moderate bill outcomes, which the House then adopts. The reverse is not true. The evidence suggests that coalition sizes generally increase, but there is mixed evidence this is due to the distribution of particularized goods.

Evidence for Party Theory   .

One of the key questions about postpassage resolution is whether the majority party can use its influence over the agenda to dictate outcomes to the standing committees and their membership, creating more partisan and more extreme policy outcomes. The analysis of conference committees yielded no evidence of this, but there have been suggestions that the floor process necessary to amendment trade empowers the majority party leadership. As with conferences, I test whether an increase in minority party membership in the winning coalition on passage causes a reduction in minority party support during the amendment trading process.

Both models in table 7.6 include an indicator for the percentage of the minority party that supports the bill, an indicator for whether or not the bill was bipartisan (defined as a bill that receives support from more than 50 percent of the minority party), and an interaction between the two. An increase in minority support is predicted to reduce minority support after conference, but the real test of majority party influence is whether bipartisan bills become partisan ones during reconciliation (this effect would be indicated by negative coefficients on the interaction terms).

The effects for minority support in both chambers are similar to those for overall coalition sizes in the previous results. More minority support produces a downward change in minority support after amendment trading, but, again, this only suggests that the change became smaller, not that fewer minority party members supported the legislation. This also reflects the ceiling effect of minority support. More importantly, the interaction coefficient for a bipartisan bill and minority support is not statistically significant in the House and is marginally *positive* in the Senate ($p = .087$). This suggests that,

TABLE 7.6 **Effect of minority party support on minority support after amendment trading**

Independent variables	House (1)	Senate (2)
House minority support %	−0.90**	
	(0.26)	
House bipartisan bill (yes = 1)	0.13**	
	(0.06)	
Senate minority support %		−1.14**
		(0.12)
Senate bipartisan bill		−0.13
		(0.10)
House coalition extremity	0.18	−0.08
	(0.25)	(0.07)
Senate coalition extremity	−0.75*	−0.13
	(0.42)	(0.09)
CQA article lines coverage	−0.03**	−0.01
	(0.02)	(0.01)
Appropriations bill	−0.10**	0.01
	(0.05)	(0.05)
House chamber SD	−1.12**	−0.25**
	(0.18)	(0.07)
Senate median-filibuster distance	0.67**	0.10*
	(0.11)	(0.06)
Distance between chamber medians	−0.25**	−0.12**
	(0.12)	(0.05)
House minority × bipartisan bill	−0.01	
	(0.24)	
Senate minority × bipartisan bill		0.29*
		(0.17)
Constant	1.12**	1.08**
	(0.13)	(0.04)
R^2	0.59	0.75
N	702	702

Note: The dependent variable is the difference between the percentage of the minority party that supports the bill for any bill that received a roll-call vote at either the passage or amendment trading stage in both chambers and was sent to the president, 93rd–111th Congresses. Entries are regression coefficients with clustered standard errors by congress in parentheses. Ideological extremity and distance variables are measured using common-space DW-NOMINATE scores. *$p < 0.1$; **$p < 0.05$.

in the Senate, bills with substantial minority party support gained minority party voters during the amendment trading process.

To allow for a direct comparison between these amendment trading results and those for conferencing in chapter 6, table 7.7 also examines changes in minority support under conditions of strong party government: during periods of unified chambers and for unified chambers in the

TABLE 7.7 **Effect of minority party support on minority support after amendment trading—strong party conditions**

Independent variables	Unified chamber		Unified chamber & 104th–111th Cong.	
	House (1)	Senate (2)	House (3)	Senate (4)
House minority support %	−0.68**		−1.04**	
	(0.34)		(0.36)	
House bipartisan bill	0.07		−0.47**	
(yes = 1)	(0.11)		(0.17)	
Senate minority support %		−1.06**		−0.98**
		(0.05)		(0.03)
Senate bipartisan bill		−0.20**		−0.01
		(0.08)		(0.02)
House coalition extremity	0.03	0.07	0.11	−0.004
	(0.23)	(0.04)	(0.11)	(0.003)
Senate coalition	−0.54*	−0.18**	−3.10**	0.11
	(0.29)	(0.08)	(0.55)	(0.15)
CQA article lines coverage	−0.01	−0.001	0.02	−0.001
	(0.01)	(0.003)	(0.01)	(0.001)
Appropriations bill	−0.12*	−0.02	0.06	0.001
	(0.06)	(0.02)	(0.05)	(0.001)
House chamber SD	−0.08	0.06**	1.47**	−0.08
	(0.14)	(0.02)	(0.35)	(0.08)
Senate median-filibuster distance	−0.13	−0.06**	0.28	−0.004
	(0.12)	(0.03)	(0.23)	(0.01)
Distance between chamber medians	0.18*	−0.08**	−0.72**	0.04
	(0.10)	(0.02)	(0.28)	(0.05)
House minority × bipartisan bill	−0.25		0.56*	
	(0.33)		(0.32)	
Senate minority × bipartisan bill		0.26**		0.01
		(0.13)		(0.02)
Constant	0.94**	1.01**	0.36**	1.01**
	(0.13)	(0.02)	(0.18)	(0.01)
Adj. R^2	0.44	0.37	0.47	0.39
N	585	585	149	149

Note: The dependent variable is the difference between the percentage of the minority party that supports the bill on conference and passage for any bill that received a roll-call vote at either the passage or amendment trading stage in both chambers and was sent to the president. Models 1 and 2 limit the sample to congresses in which the House and Senate were controlled by the same party, 93rd–111th Congresses. Models 3 and 4 limit the sample to any post-103rd congresses in which the House and Senate were controlled by the same party. Entries are regression coefficients with clustered standard errors by congress in parentheses. Ideological extremity and distance variables are measured using common-space DW-NOMINATE scores. *$p < 0.1$; **$p < 0.05$.

post-103rd congresses. Theories of partisan control over the amendment trading process suggest that under these two conditions the conditional relationship between the minority support and bipartisan bill variables should be negative as bipartisan bills are made more partisan. That is not the case in any of the four models, and, for the Senate during unified chambers and the House during unified chambers in the 104th Congress or after, the relationship is positive, the same finding as previously shown and evidence that bipartisan bills attracted additional minority support during amendment trading. In each of the four models, the minority support component term is negative, providing additional evidence that there is a reduction in the change in minority support at lower levels of minority support. That is, partisan bills become slightly more partisan at low levels of minority support but become more bipartisan at high levels of minority support.

Evidence for Bargaining Theory

Table 7.8 explores changes in the ideological makeup of coalitions in the House and Senate after amendment trading is used as the bargaining venue. Again, these models are identical to those used for conferencing to allow a direct comparison between the differing effects of each bargaining venue. In these models, a negative coefficient indicates a negative change in the ideological extremity of the winning coalition though not necessarily that the coalition became more moderate. To determine the actual effect, predicted values are necessary. The key test of median or pivot theory is a reduction in extremity if the winning coalition is more extreme than the other coalition and no change for the more moderate coalition as policy collapses to its ideal point.

In models 1 and 2 of table 7.8, ideological extremity on passage is modeled as a component in an interaction term. For both the House and the Senate, the results demonstrate that more extreme coalitions become more moderate after amendment trading. Further, in both models, the interaction term is not significant, indicating that the more moderate of the two winning coalitions does not change its ideological orientation after amendment trading. The component term demonstrates that when the House is more extreme (moderate coalition equals 0) it becomes more moderate, consistent with expectations. Conversely, more extreme Senate coalitions cause a positive change in House extremity, meaning that

TABLE 7.8 **Effect of coalition moderation on ideological change after amendment trading**

Independent variables	House (1)	Senate (2)
House coalition extremity	−0.71**	0.12**
	(0.05)	(0.02)
House more moderate coalition	0.003	
	(0.01)	
Senate coalition extremity	0.41**	−0.47**
	(0.08)	(0.10)
Senate more moderate coalition		−0.01**
		(0.004)
House total yea %	0.03**	0.01
	(0.01)	(0.01)
Senate total yea %	0.002	0.11**
	(0.04)	(0.04)
CQA article lines coverage	0.002	−0.002
	(0.003)	(0.002)
Appropriations bill	0.003	−0.01
	(0.01)	(0.01)
House chamber SD	0.04	−0.05*
	(0.03)	(0.03)
Senate median-filibuster distance	−0.16**	−0.01
	(0.02)	(0.03)
Distance between chamber medians	0.02	−0.03
	(0.03)	(0.04)
House extremity × more moderate	−0.05	
	(0.09)	
Senate extremity × more moderate		0.02
		(0.05)
Constant	0.01	−0.07
	(0.04)	(0.05)
R^2	0.57	0.54
N	702	702

Note: The dependent variable is the difference in ideological extremity of the winning coalition on passage and amendment trading, where higher values indicate a more extreme winning coalition, for any bill that received a roll-call vote at either the passage or amendment trading stage in both chambers and was sent to the president, 93rd–111th Congresses. Entries are regression coefficients with clustered standard errors by congress in parentheses. Ideological extremity and distance variables are measured using common-space DW-NOMINATE scores. *$p < 0.1$; **$p < 0.05$.

when the Senate has an extreme coalition it causes a positive change in House coalition extremity, similar to what occurs with conferences. The same relationship exists in the Senate; more extreme Senate coalitions on passage become more moderate, but an extreme House also changes Senate extremity. These findings, like others, are at odds with the notion that policy becomes more extreme after amendment trading.

The size of the coalition extremity coefficient for the modeled chamber is much larger than the coefficient for its counterpart, suggesting that, while extreme coalitions produce a positive ideological change, the moderating effect is much larger than the extremity effect. These results are very similar to those for conference committees, and like conferences amendment trading produces policy that is a compromise between the more moderate and the more extreme chamber but one that is very close to the moderate coalition's preference. For a sense of the substantive effects of changes in coalition extremity in both chambers simultaneously, figure 7.1 plots predicted values of coalition extremity.

The top panel predicts House change in coalition extremity as Senate coalition extremity increases. The solid top line and 95 percent confidence interval show how extremity changes when the House has a very moderate coalition (coalition extremity is at its minimum), while the bottom solid line shows how coalition extremity changes when the House coalition is very extreme. The bottom panel shows the same set of relationships for the Senate, where the x axis indicates a change in House extremity.

This figure can be compared directly to figure 6.1 in chapter 6, which showed that the House and Senate produce a slight increase in extremity in the other chamber if the winning coalition was also extreme. The predicted values here suggest amendment trading may be even more moderating than conferencing. Both the House and Senate coalitions can become more extreme but only when they are both at their most moderate. When the House is extreme, there is a dramatic moderating effect on its coalition ideology by the Senate winning coalition, even as it too becomes more extreme. Note also that these relationships are not affected by the relative coalition extremity in the other chamber. The Senate becomes more extreme only when it is very moderate and House coalition extremity increases, but the small slope of each line shows the relatively weak effect the House has on Senate extremity.

To summarize, consistent with the findings from conferencing, more extreme coalitions move to a more moderate position while only a very moderate chamber shows a positive change in extremity. Amendment trading produces legislation that achieves high levels of support from the entire chamber, suggesting that the process, like conferencing, distributes benefits to both chambers and produces bills near the more moderate coalition's preference. And, despite the conventional wisdom, amendment trading does not seem to make controversial bills more partisan or extreme in most cases and no more extreme than the bill would have been had it been reconciled in a conference. The theory suggests this is because the moderating

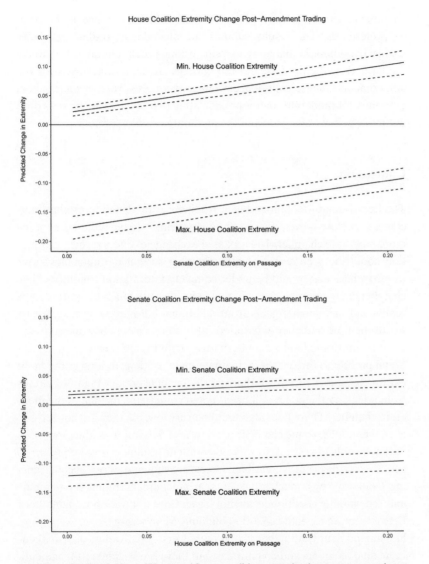

FIGURE 7.1. Predicted values of House and Senate coalition extremity change post–amendment trading based on coalition extremity pre–amendment trading. Dashed lines indicate predicted values from models 1 and 2 in table 7.8 with 95 percent confidence interval. All other variables held at their means except for appropriations, which is held at 0, and the more moderate chamber indicator, also held at 0.

chamber constrains action and does not allow the bill to move too far from its preferences. The results support the amendment trading extremity change hypothesis in that more extreme winning coalitions are substantially moderated by the process. But the findings are somewhat mixed for the amendment trading conditional extremity hypothesis. There is some gain in extremity for moderate coalitions, indicating that the iterative process does not move policy exactly to what the moderate coalition prefers.

Conclusion

The iterative nature of amendment trading was predicted to produce outcomes very close—even closer than conferencing—to the preferences of the more moderate chamber. The repeated exchange of offers reveals information about the preferences of each chamber so that the outcomes move toward where they would be under complete information conditions. The chambers may not reach exactly this point because amendment trading is costly, and incremental gains from additional bill messaging may not be worth the time and energy required. In conferencing, policy does not end up at the most moderate chamber's ideal point because there is no institutional process to force it there. In amendment trading, as long as the more extreme chamber receives a share of the benefits greater than its benefits from rejection, the policy will be accepted close to the median of the moderate chamber. These benefits should be very low, but they are not zero, so even the more extreme chamber must receive a payoff from the process.

The results also speak to why amendment trading is not the preferred venue, given its overall directional effects are similar to those of conferencing. Conferencing is much less costly than amendment trading for members and the winning coalition as a whole, as it does not use up valuable floor time or require repeated coalition building. Members of Congress may not like amendment trading because it empowers party leaders and weakens individual members and committees, but there is no evidence that amendment trading produces more ideologically divisive legislation. In fact, much like conferencing, policy moves toward the more moderate chamber because, it seems, party leaders are constrained much the same way conferees are. If they try to make policy too extreme, moderate members will reject the compromise, and the bill will fail, a situation all members want to avoid. These results are perhaps more remarkable given the sheer number of bills that the House and Senate passed by unanimous consent prior to the amendment trading process. Any change made to these bills that reduces the coalition size below unanimous consent will make the winning coalition more extreme. That the results for both chambers show moderation is a testament to just how bipartisan and accommodative the legislation created by amendment trading is.

CHAPTER EIGHT

Conclusion: Postpassage Resolution and Legislative Outcomes

I began the book by asking whether the bicameral system designed by the framers still serves its purpose effectively, at least when it comes to reaching agreement on important legislation. An increase in party strength and polarization, combined with the growth of complex policy problems, may ill suit bicameralism for modern legislating, and it is clear that bicameralism, in the American context and in other countries, makes it harder to achieve legislative successes. But how does Congress resolve differences on bills that are actually passed by both chambers? When the winning coalitions bargain over legislation, it is often not clear what factors drive success or which side will emerge with the better deal. Using insights borrowed from theories of bargaining and legislative organization, I have sought to demonstrate that coalitions and members that are more willing to reject a compromise bill are empowered during the bargaining process. This has the effect of encouraging resolution and moderating legislation when either conferencing or amendment trading is used. These results validate the institutional designs of the framers about the effects of forcing cooperation between the chambers. Interchamber resolution may make it harder to agree on how to change legislation, but, once the chambers agree on direction, bills become more moderate and a successful compromise is likely.

As Riker (1992) noted, the American system of checks and balances and separation of power—especially a two-chambered legislature distinct from the executive—is frequently seen as too slow and unresponsive. The results here may disappoint those who want our system to be more nimble and create more dramatic policy change. Responsible party theorists may have trouble with the claim that, even when the same party controls both branches, not only is legislative change slow but drastic policy changes are unlikely. Even if one chamber wants to enact dramatic change, the second chamber is always able to constrain action. This, of course, is exactly what Madison and other Federalists sought and what the Great Compromise demands.

The model and results are broadly generalizable to all bicameral legislatures with equal proposal and amending power, such as the states. Many have noted the rise of "pre-postpassage bargaining" associated with the decline in regular order and the increasing power of the party leadership. Observers have commented on the real work being done in offices and back rooms by the leadership before a conference is convened or before amendment trading even begins, with votes little more than a fait accompli. These agreements, however, must be approved by the conferees then by a majority or supermajority of the chamber. The theory and results offered here still apply in these cases, because the formal rules, rather than the actors themselves or the content of the legislation, structure the process. The agents who engage in bargaining can offer concessions or remain resolute on individual issues, but they must always receive support from the rest of the chamber in order to implement their strategy. There may not be many surprises with respect to how individual members are going to vote, but those seeking to dictate policy must be cognizant of what their members want. The findings seem generalizable then across a wide range of situations even if the textbook congressional procedures are no longer used as much as they once were.

Reviewing the Theory and Findings

Bicameral bargaining, as I have described it, is the process by which two competing chambers try to secure as large a share of the benefits as possible. These benefits are not zero-sum because both chambers are made better off, in an absolute sense, by coming to an agreement, but there are a finite amount of benefits to be divided. Thus, bargaining is a noncooperative process, though also mutually beneficial to the chambers.

While the winning coalitions in both chambers fight for their preferred legislation, they must receive more benefits from accepting than they would from rejecting the bargain to pass the compromise bill. The model demonstrates that rejection must be a real possibility in which the coalitions receive some form of benefits from rejection. If the winning coalitions received no benefits from rejection, the second-acting chamber would accept any offer made by the other coalition, which clearly does not conform to the observed congressional bargaining process. I argue that these benefits of rejection comprise the benefits to individual members of the winning coalition from electoral gains, including satisfying a different set of constituents, an important interest group, or donors. Simply put, members who are cross-pressured receive benefits from both supporting or opposing the legislation in question, and, when a coalition is composed of members who receive more benefits from rejection than acceptance, the policy offer will be rejected. Again, I make no claim that these are the *only* possible source of benefits for members when considering whether to accept or reject a policy offer as part of the winning coalition, but they seem to be the most obvious.

In Congress, talk is cheap; the victory does not go to the winning coalition that projects more confidence or is more insistent on its policy position. Despite all the rhetoric by various members, growing polarization between the parties, and increased instances of divided government and divided chambers, the procedural requirements of the chambers enforce compromise. Incrementalism, or relatively small movements from the status quo, are a direct result of the institutional rules that govern interchamber bargaining after a bill has been passed by both chambers. In this respect, conferencing and amendment trading differ in kind rather than type. Both cause policy to move away from the coalition that values rejection less and toward the coalition that values rejection more, which is the same group of legislators who are less concerned about achieving policy success. Amendment trading, not conferencing, may be even more effective in ensuring the more moderate coalition receives its preferred policy, because it requires the two chambers to update their beliefs about the other's resoluteness. As evidence that amendment trading encourages moderation, consider that it offers the more extreme coalition an opportunity to walk away at a number of different stages, which almost never happens.

The operationalization of resolute bargainers as moderate coalitions connects to theories about the willingness of members to balance competing constituent interests and electoral payoffs. Extremists, on the other hand, do not see electoral payoffs from not reaching a deal because of their level of opposition to the current policy and the lack of cross-pressure from a varied constituency, though this may not always be the case. There might sometimes be some compelling reason why more ideologically extreme members find their benefits for rejection very high and moderate members are more willing to strike a deal. In the debates over Obamacare repeal in the summer of 2017, some extreme senators (Rand Paul, Mike Lee) seemed to be the most willing to scuttle a deal, despite their intense opposition to Obamacare. In these situations, the theory is still supported if the measures used to capture high benefits of disagreement are conceptualized differently. Similarly, bargaining is not hopeless for more extreme coalitions. They can demand a larger share of the benefits if they can cultivate benefits from rejecting the compromise, perhaps through some exogenous event or process (commonly called an outside option in bargaining theory). If extreme coalitions can develop these benefits and can credibly demonstrate them, they will become stronger bargainers.

The Decline of Conferences and the Prominence of Amendment Trading

Conferences are used much less frequently than they have been in previous congresses, but this is at least partially due to the lack of important legislation passed by the House and Senate for which a conference is needed. The choice between a conference and amendment trading is the choice between a somewhat risky but far more efficient process and a less risky but far more time-consuming and difficult process. The amendment trading process, like the initial passage process, requires floor action and all of its associated difficulties. Conferencing need not be more efficient than amendment trading, but, given the realities of legislating in the modern Congress, the House and Senate prefer to avoid using floor time, if possible.

The results demonstrate the importance of having sixty votes in the Senate. Without that level of support, the Senate is unable to go to conference. The relationship between having sixty votes and using a conference does not seem to have changed in recent congresses, suggesting that determined minorities have always sought to block a conference when the legislation is important or salient. Senate Democrats changed the rules to use a conference in 2013, requiring only one motion instead of the three previously required. Democrats hoped this would decrease the costs of going to a conference, even with sixty votes, and allow the chamber to engage in conferencing more frequently. This action clearly demonstrates that Congress prefers conferencing to amendment trading, but will this lead to more conferences? It is too early to tell, but if, in the absence of the rules change, minority coalitions became more willing to force cloture votes on all three motions, then conferencing will increase. And, despite the reduction in the number of motions, the use of conferencing still requires sixty votes on passage. Further, fewer important bills are being passed, so the days of dozens of conferences per congressional session are probably gone for the immediate future.

Policy Outcomes from Conferences and Amendment Trading

Amendment trading is more time intensive and difficult for the chambers than conferencing, but it produces bills that are not drastically different from what a conference would produce. Based on the evidence here, amendment trading is not the tool of majority party control that many have suggested it is. In both conferencing and amendment trading, coalition sizes increase relative to the passage coalition in both chambers; the bills attract more minority support, and the winning coalition becomes less ideologically extreme. There is some weak evidence that this might be more true for amendment trading than it is for conferences because amendment trading allows the more moderate coalition to offer a bill that is at the limit of what the extreme coalition will accept.

Conference outcomes are largely determined by the conferees, though they are highly constrained by the willingness of the chambers to accept their offer. As shown in chapter 5, conferees exercise significant discretion when writing the compromise bill. This is important evidence that conference committees are powerful institutions that can drastically change legislation under certain conditions. When coalition majorities are small and willing to reject the bill, the conferees must be very careful about moving bills away from their preferences lest the coalition reject the conference report and cause the bill to fail. The result is that the conferees move bill outcomes between the two chambers' preferences, as measured by coalition ideology, though much closer to the more moderate coalition's preference, where the threat of rejection lies. This result most closely approximates the median or pivotal model of legislative organization, but there is evidence that some bills are distributive in nature.

Importantly, there is virtually no evidence that bills become more partisan after conference. The party leadership controls the conference committee, and party loyalists are able to secure crucial roles in the negotiations. Whether their influence is minimal or they produce party benefits in a way not observed or accounted for in the models is unknown. And, though conference bills could end up at exactly the more moderate coalition's preference, they do not. Perhaps the extent to which bills deviate from the more moderate coalition is where the party has power.

The results in chapters 6 and 7 also explain the inconsistent answers to the "Who wins?" question in conference literature. The answer is that it largely depends on which chamber must be satisfied for a particular bill. In the modern Congress, the Senate is generally more moderate, but this was not always the case and is not true for every bill. The filibuster requirement in the Senate is a powerful institutional mechanism that forces moderation from the Senate, but it is possible that the House median may be more moderate and thus the constraining member for a particular bill.

Bill Failure from Conferencing and Amendment Trading

Despite the difficulties of resolving differences, both conference committees and amendment trading are very successful. Conference failure occurs as a result of a misuse of discretion by the conferees in their proposal. Given their uncertainty about the offer each coalition will accept, conferees occasionally make offers that allocate an insufficient share of the benefits to one of the coalitions. The conferees make offers based on their prior beliefs about what each chamber will accept, and the conditions that require failure are readily observable by the conferees. Things become more difficult for the conferees when it is harder for them to identify the preferences of one of the winning coalitions. I measured conferee uncertainty through the diversity of coalition preferences, and, as preference diversity increases while coalition size decreases, bills are more likely to fail.

Failure during amendment trading presents something of a puzzle. Theoretically, the House and Senate can exchange amendments until they reach agreement, and as a result failure should never occur. Failure is rarely observed when the chambers use this venue, but in practice it may not be beneficial for the winning coalitions in each chamber to continue bargaining if the floor action required for amendment trading becomes too costly. This is expected to happen infrequently because the coalitions have already passed a bill at least once with majority support, and there may be additional passages of the bill if amendments are shuttled between the chambers multiple times. Still, a particular issue may prove more difficult to resolve than expected, or a group of members in one chamber may decide to make it too costly for the resolution process to continue.

Ideological diversity within the chambers was shown to increase the probability of bill failure, as one would expect, as it becomes more costly for a chamber to engage in amendment trading. Likewise, coalition size is an important cause of bill failure. As with conferencing, more support makes resolving differences easier and gives the negotiations room for error. Small coalitions, along with ideologically diverse coalitions, make amendment trading more difficult and lead to failure.

Remaining Questions and Future Research

Numerous questions remain about the interchamber bargaining process that I have not discussed in detail. I have minimized the role of parties in the postpassage bargaining process because bills become more moderate as compared to initial passage, and there is only weak evidence that the process has changed since the emergence of strong party government in the last decades. This is not to say parties have no role to play. Most notably, the degree of coalition extremity on passage helps determine law extremity as a result of the bargaining process. Bills are made more moderate, but the passage bill is the starting point for negotiations and sets the range of final outcomes. It is also the case that off-median bills are produced by both conferencing and amendment trading, so perhaps the parties can affect the extent to which these outcomes are moved away from the median of the more moderate coalition. Recall that conferee uncertainty about preferences is an important cause of these types of outcomes, so strong parties in a more extreme coalition can make their preferences clearer and attempt to demand more of the benefits because they reduce ideological heterogeneity. Further, by limiting the ability of the chamber to consider competing conference proposals (by the minority party, for example, which occurs in some states), the conference bill is more extreme than it would otherwise be, as competing proposals allow the majority coalition to demand policy at its ideal point, similar to how amendment trading works in Congress. I have sought to focus on how electoral incentives and institutional rules structure the interchamber bargaining process, but there seem to be ample opportunities for the parties to exert their influence, even if outcomes do not become strictly partisan.

Patience is a common determinant of bargaining strength, but it has largely been ignored here because all members operate on the same congressional time line and because there is little theory to explain its potential effects. Perhaps patience on the part of the coalitions plays a larger role than I have given it credit for. The different terms of service for the House and Senate may affect bargaining strength if, for example, a number of members of the majority are facing a difficult reelection. There is evidence that senators change their behavior when they are closer to facing the voters, so perhaps this may encourage greater impatience on the part of a Senate coalition (Shepsle et al. 2009). Or, during periods of divided chamber control, if one chamber majority believes it is in electoral trouble, it may be more desperate to cut a deal and achieve a legislative victory.

Finally, outside options are a common source of bargaining strength. These exist when some exogenous event occurs that strengthens one bargainer's hand. It is difficult in the context of Congress to imagine outside options are important because there are no other bargainers the House and Senate can turn to when striking a deal. But, if an event occurs that damages one chamber or one party, such as a scandal or national crisis, it may give one side an advantage if the other chamber becomes more willing to strike a deal.

Postpassage Bargaining in a Polarized Congress

Over the last forty years, congressional action has been characterized by partisan fighting, unorthodox lawmaking, weaker committees, and stronger leadership. One of the major themes of the book has been how these changes, especially the apparent difficulty Congress has in accomplishing even the smallest tasks, affect the resolution process and whether interchamber compromise will become increasingly unreachable. Congressional observers are pessimistic about the prospects of getting anything done as Congress lurches from one crisis to another and the necessity of two chambers, distinct and independent of each other, reaching agreement seems to make lawmaking more difficult.

The results of this study, however, should encourage readers. It may be very difficult in most circumstances for the House and Senate to agree on changing the status quo, but, when they reach that stage, they are almost always successful at ironing out the differences. And, when it comes to conferencing, winning coalition extremity actually encourages a solution because members will be unwilling to sabotage a potential legislative victory. This counterintuitive result proves the durableness and raison d'être of conferences. They are simply a very good institutional mechanism for forcing agreement between two legislative bodies. And, contrary to what might be expected, conferences by their nature reach moderate agreements.

The problem may lie in getting to conference. Though polarization has not yet fundamentally changed the dynamic imposed by the cloture requirement in the Senate, it is possible, especially if small minorities become more dedicated to blocking legislative action, that amendment trading may feature more prominently in future congresses. The implications are somewhat less sanguine for amendment trading. Differences between the coalitions produce more failure, and as the two bodies drift farther apart more rounds of amendment trading may be required; small groups of members may object to particular issues, and coalition sizes may decrease. All of these factors increase the likelihood of failure. But, like conferences, when amendment trading is successful, moderate outcomes are produced.

I argue that these middle-of-the-road outcomes produced by both conferencing and amendment trading are not likely to be fundamentally altered by an increase in polarization because they are not dependent on the composition of members or the party leadership. Only fundamental changes to the resolution rules will change the bargaining dynamic. It is true that outcomes fall between the two chambers, so, under conditions of two extreme chambers with the same policy preferences, legislation will be relatively extreme as compared to bills passed in other congresses. But this would be the case regardless of the postpassage bargaining process and reflects a shift in preferences, not the use (or misuse) of an institutional mechanism. From the framers' perspective, bicameralism produces outcomes that are generally no worse than what would be produced under a unicameral system and oftentimes are much better.

Notes

Chapter One

1. The Senate was using the budget reconciliation process to pass the bill, bypassing a potential Democratic filibuster.
2. Both quotations taken from "Senators Threaten to Block Healthcare 'Skinny Repeal' Bill," *BBC News*, July 28, 2017, http://www.bbc.com/news/world-us-canada-40748717.
3. "Senators Threaten."
4. For example, John McCain said on the floor, "I speak against this farm bill conference agreement that will serve as the basis of farm policy for the next 6 years. I oppose this legislation because it is an appalling breach of our Federal spending responsibility and could be damaging to our national integrity." Floor Statements, John McCain website, May 7, 2002, http://www.mccain.senate.gov/public/index.cfm/floor-statements?ID=fd4b15a7-e16e-de1d-679b-b96bc94f249d.
5. The 2008 version actually required two override votes as the first version sent to the president was missing approximately thirty-four pages from the bill. Congress sent a corrected version, which President Bush again vetoed, and Congress overrode again.
6. Adam Liptak, " 'We the People' Loses Appeal with People around the World," *New York Times*, February 7, 2012, http://www.nytimes.com/2012/02/07/us/we-the-people-loses-appeal-with-people-around-the-world.html?_r=0.

Chapter Two

1. As noted in *Federalist* 55 and 56, there was significant debate about whether the proposed apportionment of thirty thousand residents per member was too large or too small. *The Anti-Federalist* 3 argues that thirty-thousand-person districts were much too large, while Madison claims that by reducing the per district population the assembly would be too large, creating chaos within the body.

2. Both North Carolina and Massachusetts switched their votes. See Pope and Treier (2011) for an account of how these switches were related to the three-fifths compromise.

3. As documented by Barbara Sinclair (1997), there has been a rise in procedural actions which do not conform to the traditional rules of the chamber, what she calls "unorthodox lawmaking."

4. Erik Wasson, "GOP Blocks Reid from Creating Conference Committee on Budget," *The Hill*, April 23, 2013, http://thehill.com/policy/finance/295477-reid-to -seek-consent-to-convene-budget-conference-/.

5. There is some evidence that high levels of partisanship or polarization may have the simultaneous effect of speeding up action in the House and slowing down action in the Senate.

6. Mike Madden, " 'There's a Lot of Anger at the Senate': House Democrats Think They've Figured Out the Problem with Healthcare Reform: The Senate," *Salon.com*, January 21, 2010, http://www.salon.com/2010/01/22/filibuster_5/.

7. Madden, "There's a Lot of Anger."

8. Pulling a different House bill off the calendar and then using the modified version as a legislative vehicle in the Senate can present a challenge when measuring how long it takes bills to move through the process. Elapsed time from committee reporting to floor action and passage is sometimes used as a way of capturing gridlock or the costs of negotiating (Hughes and Carlson 2015; Taylor 2014; Woon and Anderson 2012), but depending on how the elapsed time measure is constructed it may not be valid across chambers because of changes to the bill numbers that contain the same content or, conversely, entirely different substantive language may be inserted into a different bill.

9. In 1972, the House adopted a rule to allow it to delete Senate provisions that violate the House's germaneness requirement. If the rule is used, and the House deletes something from the conference report, the process reverts to amendment exchanges. The House and Senate can also pass a concurrent resolution which modifies the conference report. Prior to the rule, the House had repeatedly felt that the Senate abused its lack of a germaneness rule to force things through the House that had not been fully considered by the body. When given a choice between rejecting the entire bill or accepting a few nongermane provisions, the House was frequently forced to grudgingly accept the bill (Oleszek 1996; Smith and Flathman 1989).

10. Determining which legislators are in agreement with the legislation has been an issue both chambers have struggled with. Various reforms have been proposed to address exactly how the presiding officer or committee chair determines which legislators agree with the bill. The standard most commonly used is whether or not the legislator voted in favor of the bill on final passage (Oleszek 1974).

11. The other reforms included preventing filibusters on motions to proceed and limiting the number of hours for debate on certain presidential nominees after cloture has been invoked.

12. Personal conversation with the author, May 22, 2009, Boulder, CO.

13. Logrolling is the practice of trading votes among members to ensure sufficient support for individual projects.

14. Emily Pierce and Jennifer Yachnin, "Tactical Skirmishes Intensified in 110th Congress," *Roll Call*, January 22, 2008, B-16; quoted in Oleszek 2008, 4.

15. Postpassage bargaining categories are taken from the actions assigned to bills by Congress.gov, which tracks which bills pass through each stage of the legislation process. See chapter 4 for additional details.

16. DW-NOMINATE scores are a measure of the ideology of individual members of Congress. The scores are based on the voting behavior of members relative to other members and are commonly used to measure both individual and collective ideology over time. The "common space" versions of these scores allow for direct comparisons in ideology across chambers.

17. Moderates, as defined by Keith Poole's Voteview.com, are identified as those members with DW-NOMINATE scores between –.25 and .25. See http://voteview .com/Political_Polarization_2014.htm, accessed June 25, 2015.

18. Evaluating the relative importance of bills and laws has been an important area of research for congressional scholars though significant controversy about approaches and methods remains. See Clinton and Lapinski (2006) and Grant and Kelly (2008) for summaries of this literature.

19. Frank R. Baumgartner and Bryan D. Jones, "Policy Agendas Project," 2013, http://www.policyagendas.org/, accessed June 4, 2015.

20. A larger share of the federal budget has been dedicated to nondiscretionary or mandatory spending, which, technically defined, is funding for any program that is automatically renewed and does not need annual congressional action to continue to receive federal money. The largest mandatory spending item is Social Security.

21. Specifically, Article I, Section 9, Clause 7 says, "No money shall be drawn from the Treasury but in consequence of Appropriations made by law."

22. As of this writing, the most recent Farm Bill was officially known as the Agriculture Act of 2014, while the Surface Transportation Bill was called the Fixing America's Surface Transportation Act during the 2015 reauthorization.

23. Appropriations bills are identified as those which contain some variant of the word "appropriate" in their title. Because appropriations bills are stand-alone legislation, authorizing legislation does not contain appropriations. Additional details of the data-collection process are described in chapter 4.

24. Though a number of early works make reference to Schelling's (1960) seminal book on bargaining (for example, Pressman 1966 and Volger 1970).

25. The Legislative Reorganization Act of 1970, which weakened the seniority system and gave rank-and-file members more control over committee processes may have been the beginning of the end of the textbook Congress. Other possible dates include the election of Ronald Reagan in 1980, which is a symbolic, if not a substantive, marker of the end of the New Deal coalition.

26. It can be shown formally that in a one-dimensional space with an odd number of legislators, outcomes will converge to the median voter as two coalitions compete to pass their preferred policy (see Black 1948 and Downs 1957).

Chapter Three

1. The technical term *noncooperative bargaining* describes processes that produce mutually beneficial outcomes between players with diverging interests. This contrasts with *cooperative bargaining* (also known as the Nash bargaining solution), which characterizes outcomes in a normative sense; for instance, by asking "What is the fair outcome?" (see McCarty and Meirowitz 2007). Noncooperative bargaining does not imply that shared party control of chambers allows the party leadership to "cooperate" with each other. This approach is consistent with recent literature that treats the process not as a mutually agreeable distribution of public good but as a noncooperative exercise where chambers protect their preferences and try to compel acquiescence by the other chamber. See Ansolabehere, Snyder Jr., and Ting (2003), McQuillan and Ortega (1992), and Rogers (1998). See Tsebelis and Money (1997) for a detailed discussion about whether interchamber bargaining is best characterized as a cooperative or noncooperative process.

2. For stylistic purposes, I refer to the bargainers as coalitions, chambers, or majorities interchangeably.

3. Though coalitions could engage in bargaining when no benefits from agreement exist, the result is trivial. The status quo is always preferred to any offer made by the other chamber. See Muthoo (2000) for a straightforward explanation.

4. O'Keefe, Ed. "The House Has Voted 54 times in Four Years on Obamacare. Here's the Full List," *Washington Post*, March 21, 2014, http://tinyurl.com/qb3btpj.

5. The passage of bills for purely symbolic reasons is an important way members of Congress can position-take, and a significant literature exists on how members of Congress use roll-call voting and bill introduction to establish ideological records. See Ansolabehere, Snyder Jr., and Stewart III (2001), Lazarus (2013), and Mayhew (1974, 2001).

6. Also see Cox and McCubbins (1997) and Schickler and Rich (1997a, 1997b).

7. "Sen. Jeff Merkley on the (Surprisingly Nontrivial) Chances for Filibuster Reform," *Grist*, November 30, 2012, http://grist.org/politics/sen-jeff-merkley-on-the-surprisingly-nontrivial-chances-for-filibuster-reform/.

8. I do not differentiate between the House and Senate. In the theory, chamber one makes the first offer, and, although the Constitution specifies that bills raising revenue must originate in the House, in practice the Senate is able to get around this requirement. There is no important strategic advantage in being the first chamber to make an offer. This mirrors what seems to occur in Congress, as majorities are not observed racing to pass legislation first.

9. The theory is based on a Rubenstein (1982) bargaining model.

10. These are among the most important bills as measured by the Clinton-Lapinski index (Clinton and Lapinski 2006).

11. To introduce bargaining over the bargaining venue needlessly complicates the theory and models a process tangential to the question examined here.

12. The chambers can also offer conferee instructions, but these are nonbinding and there is no evidence they constrain the conference committee.

13. During recent negotiations on the Farm Bill renewal, Debbie Stabenow, the chairwoman of the Senate Agriculture Committee, stated her urgency, saying, "We're anxious to go. I am very concerned that the process begin this week." David Rogers, "Senate Pushes House to Begin Farm Bill Conference," *Politico*, July 15, 2013, https://www.politico.com/story/2013/07/senate-house-farm-bill-conference-094236.

14. This seems likely given that the conferees must be in favor of the bill according to the rules of each chamber. There is also little evidence that conferees use their power to intentionally induce rejection by the chambers.

Chapter Four

1. The 111th Senate had fifty-eight Democrats and two independents who caucused with the Democrats prior to the death of Edward Kennedy and the subsequent election of Republican Scott Brown.

2. Within-chamber disagreement also captures the difficulty of constructing around a compromise bill a winning coalition that may consist of members not necessarily in the original winning coalition.

3. Prior to 1975, the cloture threshold was two-thirds of members voting, while since the rule change it is sixty votes regardless of how many senators vote (see Wawro 2010). The variable used in the analysis is coded as sixty votes for bills passed after 1973, and sixty-seven votes for bills passed in 1973.

4. The vast majority of bills that receive at least one line of coverage are written about extensively.

5. I can use bills up to the 113th Congress for descriptive purposes, but, as noted, the *CQA* article lines variable goes only to the 111th Congress. Thus, empirical models which include the *CQA* variable are limited to the 93rd through 111th Congresses.

6. In these situations, amendment trading is almost always an afterthought in that it is used to clean up any remaining discrepancies between the bills and allow the House to avoid violating its germaneness rules. There is little evidence to suggest that amendment trading after a conference has a systematic, substantive effect on bill outcomes.

7. As noted in chapter 2, some bills serve as vehicles for other bills when they are pulled off the calendar and have the entire text deleted and replaced. This presents a measurement challenge in that it is very difficult to identify, across the data set,

different legislative vehicles. Many of the vehicles are initially passed with unanimous consent, so they will be excluded from these analyses. Further, in other empirical tests, these bills would bias the results in a more conservative direction, making it more difficult to find the hypothesized relationships. An initial sample of all bills suggests it is relatively rare for a bill to be pulled off the calendar and have entirely different text inserted. More commonly, the Senate will insert its own text into the House version.

8. To ensure the exclusion of these bills does not bias the results I reestimated all models using only those bills which received a vote in the Senate and coded the corresponding unanimous consent vote in the House as passed with 100 percent support. The results (not shown) are consistent with the empirical results in the text. In most of the reestimated models, the results are stronger than those discussed in the text, suggesting excluding bills without a roll-call vote in either chamber is a more conservative test of the theory. The exclusion of unanimous consent votes is consistent with other studies of roll-call votes that exclude noncompetitive votes and with Krehbiel and Woon's (2005) characterization of nonclose votes as nonstrategic votes. See, for example, Wright's (2004) study of state roll-call voting, which excludes those with support from greater than 95 percent of members; see also McGrath, Rogowski, and Ryan (2015), who also use a 95 percent cutoff, and Masket (2008) and Snyder and Groseclose (2000), who use a 65 percent cutoff. That cutoff is too low for the purposes here, given that the vast majority of votes, especially in the Senate, are passed with greater than 65 percent support.

9. In table 4.2, the *CQA* lines dichotomous variable is used because of the number of extremely high-value bills which distort the mean.

10. The descriptive data above show 749 bills through the 113th Congress, but the 112th and 113th are not used in the analysis because some variables are missing for those years.

11. Six bills rejected by the House but later passed are excluded from the data.

12. The total support and majority share variables are correlated, as one would expect, but there are some important differences between the two concepts. Both capture the importance of coalition building across diverse sets of members. In the Senate, majority party support is correlated with overall support at .55, while in the House the two correlate at .48. It is possible (and common) to have high majority party support and low overall chamber support and (rarely) high overall chamber support and low majority party support.

13. All other variables are held at their means other than appropriations (set to 0) and public law (set to 1).

Chapter Five

1. I make no assumptions as to whether the legislative outcome reflects the policy preferences of the chamber median or represents outlying policy, either the party's or a group of legislative policy demanders.

2. The logic here is very similar to that surrounding veto bargaining: vetoes shape legislative outcomes even though vetoes are rarely used (see Cameron 2000).

3. It is probable that members sometimes do not vote sincerely but instead vote strategically. Poole and Rosenthal (1997) specifically suggest that logrolling legislators may support a bill they would otherwise not based on their ideological position. This should not affect the measure here because I examine vote switching rather than a single vote. If members are logrolling, they are unlikely to vote yes and then to vote no if the legislative substance remains similar when the bill returns from conference. Further, a member may oppose a bill hoping to support a better alternative, but it is unclear whether the same member would then vote yes when the bill returned from conference.

4. As noted above, this is exceedingly rare.

5. Both component terms are positive and statistically significant (House yea percentage at the .1 level) though these terms do not have a meaningful substantive interpretation.

Chapter Six

1. This assumes open proposal rights. Otherwise, an actor can make a take-it-or-leave-it offer, and the median decides between only the proposed offer and the status quo.

2. When uncertainty is high and coalition sizes are low, the conferees may propose an unacceptable offer (see chapter 5 for details).

3. Vander Wielen (2010) is an important exception.

4. There is no theoretical reason to expect the more moderate chamber to move closer to the status quo, as the conferees have no incentive to make an offer that allocates additional benefits to a larger winning coalition within a chamber.

5. A bill cannot reach the conference stage if fewer than .5 of members voting support it on passage.

6. I do not subset the data by controversial vote as that is meant to capture bill importance, and appropriations bills in general are assumed to be important.

7. The number of observations in these analyses are smaller than the number in the difference-of-means tests because only bills which have both House and Senate data are included. The difference-of-means tests above include all bills even if the bill was passed in one chamber with unanimous consent votes on both passage and conference. This is necessary because some control variables require data from the passage vote in the other chamber.

8. Unless otherwise noted, all predicted values are calculated at the mean of all variables except appropriations, which is set to 0.

9. Note also that the moderate coalition indicator for the Senate is negative and statistically significant. This effect cannot be interpreted because the Senate cannot be more moderate when House extremity equals zero.

10. There is evidence from the states that allowing a competing proposal from the losing coalition (which more closely reflects true median voter theory) produces more moderate outcomes as compared to states that do not allow a competing proposal (see Ryan 2014).

Chapter Seven

1. And, in the bargaining model, if a winning coalition does not receive some benefits from rejection, the result is trivial because any offer will be accepted by the chamber receiving the first offer.

2. On difficult votes, the party leadership may also seek to keep details of the bill secret to prevent interests from organizing against it (Curry 2015). This is possible during the amendment trading process but not during conferencing.

3. For example, see Susan Davis and Richard Wolf, "U.S. Senate Goes 'Nuclear,' Changes Filibuster Rules," *USA Today*, November 21, 2013, http://www.usa today.com/story/news/politics/2013/11/21/harry-reid-nuclear-senate/3662445/.

4. In many cases, the House objects to a certain part of the conference because it violates its germaneness rule. House rules now allow the House to reject that portion alone and force the chambers to amendment trade on those provisions to which the House objects.

5. This is the maximum number of exchanges in the data set for H.R. 3128 in the 99th Congress, the Consolidated Omnibus Budget Reconciliation Act of 1985.

6. Though the predicted probabilities of failure are statistically significant, the differences in effect sizes are themselves not statistically significant.

References

Abramowitz, Alan, Brad Alexander, and Matthew Gunning. 2006. "Don't Blame Redistricting for Uncompetitive Elections." *PS: Political Science and Politics* 39(1):87–90.

Adler, E. Scott. 2002. *Why Congressional Reforms Fail: Reelection and the House Committee System.* Chicago: University of Chicago Press.

Adler, E. Scott, and John Wilkerson. 2007. "A Governing Theory of Legislative Organization." Prepared for the annual meetings of the American Political Science Association, Chicago, August 29–September 2.

———. 2012. *Congress and the Politics of Problem Solving.* New York: Cambridge University Press.

Aldrich, John H. 1995. *Why Parties?* Chicago: University of Chicago Press.

———. 2000. "Southern Parties in State and Nation." *Journal of Politics* 62(3): 643–670.

Aldrich, John H., and David W. Rohde. 1997. "The Transition to Republican Rule in the House: Implications for Theories of Congressional Politics." *Political Science Quarterly* 112(4):541–567.

———. 1998. "Measuring Conditional Party Government." Presented at the Annual Meeting of the Midwest Political Science Association, Chicago.

———. 2000. "The Republican Revolution and the House Appropriations Committee." *Journal of Politics* 62(1):1–33.

Ansolabehere, Stephen, and Philip Edward Jones. 2010. "Constituents' Response to Congressional Roll Call Voting." *American Journal of Political Science* 54(3): 583–597.

Ansolabehere, Stephen, James M. Snyder, Jr., and Charles Stewart, III. 2001. "Candidate Positioning in U.S. House Elections." *American Journal of Political Science* 45(1):136–159.

Ansolabehere, Stephen, James M. Snyder Jr., and Michael M. Ting. 2003. "Bargaining in Bicameral Legislatures: When and Why Does Malapportionment Matter?" *American Political Science Review* 97(3):471–481.

Arnold, R. Douglas. 1990. *The Logic of Congressional Action*. New Haven, CT: Yale University Press.

Bach, Stanley. 2003. *Platypus and Parliament: The Australian Senate in Theory and Practice*. Canberra: Department of the Senate.

Baron, David P., and John A. Ferejohn. 1989. "Bargaining in Legislatures." *American Political Science Review* 89(4):1189–1206.

Binder, Sarah. 2003. *Stalemate: Causes and Consequences of Legislative Gridlock*. Washington, DC: Brookings Institution Press.

Black, Duncan. 1948. "On the Rationale of Group Decision-Making." *Journal of Political Economy* 56(1):23–34.

Black, Duncan, Robert Albert Newing, Iain McLean, Alistair McMillan, and Burt L. Monroe. 1958. *The Theory of Committees and Elections*. New York: Cambridge: University Press.

Bosso, Christopher. 2017. *Framing the Farm Bill: Interests, Ideology, and the Agricultural Act of 2014*. Lawrence: University of Kansas Press.

Box-Steffensmeier, Janet, Josh M. Ryan, and Anand Edward Sokhey. 2015. "Examining Legislative Cue-Taking in the US Senate." *Legislative Studies Quarterly* 40(1):13–53.

Bradbury, John Charles, and W. Mark Crain. 2002. "Bicameral Legislatures and Fiscal Policy." *Southern Economic Journal* 68(3):646–659.

Brady, David, Richard Brody, and David Epstein. 1989. "Heterogeneous Parties and Political Organization: The U.S. Senate, 1880–1920." *Legislative Studies Quarterly* 14(2):205–223.

Brady, David, and David Epstein. 1997. "Intraparty Preferences, Heterogeneity, and the Origins of the Modern Congress: Progressive Reform in the House and Senate, 1890–1920." *Journal of Law, Economics, and Organization* 13(1):26–49.

Brady, David W., Hahrie Han, and Jeremy C. Pope. 2007. "Primary Elections and Ideology: Out of Step with the Primary Electorate." *Legislative Studies Quarterly* 32(1):79–105.

Brewer, Mark D., Mack D. Mariani, and Jeffrey M. Stonecash. 2002. "Northern Democrats and Party Polarization in the U.S. House." *Legislative Studies Quarterly* 27(3):423–444.

Burden, Barry C. 2001. "The Polarizing Effect of Congressional Primaries." In *Congressional Primaries and the Politics of Representation*, edited by Peter F. Galderisi, Marni Ezra, and Michael Lyons, 95–115. New York: Rowman and Littlefield.

Cameron, Charles M. 2000. *Veto Bargaining*. Cambridge: Cambridge University Press.

Canes-Wrone, Brandice, David W. Brady, and John F. Cogan. 2002. "Out of Step, Out of Office: Electoral Accountability and House Members' Voting." *American Political Science Review* 96(1):127–140.

Cann, Damon M. 2008. *Sharing the Wealth: Member Contributions and the Exchange*

Theory of Party Influence in the U.S. House of Representatives. Albany: State University of New York Press.

Carson, Jamie L., Gregory Koger, Matthew J. Lebo, and Everett Young. 2010. "The Electoral Costs of Party Loyalty in Congress." *American Journal of Political Science* 54(3):598–616.

Clinton, Joshua D., and John S. Lapinski. 2006. "Measuring Legislative Accomplishment, 1877–1994." *American Journal of Political Science* 50(1):232–249.

Collie, Melissa P. 1988. "Universalism and the Parties in the U.S. House of Representatives, 1921–1980." *American Journal of Political Science* 32(4):865–883.

Cox, Gary W. 2000. "On the Effects of Legislative Rules." *Legislative Studies Quarterly* 25(2):169–192.

———. 2006. The Organization of Democratic Legislatures. In *Oxford Handbook of Political Economy*, edited by Barry R. Weingast and Donald Wittman, 141–161. Oxford: Oxford University Press.

Cox, Gary W., Thad Kousser, and Mathew D. McCubbins. 2010. "Party Power or Preferences? Quasi-Experimental Evidence from American State Legislatures." *Journal of Politics* 72(3):799–811.

Cox, Gary W., and Mathew D. McCubbins. 1993. *Legislative Leviathan: Party Government in the House*. Berkeley: University of California Press.

———. 1997. "Toward a Theory of Legislative Rules Changes: Assessing Schickler and Rich's Evidence." *American Journal of Political Science* 41(4):1376–1386.

———. 2005. *Setting the Agenda: Responsible Party Government in the US House of Representatives*. Cambridge: University of Cambridge Press.

Crespin, Michael H., and David Rohde. 2010. "Dimensions, Issues, and Bills: Appropriations Voting on the House Floor." *Journal of Politics* 72(4):976–989.

Curry, James M. 2015. *Legislating the Dark: Information and Power in the House of Representatives*. Chicago: University of Chicago Press.

Cutrone, Michael, and Nolan McCarty. 2006. "Does Bicameralism Matter?" In *Oxford Handbook of Political Economy*, edited by Barry Weingast and Donald Wittman, 180–199. New York: Oxford University Press.

Davis, Christopher M. 2014. "The Legislative Process on the House Floor: An Introduction." Washington, DC: Congressional Research Service.

Den Hartog, Chris, and Nathan W. Monroe. 2011. *Agenda Setting in the U.S. Senate: Costly Consideration and Majority Party Advantage*. New York: Cambridge University Press.

Diermeier, Daniel, and Roger B. Myerson. 1999. "Bicameralism and Its Consequences for the Internal Organization of Legislatures." *American Economic Review* 89(5):1182–1196.

Downs, Anthony. 1957. *An Economic Theory of Democracy*. New York: Harper Collins.

Druckman, James M., Lanny W. Martin, and Michael F. Thies. 2005. "Influence without Confidence." *Legislative Studies Quarterly* 30(4):529–548.

Epstein, David, and Sharyn O'Halloran. 1996. "The Partisan Paradox and the US Tariff, 1877–1934." *International Organization* 50(2):301–324.

Fearon, James D. 1995. "Rationalist Explanations for War." *International Organization* 49(3):379–414.

Fenno, Richard F. 1966. *The Power of the Purse: Appropriations Politics in Congress*. Boston: Little, Brown.

————. 1973. *Congressmen in Committees*. Boston: Little, Brown.

Ferejohn, John A. 1974. *Pork-Barrel Politics*. Stanford, CA: Stanford University Press.

Fiorina, Morris, Samuel Abrams, and Jeremy C. Pope. 2005. *Culture Wars? The Myth of a Polarized America*. New York: Pearson Longman.

Fleisher, Richard, and John R. Bond. 2004. "The Shrinking Middle in the US Congress." *British Journal of Politics* 34(3):429–451.

Grant, J. Tobin, and Nathan J. Kelly. 2008. "Legislative Productivity of the U.S. Congress, 1789–2004." *Political Analysis* 16(3):303–323.

Groseclose, Tim. 1996. "An Examination of the Market for Favors and Votes in Congress." *Economic Inquiry* 34(2):320–340.

Groseclose, Tim, and James M. Snyder. 1996. "On Buying Supermajorities." *American Political Science Review* 90(2):303–315.

Hamilton, Alexander, James Madison, and John Jay. 1961. *The Federalist Papers*. Edited by Clinton Rossiter. New York: Signet Classics.

Hammond, Thomas H., and Gary J. Miller. 1987. "The Core of the Constitution." *American Political Science Review* 81(4):1155–1174.

Heckman, James J. 1976. "The Common Structure of Statistical Models of Truncation, Sample Selection and Limited Dependent Variables and a Simple Estimator for Such Models." *Annals of Economic and Social Measurement* 5(4):120–137.

Heller, William B. 2007. "Divided Politics: Bicameralism, Parties, and Policy in Democratic Legislatures." In *Annual Review of Political Science*, vol. 10, 245–269. Palo Alto, CA: Annual Reviews.

Hinckley, Barbara. 1972. "Coalitions in Congress: Size and Ideological Distance." *Midwest Journal of Political Science* 16(2):197–207.

Hughes, Tyler, and Deven Carlson. 2015. "Divided Government and Delay in the Legislative Process: Evidence from Important Bills, 1949–2010." *American Politics Research* 43(5):771–792.

Hurwitz, Mark S., Roger J. Moiles, and David W. Rohde. 2001. "Distributive and Partisan Issues in Agricultural Policy in the 104th House." *American Political Science Review* 95(4):911–922.

Jacobson, Gary. 2000. *Party Polarization in National Politics: The Electoral Connection*. Washington, DC: CQ Press.

Jenkins, Jeffrey A., and Nathan W. Monroe. 2012. "Buying Negative Agenda Control in the U.S. House." *American Journal of Political Science* 56(4):897–912.

Jenkins, Jeffery A., and Michael C. Munger. 2003. "Investigating the Incidence of Killer Amendments in Congress." *Journal of Politics* 65(2):498–517.

Jones, David R. 2003. "Position Taking and Position Avoidance in the U.S. Senate." *Journal of Politics* 65(3):851–863.

Kaiser, Robert G. 2013. *Act of Congress: How America's Essential Institution Works, and How It Doesn't.* New York: Alfred A. Knopf.

Kernell, Sam. 1973. "Is the Senate More Liberal than the House?" *Journal of Politics* 35(2):332–366.

Kiewiet, D. Roderick, and Mathew D. McCubbins. 1991. *The Logic of Delegation: Congressional Parties and the Appropriations Process.* Chicago: University of Chicago Press.

King, Gary, Robert O. Keohane, and Sidney Verba. 1994. *Designing Social Inquiry.* Princeton, NJ: Princeton University Press.

Kirkland, Justin H. 2014. "Ideological Heterogeneity and Legislative Polarization in the United States." *Political Research Quarterly* 67(3):533–546.

Koger, Gregory. 2010. *Filibustering: A Political History of Obstruction in the House and Senate.* Chicago: University of Chicago Press.

Krehbiel, Keith. 1995. "Cosponsors and Wafflers from A to Z." *American Journal of Political Science* 39(4):906–923.

———. 1998. *Pivotal Politics.* Chicago: University of Chicago Press.

Krehbiel, Keith, Kenneth A. Shepsle, and Barry R. Weingast. 1987. "Why Are Congressional Committees Powerful?" *American Political Science Review* 81(3):929–945.

Krehbiel, Keith, and Jonathan Woon. 2005. "Selection Criteria for Roll Call Votes." *Research Paper Series: Stanford Graduate School of Business.* Prepared for the meetings of the American Political Science Association, Washington, DC.

Krutz, Glen S. 2000. "Getting around Gridlock: The Effect of Omnibus Utilization on Legislative Productivity." *Legislative Studies Quarterly* 25(4):533–549.

———. 2001. *Hitching a Ride: Omnibus Legislating in the US Congress.* Columbus: Ohio State University Press.

Layman, Geoffrey C., and Thomas M. Carsey. 2002. "Party Polarization and 'Conflict Extension' in the American Electorate." *American Journal of Political Science* 46(4):786–802.

Layman, Geoffrey C., Thomas M. Carsey, and Juliana Menasce Horowitz. 2006. "Party Polarization in American Politics: Characteristics, Causes, and Consequences." *Annual Review of Political Science* 9(1):83–110.

Lazarus, Jeffrey. 2013. "Issue Salience and Bill Introduction in the House and Senate." *Congress and the Presidency* 40(3):215–229.

Lazarus, Jeffrey, and Nathan Monroe. 2007. "The Speaker's Discretion: Conference Committee Appointments in the 97th through 106th Congresses." *Political Research Quarterly* 60(4):593–606.

Lebo, Matthew J., Adam J. McGlynn, and Gregory Koger. 2007. "Strategic Party Government: Party Influence in Congress, 1789–2000." *American Journal of Political Science* 51(3):464–481.

Lee, Frances E. 2000. "Senate Representation and Coalition Building in Distributive Politics." *American Political Science Review* 94(1):59–72.

Lijphart, Arend. 1999. *Patterns of Democracy: Government Forms and Performance in Thirty-Six Countries*. New Haven, CT: Yale University Press.

Lipset, Seymour Martin, and Jason M. Lakin. 2004. *The Democratic Century*. Norman: University of Oklahoma Press.

Longley, Lawrence D., and Walter J. Oleszek. 1989. *Bicameral Politics: Conference Committees in Congress*. New Haven, CT: Yale University Press.

Madonna, Anthony. 2011. "Winning Coalition Formation in the U.S. Senate: The Effects of Legislative Decision Rules and Agenda Change." *American Journal of Political Science* 55(2):276–288.

Manley, John F. 1970. *The Politics of Finance: The House Ways and Means Committee*. Boston: Little, Brown.

Masket, Seth E. 2008. "Where You Sit Is Where You Stand: The Impact of Seating Proximity on Legislative Cue-Taking." *Quarterly Journal of Political Science* 3(3):301–311

Mayhew, David R. 1974. *Congress: The Electoral Connection*. New Haven, CT: Yale University Press.

———. 1991. *Divided We Govern: Party Control, Lawmaking, and Investigations 1946–1990*. New Haven, CT: Yale University Press.

———. 2001. "Observations on Congress: The *Electoral Connection* a Quarter Century after Writing It." *PS: Political Science and Politics* 34(2):251–252.

McCarty, Nolan, and Adam Meirowitz. 2007. *Political Game Theory: An Introduction*. Cambridge: Cambridge University Press.

McCarty, Nolan, Keith T. Poole, and Howard Rosenthal. 2006. *Polarized America: The Dance of Ideology and Unequal Riches*. Cambridge, MA: MIT Press.

McGrath, Robert J., Jon Rogowski, and Josh M. Ryan. 2015. "Gubernatorial Veto Powers and the Size of Legislative Coalitions." *Legislative Studies Quarterly* 40(4):571–598.

McQuillan, Lawrence J., and Lydia D. Ortega. 1992. "Conference Committee Participation and Party Loyalty." *Public Choice* 64(4):485–494.

Minkoff, Scott L., and Josh M. Ryan. 2012. "The Appropriations Policy as Policy Tool." Paper presented at the Midwest Political Science Association's Annual Meeting, Chicago.

Morrow, James D. 1989. "Capabilities, Uncertainty and Resolve: A Limited Information Model of Crisis Bargaining." *American Journal of Political Science* 33(4):941–972.

———. 1992. "Signaling Difficulties with Linkage in Crisis Bargaining." *International Studies Quarterly* 36(2):153–172.

Muthoo, Abhinay. 2000. "A Non-technical Introduction to Bargaining Theory." *World Economics* 1(2):145–166.

Muthoo, Abhinay, and Kenneth A. Shepsle. 2008. "The Constitutional Choice of Bicameralism." In *Institutions and Economic Performance*, edited by Elhanan Helpman, 249–291. Cambridge, MA: Harvard University Press.

Oleszek, Walter J. 1974. "House-Senate Relationships: Comity and Conflict." *Annals of the American Academy of Political and Social Science* 411(1):75–86.

———. 1996. *Congressional Procedures and the Policy Process*. 4th ed. Washington, DC: CQ Press.

———. 2007. *Congressional Procedures and the Policy Process*. 7th ed. Washington, DC: CQ Press.

———. 2008. "Whither the Role of Conference Committees: An Analysis." Washington DC: Congressional Research Service.

Peress, Michael. 2013. "Estimating Proposal and Status Quo Locations Using Voting and Cosponsorship Data." *Journal of Politics* 75(3):613–631.

Polsby, Nelson W. 1968. "The Institutionalization of the U.S. House of Representatives." *American Political Science Review* 62(1):144–168.

Poole, Keith, and Howard Rosenthal. 1997. *Congress: A Political-Economic History of Roll Call Voting*. New York: Oxford University Press.

Pope, Jeremy C., and Shawn Treier. 2011. "Reconsidering the Great Compromise at the Federal Convention of 1787: Deliberation and Agenda Effects on the Senate and Slavery." *American Journal of Political Science* 55(2):289–306.

Powell, Robert. 1996. "Stability and the Distribution of Power." *World Politics* 48(2):239–267.

———. 1999. *In the Shadow of Power: States and Strategies in International Politics*. Princeton, NJ: Princeton University Press.

Pressman, Jeffrey L. 1966. *House vs. Senate: Conflict in the Appropriations Process*. New Haven, CT: Yale University Press.

Reiter, Dan. 2004. "Exploring the Bargaining Model of War." *Perspectives on Politics* 1(1):27–43.

Riddick, Floyd Millard, and Alan S. Frumin. 1992. *Riddick's Senate Procedure: Precedents and Practices*. No. 101. US Government Printing Office.

Riker, William H. 1962. *The Theory of Political Coalitions*. New Haven, CT: Yale University Press.

———. 1992. "The Justification of Bicameralism." *American Political Science Review* 13(1):101–116.

Rogers, James R. 1998. "Bicameral Sequence: Theory and State Legislative Evidence." *American Journal of Political Science* 42(4):1025–1060.

Rohde, David W. 1991. *Parties and Leaders in the Postreform House*. Chicago: University of Chicago Press.

Rubenstein, Ariel. 1982. "Perfect Equilibrium in a Bargaining Model." *Econometrica* 50(1):97–109.

Ryan, Josh M. 2014. "Conference Committee Proposal Rights and Policy Outcomes in the States." *Journal of Politics* 76(4):1059–1073.

———. 2018. "Constructing Congressional Activity: Uncertainty and the Dynamics of Legislative Attention." *Political Science Research and Methods* 6(2):299–321. https://doi.org/10.1017/psrm.2015.66.

Rybicki, Elizabeth. 2003. "Unresolved Differences: Bicameral Negotiations in Congress, 1877–2002." Paper presented at the History of Congress Conference, University of California at San Diego, December 5–6.

———. 2007. "The Development of Bicameral Resolution Procedures in the U.S. Congress." PhD diss., University of Minnesota.

Schelling, Thomas C. 1960. *The Strategy of Conflict*. Cambridge, MA: Harvard University Press.

Schickler, Eric. 2001. *Disjointed Pluralism: Institutional Innovation and the Development of the U.S. Congress*. Princeton, NJ: Princeton University Press.

Schickler, Eric, and Andrew Rich. 1997a. "Controlling the Floor: Parties as Procedural Coalitions in the House." *American Journal of Political Science* 41(4): 1340–1375.

———. 1997b. "Party Government in the House Reconsidered: A Response to Cox and McCubbins." *American Journal of Political Science* 41(4):1387–1394.

Shell, Donald. 2001. "The History of Bicameralism." *Journal of Legislative Studies* 7(1):5–18.

Shepsle, Kenneth A. 1974. "On the Size of Winning Coalitions." *American Political Science Review* 68(2):505–518.

———. 1989. "The Changing Textbook Congress." In *Can the Government Govern?*, edited by John E. Chubb and Paul E. Peterson, 238–266. Washington, DC: Brookings Institute Press.

Shepsle, Kenneth A., Robert P. Van Houweling, Samuel J. Abrams, and Peter C. Hanson. 2009. "The Senate Electoral Cycle and Bicameral Appropriations Politics." *American Journal of Political Science* 53(2):343–359.

Shepsle, Kenneth, and Barry Weingast. 1981. "Structure-Induced Equilibrium and Legislative Choice." *Public Choice* 37(3):503–519.

———. 1987. "Institutional Foundations of Committee Power." *American Political Science Review* 81:85–103.

———. 1989. Penultimate Power: Congress Committees and the Legislative Process. In *Home Style and Washington Work*, edited by Morris P. Fiorina and David W. Wohde, 199–217. Ann Arbor: University of Michigan Press.

———. 1994. "Positive Theories of Congressional Institutions." *Legislative Studies Quarterly* 19(2):149–179.

Sinclair, Barbara. 1983. *Majority Leadership in the U.S. House*. Baltimore: Johns Hopkins University Press.

———. 1994. "House Special Rules and the Institutional Design Controversy." *Legislative Studies Quarterly* 19(4):477–494.

———. 1997. *Unorthodox Lawmaking: New Legislative Processes in the US Congress*. Washington, DC: CQ Press.

———. 2006. *Party Wars: Polarization and the Politics of National Policy Making*. Norman: University of Oklahoma Press.

———. 2012. "Ping Pong and Other Congressional Pursuits: Party Leaders and Postpassage Procedural Choice." In *Party and Procedure in the United States Congress*, edited by Jacob R. Strauss, 231–252. Lanham, MD: Rowman and Littlefield.

Smith, Steven S. 1988. "An Essay on Sequence, Position, Goals, and Committee Power." *Legislative Studies Quarterly* 13(2):151–176.

———. 1989. *Call to Order: Floor Politics in the House and Senate*. Washington, DC: Brookings Institute.

Smith, Steven S., and Marcus Flathman. 1989. "Managing the Senate Floor: Complex Unanimous Consent Agreements since the 1950s." *Legislative Studies Quarterly* 14(3):349–374.

Smith, Steven S., Ian Ostrander, and Christopher M. Pope. 2013. "Majority Party Power and Procedural Motions in the U.S. Senate." *Legislative Studies Quarterly* 38(2):205–236.

Snyder, James M., Jr., and Tim Groseclose. 2000. "Estimating Party Influence in Congressional Roll Call Voting." *American Journal of Political Science* 44(2): 192–211.

Squire, Peverill. 2006. "Historical Evolution of Legislatures in the United States." *Annual Review of Political Science* 9:19–44.

———. 2012. *The Evolution of American Legislatures: Colonies, Territories, and States, 1619–2009*. Ann Arbor: University of Michigan Press.

Steiner, Gilbert Y. 1951. *The Congressional Conference Committee: Seventieth to Eightieth Congresses*. Urbana: University of Illinois Press.

Strom, Gerald S., and Barry S. Rundquist. 1977. "A Revised Theory of Winning in House-Senate Conference Committees." *American Political Science Review* 71(2):448–453.

Taylor, Andrew J. 2014. "Bill Passage Speed in the US House: A Test of a Vote Buying Model of the Legislative Process." *Journal of Legislative Studies* 20(3): 285–304.

Theriault, Sean M. 2008. *Party Polarization in Congress*. New York: Cambridge University Press.

Theriault, Sean M., and David W. Rohde. 2011. "The Gingrich Senators and Party Polarization in the U.S. Senate." *Journal of Politics* 73(4):1011–1024.

Tsebelis, George. 2002. *Veto Players: How Political Institutions Work*. Princeton, NJ: Princeton University Press.

Tsebelis, George, and Jeannette Money. 1997. *Bicameralism*. Cambridge: Cambridge University Press.

Vander Wielen, Ryan J. 2010. "The Influence of Conference Committees on Policy Outcomes." *Legislative Studies Quarterly* 35(4):487–518.

Vander Wielen, Ryan J., and Steven S. Smith. 2011. "Majority Party Bias in U.S. Congressional Conference Committees." *Congress and the Presidency* 48(3): 271–300.

Volger, David J. 1970. "Patterns of One House Dominance in Congressional Conference Committees." *Midwest Journal of Political Science* 14(2):303–320.

Wawro, Gregory. 2010. "The Filibuster and Filibuster Reform in the U.S. Senate, 1917–
1975." Testimony before the Senate Committee on Rules and Administration.
April 27. http://www.columbia.edu/~gjw10/rules_committee_statement_final.pdf.

Wawro, Gregory J., and Eric Schickler. 2004. "Where's the Pivot? Obstruction and
Lawmaking in the Pre-cloture Senate." *American Journal of Political Science*
48(4):758–774.

———. 2006. *Filibuster: Obstruction and Lawmaking in the U.S. Senate*. Princeton,
NJ: Princeton University Press.

Weingast, Barry R., and William Marshall. 1988. "The Industrial Organization of
Congress; or, Why Legislatures, Like Firms, Are Not Organized as Markets."
Journal of Political Economy 91(1):132–163.

Wilkerson, John D. 1999. " 'Killer' Amendments in Congress." *American Political Science Review* 93(3):535–552.

Wilson, Woodrow. 1885. *Congressional Government*. Cleveland, OH: Meridian.

Wolfensberger, Donald. 2008. "Have House-Senate Conferences Gone the Way of
the Dodo?" Wilson Center. Published July 7, 2011. https://www.wilsoncenter.org
/publication/have-house-senate-conferences-gone-the-way-the-dodo.

Woon, Jonathan, and Sarah Anderson. 2012. "Political Bargaining and the Timing
of Congressional Appropriations." *Legislative Studies Quarterly* 37(4):409–436.

Wright, Gerald. 2004. *Representation in America's Legislatures*. National Science
Foundation Grant. http://www.indiana.edu/~ral/. Accessed February 5, 2018.

Index

Affordable Care Act (ACA). *See* Patient Protection and Affordable Care Act

amendment trading: bill failure in, 62–63, 156–58, 161–64, 185–86; choice of, 52–54, 57–59; coalition changes after, 158–60, 164–67, 169–70, 178–79, 184; with conference committees, 23–24, 34, 160, 193; examples of, 52, 68–69, 157–58; ideological changes after, 159, 167–69, 171–79, 184; measurement of, 77–78, 160–61; outcomes from, 9–11, 62–63, 123, 154–56; process of, 8–11, 19, 24, 196; theory of, 4, 10–11, 38–39, 45, 49–50, 62–67, 69–72, 74, 76–77, 80, 87, 93–94; use in Congress, 16–18, 24–27, 29–31, 34, 40–41, 46, 88–91, 122–23, 183

American colonies, 9, 14–15

appropriations: and amendment trading, 76, 157–58, 164, 170–73, 175; in Australia, 12; and coalition size, 138–40; in conference committees, 20, 31–36, 70, 76, 102–3, 123; distributive theory and, 76, 80, 130, 132, 135, 138–40, 143, 150–52; effect on coalition size, 142–43; effect on conferencing, 88–92; effect on ideology, 118, 150–51; effect on minority support, 145–47; effect on postpassage bargaining, 10, 35, 85–86, 88–90; effect on vote switching, 109, 115; examples of, 8–69, 105, 135, 157–58; measurement of, 79–80, 108, 191; parties and, 38; procedures for, 31–32, 78, 80, 191, 195; "who wins?," 123

authorization, 2–4, 31–32, 191

bargaining: amendment trading as venue for, 34, 174–79; avoiding, 57–59; bills eligible for, 81–83; causes of failure in, 59–61, 62–63, 196; changes as a result of, 2, 7–8; competing theories on outcomes from, 124–32; conditions to use, 19, 26–31, 33–34, 52, 54, 56–57, 64, 68–69, 71–73, 83–87, 121, 160, 180–81, 186–87, 191; conferee selection and, 23–25; conferences outcomes and, 123–25, 129–33, 147–53; congressional actors and, 45–46; costs in conference of, 52, 81–83; definition of, 46–47; disagreement benefits from, 47–48; divided government and, 37; evidence for, 88–93; failure in, 44; future questions and 187–88; moderate chambers and amendment trading for, 62–65, 155–58; moderation and conference outcomes in, 62–65; patience in, 186–87; postpassage resolution and, 26–27, 29; predictions from, 71–73, 124; predictions of outcomes from, 61–62; predictors of, 76–77; preference for the status quo, 192; procedural changes to process in Congress, 16–17; research on outcomes from, 35–36, 123–24; Senate filibuster and, 74, 87; Senate support and, 73–75; sequence of, 51–52, 54; strength in, 4, 9, 33, 37, 110, 121, 123; strength in conference for, 4, 33–34; summary of in Congress, 64, 70–71, 101; theoretical costs of, 48–51; theoretical evidence of, 147, 152, 175–80; theory of in Congress, 10–11, 30, 35–36, 39–44,